Irreconcilable Differences?

Irreconcilable Differences?

Fostering Dialogue among Philosophy, Theology, and Science

Edited by
JASON C. ROBINSON
and DAVID A. PECK

Foreword by Brian McLaren

PICKWICK Publications • Eugene, Oregon

IRRECONCILABLE DIFFERENCES?
Fostering Dialogue among Theology, Philosophy, and Science

Copyright © 2015 Wipf and Stock Publishers. All rights reserved. Except for brief quotations in critical publications or reviews, no part of this book may be reproduced in any manner without prior written permission from the publisher. Write: Permissions, Wipf and Stock Publishers, 199 W. 8th Ave., Suite 3, Eugene, OR 97401.

The epigraph comes from Blaise Pascal, *Pensées*, trans. and introd. A. J. Krailsheimer, Penguin Classics (Harmondsworth, UK: Penguin, 1968)

Pickwick Publications
An Imprint of Wipf and Stock Publishers
199 W. 8th Ave., Suite 3
Eugene, OR 97401

www.wipfandstock.com

ISBN: 978-1-4982-0004-2

Cataloguing-in-Publication Data

Irreconcilable differences? : fostering dialogue among theology, philosophy, and science / edited by Jason Robinson and David Peck.

xxii + 222 p. ; 23 cm. Includes bibliographical references.

ISBN 13: 978-1-4982-0004-2

1. Religion and science. 2. Religion and philosophy. I. Robinson, Jason. II. Peck, David. III. McLaren, Brian. IV. Title.

BL 240 I7 2015

Manufactured in the U.S.A.   02/24/2015

"If we submit everything to reason our religion will be left with nothing mysterious or supernatural. If we offend the principles of reason our religion will be absurd and ridiculous... There are two equally dangerous extremes: to exclude reason, to admit nothing but reason."

—Blaise Pascal

Contents

Contributors | ix
Foreword by Brian McLaren | xiii
Acknowledgments | xv
Introduction | xvii

Part 1: Philosophy and Theology

1 The Superiority of Theology over Philosophy | 3
 —Jean Grondin

2 Philosophy/Theology/Religion | 12
 —Gary B. Madison

3 Philosophy and Faith | 20
 —Henry Pietersma

4 The Understanding of Being: The Case of St. Anselm | 28
 —Graeme Nicholson

5 Reformers, Philosophers, Kierkegaard, and the *Akedah Yitzakh* | 48
 —Victor A. Shepherd

6 A Phenomenological Analysis of Basic Concepts Shared by Evolutionary Theory and Intelligent Design | 61
 —Jeff Mitscherling

7 Faith in Reason and Faithful Reasoning: Polanyi's Fiduciary Program as Common Ground between Philosophy and Theology | 75
 —Martin X. Moleski, SJ

8 Religion and Philosophy: Same Content, Different Form—What Does Hegel Mean? | 88
 —Jay Lampert

9 "Truth Is Subjectivity": The Religious and the Secular within the Bounds of Kierkegaard and Kant | 105
   —Brayton Polka

10 We Have Never Been Secular: The Politics of Reading Scripture and Practicing Theology | 117
   —Mark Alan Bowald

11 Why Spinozists and Kierkegaardians Should Love Each Other | 135
   —Michael Strawser

Part 2: Science and Theology

12 Thinking of Everything: Scientific and Theological Challenges of the Multiverse | 151
   —Robert B. Mann

13 Galileo's Hermeneutical Model: The Reconciliation of Scripture and Science | 174
   —Jennifer Hart Weed

14 Philosophical Hermeneutics and the Natural Sciences: A Conflict in Progress | 184
   —Jason C. Robinson

15 Muhammad Iqbal: A Reformist Islamic Philosophy of Science | 205
   —H. Chad Hillier

Contributors

Mark Alan Bowald is Associate Professor and Chair in the department of Religion and Theology at Redeemer University College. He is the General Editor for the interdisciplinary journal *Christian Scholar's Review*. His research focuses on philosophical and theological hermeneutics and on religion and popular culture, especially religion and film.

Jean Grondin is Professor of Philosophy at the Université de Montréal. His books, which have been translated into fifteen languages, include *Introduction to Metaphysics*, *La philosophie de la religion*, *Hans-Georg Gadamer: A Biography*, and *Introduction to Philosophical Hermeneutics*. His work has earned him numerous awards, among them the Killam Prize, the Molson Prize, and the Konrad-Adenauer Award.

H. Chad Hillier is Lecturer in the Department of Society, Culture, and Environment at Wilfrid Laurier University. He specializes in global cultures, religions, and political philosophy and has recently edited *Muhammad Iqbal: Essays on the Reconstruction of Modern Muslim Thought*.

Jay Lampert, Professor of Philosophy at the University of Guelph and Associate Professor of Philosophy at Duquesne University. His books include *Synthesis and Backward Reference in Husserl's Logical Investigations*, *Deleuze and Guattari's Philosophy of History*, and *Simultaneity and Delay*. His current book project concerns the conception of the future presupposed in open-ended decision-making. He has written on such philosophers as Hegel, Husserl, Gadamer, Derrida, Deleuze, and Marion.

Gary B. Madison is Professor Emeritus of Philosophy at McMaster University. He studied under Paul Ricoeur and was a close friend of Hans-Georg Gadamer, with whom he worked to promote the cause of philosophical hermeneutics in North America. His writings, now housed in the William A. Blakley Library at the University of Dallas, include *On Suffering:*

Philosophical Reflections on What It Means to Be Human, *Understanding: A Phenomenological-Pragmatic Analysis*, *The Hermeneutics of Postmodernity: Figures and Themes*, and *The Politics of Postmodernity: Essays in Applied Hermeneutics*, as well as many articles, reference works, and edited collections.

Robert B. Mann is Professor of Physics and Applied Mathematics at the University of Waterloo, has been a visiting professor at Harvard, Cambridge, the Kavli Institute for Theoretical Physics, MacQuarrie University, the Université de François Robillard at Tours, and the University of Queensland. Author of over 350 papers on black holes, cosmology, and particle and quantum physics, he is the recipient of a Fulbright Fellowship, Teaching Excellence awards from the Ontario Undergraduate Student Alliance and the University of Waterloo, and Outstanding Referee Awards. He is a past President of the Canadian Association of Physicists and served on the Advisory Board of the John Templeton Foundation.

Jeff Mitscherling is Professor of Philosophy at the University of Guelph. He has also taught at the University of Saskatchewan, the University of Western Ontario, McGill University, the Jagiellonian University, and the International Academy of Philosophy. He is the author of *Roman Ingarden's Ontology and Aesthetics*, *The Author's Intention* (with Tanya DiTommaso and Aref Nayed), *The Image of a Second Sun: Plato on Poetry, Rhetoric, and the Technē of Mimēsis*, and *Aesthetic Genesis: The Origin of Consciousness in the Intentional Being of Nature*, as well as numerous articles.

Martin X. Moleski, SJ is Professor of Religious Studies and Theology at Canisius College, Buffalo. He is the author of *Personal Catholicism: The Theological Epistemologies of John Henry Newman and Michael Polanyi* and co-author, with William Scott, of *Michael Polanyi: Scientist and Philosopher*.

Graeme Nicholson is Professor Emeritus of Philosophy at the University of Toronto. He is the author of *Seeing and Reading*, *Illustrations of Being*, and (more recently) *Justifying Our Existence: An Essay in Applied Phenomenology* and *Plato's Phaedrus: The Philosophy of Love*. He has also produced many other publications in ontology, hermeneutics, and anarchism, and is currently completing a study of Heidegger's *On the Essence of Truth*.

Henry Pietersma is Professor Emeritus of Philosophy at the University of Toronto. His publications include *Phenomenological Epistemology* and numerous articles on Brentano, Husserl, Heidegger, Marcel, and Merleau-Ponty.

Brayton Polka is Professor Emeritus of Humanities and of Social and Political Thought at York University, Toronto. He is the author of several books and numerous smaller studies on hermeneutics, showing that interpretation is the covenantal relationship *par excellence*. In addition to general studies applying his hermeneutical theory to the relationship between religion and philosophy, he has authored more specialized, interpretive studies of Freud, Spinoza (in two volumes), and Shakespeare. His most recent book is *Rethinking Philosophy in Light of the Bible: From Kant to Schopenhauer*.

Victor A. Shepherd is Professor of Systematic and Historical Theology at Tyndale University College and Seminary and Adjunct Professor of Theology at the University of Toronto, has also taught at Memorial University of Newfoundland and McMaster University. His publications include *Mercy Immense and Free: Essays on Wesley and Wesleyan Theology*, *A Ministry Dearer than Life: The Pastoral Legacy of John Calvin*, *Interpreting Martin Luther*, and *The Nature and Function of Faith in the Theology of John Calvin*. His forthcoming book is *The Committed Self: An Introduction to Existentialism for Christians*.

Michael Strawser is Chair of the Department of Philosophy and Associate Professor of Philosophy at the University of Central Florida. He has published *Both/And: Reading Kierkegaard from Irony to Edification* and *Asking Good Questions: Case Studies in Ethics and Critical Thinking* (with Nancy Stanlick), and is currently working on a book titled *Kierkegaard and the Philosophy of Love*. Dr. Strawser is Senior Editor of the online journal *Florida Philosophical Review*.

Jennifer Hart Weed is Associate Professor of Philosophy at the University of New Brunswick. She has published "Aquinas on the Forced Conversion of Jews: Belief, Will and Toleration" as well as many other articles on the thought of St. Thomas Aquinas. Her research interests include medieval metaphysics, philosophy of science, and the relation between philosophy and theology.

Foreword

For the last several years I've been increasingly involved in the seemingly intractable conflict in Israel–Palestine. Many see the interests of the two groups to be irreconcilable. One side will win and the other will lose; the only question is which will be which.

But others of us see it differently. We don't believe Israelis can win if Palestinians lose, nor can Palestinians win if Israelis lose. We agree with the Israeli women who read an official Israeli sign forbidding Israelis to venture into "Area A" of Palestinian territory. They covered the official sign with one refusing apartheid and encouraging mutual hospitality: "Refuse to be enemies!" it said.

One could make the case that theology, and especially Christian theology, has been similarly embattled over the last five hundred years or so. Its opponent has been science. With Copernicus and Galileo, church authorities entered into a contest with astronomy. With Martin Luther and Henry VIII, authorities faced the challenge of political independence and autonomy, defending the divine right of kings and popes against the upstart claims of parliaments, congresses, and constitutions. With Darwin, the conflict was over evolution, and later conflicts centered on feminism, colonialism, segregation, poverty, the environment, and LGBT equality. To be religious, it seems, has meant to be in relentless conflict.

Less strident perhaps, but no less real—and, one could argue, even more longstanding—the conflict between philosophy and theology has simmered, usually on the back burner. From Tertullian's "What hath Athens to do with Jerusalem?" in the early third century to the challenges of the New Atheists today, the conflict has at times boiled over. Sometimes philosophers have been on the offense, seeking to attack indefensible positions and purge unreasonable claims. At other times, theologians have launched the attack through inquisitions and restrictions on free speech in institutions over which they held sway.

The question today: can theologians, philosophers, and scientists refuse to be enemies? Can we dare to believe that there is a common good to which the contributions of each are needed, and from which all can derive benefit?

I have skin in this game. I am a committed Christian, a former pastor, and a writer on the intersection of theology and contemporary life. I am also a lover of science, a nerd who watches TV science and nature programs "religiously," whose interests span from cosmology to astrophysics to evolutionary biology to herpetology to ornithology to paleontology to neurobiology to ecology.

Not only that, but I've always loved philosophy. As a boy in middle school, I started writing (without really knowing it) philosophical dialogues. As an undergraduate, I devoured Sartre and Camus; then I did graduate work on Kierkegaard and Marcel. I continue to read philosophy today: in recent years, Jacques Derrida, Jack Caputo, Michael Polanyi, and Richard Kearney.

That's why I was so pleased to read this book and see leaders from all three communities—theologians, scientists, and philosophers—pull a stool up to the bar at the neighborhood pub, so to speak, and talk as friends about how we're going to get along in the future.

I imagine there will always be fighters who square off from their opposing corners to do battle. Some of them will criticize any who dare to "fraternize with the enemy." To them difference means danger, and there is no reconciliation, only victory and defeat. But thank God (or evolution, or human wisdom, or all of the above), there will also be others of us who believe that the *logos* or inherent logic of the universe works in the direction of reconciliation, understanding, and peace rather than polemics. For us, a book like this represents a win-win-win.

We will find ourselves grateful not only to those who wrote these offerings for mutual understanding, but also for all who read them, ponder them, and spread their good influence.

Brian McLaren

Acknowledgments

We are deeply indebted to everyone who contributed to the conferences we always hoped would one day evolve into a book. Besides those already named in the text, there are others we would like to thank as well: Darryl Murphy, a mutual friend, good guy, and outstanding conference supporter; the many faculty and friends who encouraged us along the way; Theo Plantinga, who pushed us to take the next step; Debbie Sawczak for her invaluable editorial work, and Victor Shepherd for his generous support throughout. A big thanks to Brian McLaren for taking the time out of his schedule to read and then introduce our book. We regret that we were unable to include every conference presentation in the book. There are many reasons for this, most of which have nothing to do with the quality of the presentations. We would like to emphasize our indebtedness to every presenter and to conference attendees for their interest, feedback, and enthusiasm. And with an appreciation that we cannot convey adequately with words, we want to thank our wives and families for all their unconditional support and encouragement.

Introduction

If the unexamined life is not worth living, as Socrates so famously proclaimed, then perhaps the unexamined conversation is not worth pursuing. In the spirit of sincere and conscientious dialogue, it is with great pleasure that we offer this book. In it you will find a selection of presentations from an annual conference held over four consecutive years at McMaster University and the University of Guelph, as well as five other papers delivered elsewhere (those by Hillier, Robinson, Bowald, Strawser, and Polka) that contributed important ideas to the book. What makes the collection unique is that it represents the extensive expertise and experience of accomplished thinkers from three different disciplines—philosophy, theology, and science—that on the surface seem completely at odds with one another. Our hope is that readers will participate in the challenges presented in this text by reading about some of the most powerful current debates and problems in the evolving relationships between philosophy, theology, and science. To some scholars the prospect of dialogue among these disciplines looks bleak and unattainable due to irreconcilable differences; to others the future looks bright, but fraught with conceptual and pragmatic issues that we must address if there is to be progress. Are these disciplines destined for mutual collaboration, healthy convergence, or exclusionary conquest?

As conference organizers and editors we saw the importance of such conversation several years ago. Standing in the hallways of the University of Guelph we talked about how odd it was that philosophy and theology seemed unrelated today, and that so few seemed to be having conversations that sought to connect these ancient disciplines. We were both finishing our Masters degrees in philosophy at the time and wondered about the possibility of a conference whose primary purpose would be to gather as many distinct voices as possible around the same table. Our conviction was simple: someone had to take the initiative to create an opportunity for dialogue. Naiveté and enthusiasm guided us through the initial stages of planning the conference; we had no idea what it might actually look like, or whom we would invite. We also had no idea that the series of four conferences that eventually materialized would help to radically reshape many of our own beliefs and assumptions about the world, the divine, and the God hypothesis.

Initially our sense of adventure allowed us to envision only one conference, grounded in completely open and unfettered conversation. We assumed the dialogue would be difficult. Could we expect these experts to have much to say to each other? Would they be anything more than passing ships in the night, talking past one another? The intimidation factor was significant, too: many of those we invited to speak were either distant inspirations to us—scholars with impressive credentials whose books occupied privileged spaces on our bookshelves—or personal mentors and supervisors in our own degree programs.

One year later we had our first open, public, and free event at McMaster Divinity College. We called it "Irreconcilable Differences?" and included a longish subtitle, "Fostering Dialogue between Philosophy and Theology"; in subsequent years we added "Science," realizing that these three fields addressed related questions and were therefore natural dialogue partners. After that first event the venue switched to the University of Guelph. We'd like to note here that both McMaster Divinity College and the University of Guelph were generous in funding these events. Given the ongoing budget dilemma faced by so many departments and institutions, this willingness to help came as both a great encouragement and a delightful surprise.

The administrative and procedural tasks involved in finding a place for philosophers, theologians, and scientists to feel comfortable seemed initially daunting. Looking back, however, it is clear that what we took to be a challenging format, the combining of different worlds so to speak, was actually quite natural: these were not entirely distinct and separate worlds, but complementary and supporting disciplines. In fact, the proverbial fit needed no forcing on our part, only the space for an open forum. This kind of space is hard to find. We believe that in the spirit of complementarity academic institutions should give practical encouragement to open-structured, free dialogue at all levels. It's time to do a little more interdisciplinary listening.

To be frank, in retrospect, we got lucky. These highly accomplished, internationally respected and well-known scholars took a chance on us relative newbies in the academic community. They came prepared for open, vulnerable conversation, prepared not to exclude the other but to speak and listen. Theology, philosophy, and science turned out not to be the antagonistic voices we had assumed them to be. All three disciplines have grown from the same basic desire to understand, to ask (and try to answer) big questions—a desire we believe to be evident throughout this book. Each contributor offers insight into the kinds of struggles that have engaged them in pursuing their own desire to know. As editors we found this level of existential honesty inviting and refreshing.

In many respects we are encouraged by these papers, for we began organizing the conferences after reflecting on our own experiences in theological and philosophical forums, in departments, schools, and other venues. What is science? What is philosophy? What is theology? Is one superior to the rest? What do these fields, ways of thinking, areas of investigation offer humanity? As odd as it may sound, the conferences and the compilation of this volume have had therapeutic value for us, providing an outlet for our own questions as well as those of others.

We had two main goals behind the creation of the conference and this text. First, we wanted to generate dialogue where we felt it was lacking. Second, we wanted the discussion to be as open and unencumbered as possible, which meant giving invited speakers no instruction other than to offer, in language as accessible as they could, their own insights into the ongoing conversation (or lack thereof) among philosophers, theologians, and scientists. At first some of our presenters found this lack of prescription odd. It was interesting to hear their feedback as we gave them room to breathe creatively and academically with our broadly planned forum. We believe that the loose structure lent a pronounced strength to the conferences and this text; there was no forced conformity, no pigeonholing, no status quo to maintain. One has only to take a quick glance at the table of contents to realize that what we have here is a goldmine of eclectic reflection, varied in content, tone, and scope. Had we simply assigned a topic or question, the job of participants might have been easier—and the task of publicizing the conference and gathering an audience would likely have been simplified. However, our strategy yielded very interesting results that we could not have obtained otherwise.

After each of the conferences ended, we had the rare privilege of witnessing how the different presenters interacted companionably over dinner. It's important for our readers to know that the public face of sincere dialogue and exchange continued on in more intimate settings. As different as these scholars were in training, research interest, and personal conviction and belief, their conversations continued long into the night. Theologians, philosophers, and scientists have more in common and far more to discuss together than most of us realize.

Some of the papers in this collection will come across as academic, while others are very conversational. We wrestled with what to do with such diverse presentation styles, but ultimately we chose to let the papers stand and the chips to fall where they may, believing that the imposition of major structural revisions would compromise the spirit of the conferences. The only requirement we made of our speakers was that they guard against using too much jargon or specialized terminology so as to make the conversation inclusive, but it is a challenge for authors to convey ideas without heavy reliance on the cognitive shortcuts afforded by the esoteric vocabulary of their respective fields. Nevertheless, we are convinced that genuine dialogue requires a willingness to hear and be heard—and that means not condescending, but building a common language where there might otherwise be none. We trust our decisions will offer readers an experience that is interesting, engaging, and accessible.

The first three contributions in the first section, "Philosophy and Theology," are uniquely personable and inviting: Grondin, Madison, and Pietersma speak to readers as if they are in the same room with them, with little to no academic jargon to get in the way of the conversation. Their contributions come across in the written medium very much like they did when we first heard them at the conference. What should strike readers even more is that these papers are grounded in the unique experiences, convictions, and concerns that the authors have gathered over many years of reflection and dialogue with others who have also invested a great deal of their lives in pursuing similar questions.

What is the primary task of theology today? Is it to confront the spread of religious fundamentalism and the idolization of science? Is it to find clarity through philosophical conceptions and vocabulary? Is it to establish itself as separate from philosophy and other forms of human understanding? Is theology superior to philosophy, or vice versa? What is the role of hermeneutics (interpretation theory) in theology? Or even more foundational, What is hermeneutics today?

One of the lessons to be learned from Grondin, Madison, and Pietersma is that we must remain open to new questions. This is perhaps the main argument of modern (certainly Gadamerian) hermeneutics. That is, to really learn about the new, the unknown, we must be vulnerable and open to "the other" through the sincere and sometimes dangerous act of asking questions. However one decides to answer certain questions, the ability to continue interrogating and learning about that which may confront and destabilize our assumptions remains paramount.

The papers in the rest of the first section are slightly more traditional in form and presentation than the first three. Like the others, these authors offer us insight into problems and questions with which they have long struggled. Nicholson, Moleski, Shepherd, Mitscherling, Lampert, Polka, Bowald, and Strawser invite us to a new conception of the nature and roles of philosophy and theology, and of the relationship between them. Perhaps we should understand them through an examination of the structure of human understanding itself, or think of them in terms of the kinds of things they may and may not be able to do. Either way they have a practical, everyday edge.

These papers continue to challenge our interpretive assumptions, that is, our hermeneutical beliefs. How might we have a theological or philosophical hermeneutics? May we apply a philosophical way of interpreting the world, self, and God to theology, or vice versa? Which might have more promise? Such questions invite us to rethink our most cherished beliefs about the possibilities of understanding and about "being" human. To help guide the investigation you will hear from many different voices including, but not limited to, Anselm, Heidegger, Polanyi, Kierkegaard, and Hegel.

Readers should take care to notice how seamlessly these authors, relying on thinkers from almost every time period, are able to weave together complex ideas. As junior scholars ourselves, struggling to develop competencies that these contributors have mastered, we greatly appreciate those capable of offering insight into Hegel's thinking one minute, and then Kant, Heidegger, or Anselm the next. Moreover, we are continually inspired by the uniqueness of each author's approach to ancient questions.

Mitscherling argues for a novel perspective on the ongoing debate between evolutionary theory and intelligent design. By looking at the matter through the perspective of a realist phenomenology, he produces new insights into how we might better conceive of the issues. Too often proposed dialogue on this matter seems to end abruptly or disintegrate into more deeply entrenched positions instead of producing enlightenment. Perhaps through the lens of a realist phenomenology we might be able to rethink some of our basic assumptions and begin to have more healthy and productive conversations.

In the second section, "Science and Theology," readers are asked to rethink the dynamic that exists between theology and science. How should we conceive of these two forms of human thought and practice? The historical portrait of science and theology discloses a relationship not nearly as antagonistic as many have believed, and yet, especially today, the tension between theology and science—or perhaps more accurately religion and science?—is palpable.

Mann challenges traditional theological perspectives through an examination of major themes in the theory of the multiverse. He proposes that some of the challenges confronting theology in this theory—such as the idea that our own universe is but a small part of a much larger structure—may ultimately mean that theology and science are not reconcilable. There may be deep antagonisms that may never be resolved.

Weed closely examines Galileo's method of interpretation with the ultimate goal of discerning whether his approach might offer insight into the current debates between theology and science. Galileo is easily one of the most famous examples used to show the potential for conflict between science and theology. But was the conflict really between science and theology? Are the two incompatible for Galileo? Are theology and science able to support or supplement one another, or must we approach them differently? Is human reason a substitute for faith?

Robinson encourages dialogue between philosophical hermeneutics and the natural sciences. He does this by laying out some of the key themes of progress for both. To help define what each means by progress, Robinson challenges the traditional notion of objectivity as necessarily superior to subjectivity. Agreeing with Heidegger and Gadamer, he argues that we must find the right place for scientific and technological activities such that we do not surrender our natural mode of understanding for artificial and inhibiting forms of investigation such as foundational-objectivity.

In his paper on the Indian-Muslim thinker Muhammad Iqbal, Hillier outlines the influential reformist's interrogation of scientific naturalism/materialism, an ideological system that Iqbal finds inconsistent with religion. In his response to the perceived epistemological crisis occurring within Islam at the time, Iqbal assesses the challenge posed by modernity, believing that any resolution to the crisis would require an authentic assimilation of Western knowledge to the Qur'anic worldview. Hillier shows how Iqbal draws upon various systems of natural philosophy (e.g., Bergsonian-Whiteheadian) and psychology (e.g., Gestalt) to articulate an understanding of science that takes a more holistic and genuine account of human experience. In doing so, Iqbal adds an Islamic voice to the critics of philosophical and scientific naturalism at the beginning of the twentieth century.

Aquinas, through his interpretation of Aristotle, led us to believe that metaphysics and physics were not necessarily so separate and distinct. Intuitively that sounds about right. Why can they not speak to each other? Can't we learn from the other—and from the other discipline? Listening to others presupposes trust, the willingness to imagine the possibility of common ground, and the courage to let go of the illusions of objectivity and certainty to which many traditional thinkers have clung. We believe *Irreconcilable Differences?* is a testament to such trust, willingness, and courage. Unanimity isn't necessary when it comes to first principles, but we believe open collaboration is. We are hopeful that others will continue to look for ways to bridge the academic, social, relational, and political gaps in all that they do.

Part 1

Philosophy and Theology

1

The Superiority of Theology over Philosophy

JEAN GRONDIN

The chance to take part in a dialogue between philosophy and theology is an opportunity one cannot miss. I am for the most part a philosopher, but have always had a profound admiration for theology; call it a secret crush. Back in the 70s I had the privilege of studying not only philosophy, but also Greek philology and theology, at the University of Tübingen. If I can brag about something in life, it is that I had outstanding theology teachers: Hans Küng, Walter Kasper, Jürgen Moltmann, Gerhard Ebeling, Eberhard Jüngel, and Herbert Haag. You may think I mean to impress you with those names, but I am myself overwhelmed by the quality of teachers I had. I thoroughly admire them and their discipline, although it is not mine.

It is often said that a dialogue must be conducted between equals. In our society we are thoroughly enamored with the notion that we are all equal—which is all well and good in a democratic society, but is not always true in dialogue, or in life in general. For my part I have learned most from dialogues with teachers and other thinkers who are brighter and more knowledgeable than I am, and there are many of these (a fact of which any reader will be convinced by the end of this paper). If the same holds for life in general, it is because I also prefer to listen to singers who sing better than

I do; and when I am dealing with a plumber, I prefer him or her to be more knowledgeable about certain things than I am.

So it is with my relation to theology, and perhaps the relation of philosophy to theology in general. I always had the feeling I was dealing with a better, superior discipline, as it was already called in the traditional university system with its four faculties: law, medicine, the "inferior faculty" (i.e., philosophy), and the *superior facultas* (theology). Not that I want to trade disciplines, because philosophy is the only discipline I can really practice; but I feel like the long-distance runner who enjoys his grueling sport, but who readily admits that hockey is, for many reasons, a more interesting sport.

All this might sound like an irrational admiration, so I thought I might try to formulate the reasons for it. Hence I will give you, in truly boring philosophical fashion, seven (debatable) reasons why I believe theology is superior to philosophy.

It may be that I have a somewhat idealized view of theology. I am fully aware of that; indeed, I would say that much of the theological work of the last two decades is actually rather disheartening. But one of the reasons for the current state of theology, I would contend, is that theologians have traded some of their best traditions for philosophical fads. A look at the curriculum of a theology faculty nowadays would seem to confirm this. My polite warning to theologians would be: I am not sure that the fashionable theology-is-dead type of discourse is of real interest to anybody, either to theologians themselves or to practitioners of other sciences. I think, on the contrary, that theologians have every reason to be very proud of the much-maligned traditions of their discipline.

Here are my seven reasons for the superiority of theology over philosophy. They go from the more mundane, "sociological" reasons to what I hope are more essential ones. Let us start with the most trivial reasons, while noting that the trivial is also very real.

THEOLOGY INTERESTS MORE PEOPLE THAN PHILOSOPHY.

This may sound trite, but it is nevertheless a fact. To begin with, everybody—and I am speaking here of normal people—has an idea of what theology is about: it deals with matters of faith, God, life after death, ritual, etc. This is not the case with philosophy. To be sure, the word "philosophy" is often used loosely in common parlance—as, for example, when one speaks about the "philosophy" of the coach of this or that hockey team—but people don't really know what *philosophers* do. As most of you can testify, we can't even explain to our own families and children what it is we are doing. And if we show them the books we write, in most cases they cannot read them. This is not true in the same way or to the same extent, at least in my experience, of theology. People know what theological debates are about and can relate to them. You can put almost anybody in a theology conference, and chances are they will understand at least something of what is being said. The same does not hold for philosophy conferences.

Furthermore, everyone has strong views about theological matters. Either they are believers or they aren't, and if they aren't, they nevertheless have strong views on organized religion, faith, and the church. A result of this is that theological issues attract a very wide public—helping to explain, for instance, the success of Dan Brown's bestseller, *The Da Vinci Code*. It is also true that everybody follows the election of a pope, and important news magazines will devote their title issues to figures like Muhammad, Moses, Jesus Christ, the Virgin Mary, or Maria Magdalena. I even remember an issue of *Time* magazine recently devoted to the angels, and one, at the end of 2005, devoted to Saint Joseph, a rather obscure figure of whom we know so little, but who nevertheless sparks interest. For some reason, I cannot imagine an issue of *Time* magazine devoted to Kant, Derrida, or Gadamer. So it is a fact: philosophy might have its intrinsic merits (and I believe it does), but people are generally more interested in theological matters, which also happen to be more accessible.

THEOLOGY IS MORE RELEVANT THAN PHILOSOPHY TO CURRENT WORLD EVENTS.

Religion and theology have often been proclaimed dead, but one need not look very far to discover that current world events are shaped by religious issues and divisions. One immediately thinks, of course, of the rise of fundamentalism in Islam and the Middle East. But this presence of religion can also be felt even in the United States, where the Religious Right plays an important role in electing presidents and naming judges to the Supreme Court. I think theologians are better equipped than philosophers to deal with these matters: they can explain to us why cartoons of Muhammad raise such a ruckus in the Middle East, what it is that the Chinese are destroying in Tibet, why peace is so difficult to reach in Northern Ireland, what divides the Shiites from the Sunnis, and why we encounter, to a certain extent, similar persistent divisions between Protestants, Catholics, and Orthodox believers (as in the former Yugoslavia). One can also think of the impact of liberation theology on political events in Latin America. And who can forget the important role played by the Pope in bringing down communism (the invention, by the way, of a philosopher)? In this, John Paul II outdid the CIA, the U.S. Defense Department, NATO, the Comintern, and all the think tanks and leaders of the world. Small wonder that all the world leaders (rightly humbled) attended his funeral in 2005. It is hard to imagine philosophers playing such an influential role, and when philosophers do act on the public stage, their actions are mostly disastrous. It is pointless to remind everybody here of Heidegger's involvement with Hitler, or of Lukács and Sartre, both defenders of Stalin, to say nothing of Michel Foucault, an admirer of Mao and the Ayatollah Homeini. I will not dwell on this chapter, painful as it is for philosophers (I do not want to rub it in), but I think it is safe to conclude that theology is far more relevant to world events than philosophy is or can ever wish to be. And theologians are taking account of this fact themselves by insisting today on the importance of inter-religious dialogue, one of the liveliest branches of theological research. In doing so they are setting an example for the rest of the world. As for philosophy, it is difficult to imagine a Heideggerian seriously discussing with an analytical philosopher on such a paramount issue as the meaning of the verb "to be."

I might recall here a personal experience where this reality began to dawn upon me. One afternoon in December 1979 I was slowly making my way to a class taught by Hans Küng. When I arrived at the auditorium, I saw thousands of noisy people in attendance, demonstrating with loudspeakers because it had just been learned that the Vatican had withdrawn Küng's *missio canonica*, the permission to teach. For weeks and months to come, the decision filled the headlines in all of Germany and even the rest of the world. The following day, a march was organized through the romantic streets of Tübingen. There were 30,000 marchers, some carrying torches, in a city of 70,000 otherwise rather quiet Swabians. I then realized: my God, theology matters to people! In fact, what happens in theology and in the church can be a world event.

THEOLOGIANS DO NOT ONLY WRITE FOR THEOLOGIANS.

This has, of course, everything to do with my two previous points, but it is still an academic singularity worth mentioning. Theologians have a readership that goes well beyond the scholarly realm of theology departments or "divinity schools," as they are sometimes called. We might delude ourselves into thinking otherwise, but philosophy professor, more often than not, write articles and books for other philosophy professors. In this regard, the German philosopher Odo Marquard once quipped that philosophers are like sock producers who only produce socks for other sock producers (the rest of the world would get its socks elsewhere). How refreshing to see that theologians have a much wider and more interested readership! I remember that when I was studying in Tübingen, the bestsellers of the time were Hans Küng's books, *Existiert Gott?* and *Christsein*. They topped the charts for months and years. And where did these books come from? They were, as I can testify, the revised text of the course lectures Küng had delivered in Tübingen. Yet ordinary people could understand them. I cannot, in my wildest dreams, imagine ordinary people being interested in the standard philosophical issue of whether our words relate to the outside world or not.

THERE IS AN OUTSIDE THEOLOGICAL WORLD FOR THEOLOGIANS.

If theologians do not write only for theologians, it is because there is a world outside academia in which theologians can be active. People who study theology often become something other than mere academics: they become priests, ministers, imams, rabbis, pastoral assistants, community workers, missionaries, counselors, even nuns. There is even a theological hierarchy in the outer world, allowing some theologians to be administrators and managers. In other words, there are other people doing theology and theological work besides career academics, people who can also write books and articles on theological topics and say meaningful things about them. In the field of philosophy, we are mostly stuck with sock producers producing socks for other sock producers. Unlike theologians, we don't have a wealth of practical and pastoral experience to draw on and address. We are happy with the ivory tower, and when we happen to come down from it, our origin shows.

THEOLOGIANS ARE BETTER TRAINED THAN PHILOSOPHERS.

This might be a tad less true today, but I had the feeling, in the course of my studies and teaching, that theologians are better schooled than philosophers. Not only are they more in touch with reality, as I have already argued; they have, in principle, a more solid upbringing than philosophers: it is obvious that serious theologians must know something of the ancient languages vital to their area of study (Greek, Latin, Hebrew, Arabic, etc.).

Most of their sacred texts are written in those languages, so a certain familiarity with them is presupposed—once again, I insist, *in principle*. Now, one could argue that this also holds for the honest philosopher, but I would say it is more obvious in the case of theologians, since philosophers today can pursue a decent career while remaining unilingual (the main language being English, the new *lingua franca*). The *Bildung*-asymmetry between philosophy and theology also shows in the fact that most theologians receive some training in philosophy (John Paul II urged Catholic theologians to do so in his encyclical *Fides et ratio*). It would be an understatement to say that philosophers today do not reciprocate this interest. Indeed, most of them actually despise theology (a disease which is, alas, also found among some theologians).

THEOLOGIANS HAVE AN IMPRESSIVE CANON AND A BLINDING ARRAY OF DOGMAS.

Theologians have all sorts of canonical and religious texts to deal with, but they also have many important specific doctrines. We have something similar in philosophy in the form of a set of enduring classical texts that all philosophers are expected to read, but this is not really comparable. They are very impressive texts, in my mind, but there is no real consensus on which ones are to be regarded as authoritative. The writings of Plato, Aristotle, Descartes, Hume, and Kant would surely fall into the category of texts considered *de rigueur*, but they enjoy no specific authoritative value as sources of truth or dogma, and their relevance is widely contested. One can easily find philosophers who honestly think that Descartes, with his division of mind and body, is responsible for all the ills that befall philosophy and modernity. Others believe Plato is to blame for the tragedy of modern technology. Whereas some will devote their entire lives to the study of Hegel's works, most philosophers in North America believe he is a lunatic. In short, in philosophy we have endless quarrels about the relative merits of our classical texts. And as for contemporary philosophy, it is safe to say that philosophers of different stripes do not read the same texts at all.

Theology has a tantalizing array of texts and pronouncements: sacred texts to start with, such as the Bible, the Torah, or the Qu'ran, but also the texts produced by councils and rabbis over the centuries, dogmatic formulations, papal encyclicals, pastoral letters, and so on—not to mention the texts and lives of the saints and mystics and church fathers, and the sacred texts of religions other than one's own. In addition to all these, theologians also have what we philosophers have: the classic writings of their theologians, such as

Augustine, Aquinas, Luther, Calvin, Schleiermacher, Barth, Bultmann, etc. It is very difficult to imagine a serious theologian completely discarding the gospel of Matthew or, heaven forbid, an imam downplaying the importance of the Qu'ran. Yet the parallel to this goes on all the time in philosophy.

We philosophers don't really have anything that could be construed as equivalent to "doctrine." And quite often, it is difficult to know what philosophers are even talking about. I keep reading articles by philosophers claiming that people have not yet grasped what Kant is talking about when he speaks about causality. The subjects of our discussions are fuzzy, fascinatingly so at times, but always in a way that makes their basic meaning contentious: what is a Platonic Idea, what is Leibniz's Monad, what is Hegel's Spirit, what is Being for Heidegger? It is very difficult to speak here of anything like "doctrine."

Theologians, for their part, have a host of doctrines to deal with, some of them outdated even for them, or perhaps re-interpreted, but still essential: Muhammad is the Prophet of God, there was a Resurrection of Jesus Christ, there are three Persons in the Trinity, the Messiah will come, etc.; challengeable doctrines, certainly, but doctrines nevertheless.

Now, many philosophers, indeed most, would joyously transform their discipline's lack of doctrine into a virtue. How cumbersome, they would sigh, for a free spirit to have to live with "sacred texts" and dogmas. Moreover, theology has the disadvantage (they would say) of having to rest on a "faith" that they can happily do without in philosophy. Indeed, many theologians would nowadays agree with such philosophers, apparently envying the "freedom from dogma" enjoyed by the discipline of philosophy. However, this issue of faith leads me to my seventh and last reason in favor of the superiority of theology over philosophy.

THEOLOGY KNOWS THAT IT RESTS ON FAITH IN SOMETHING THAT LIES BEYOND DISCOURSE.

It is true that theology rests on faith, but the outstanding strength of theology consists in the fact that it has no problem acknowledging that fundamental reliance. Its basic doctrines are indeed to be found in a *credo*, "I believe." Now, I would contend that this is equally true of philosophy, and indeed of all other sciences: they *also* rest on a set of beliefs and convictions, be it only the belief that the words they use can describe reality. Philosophy's weakness is that those beliefs are seldom recognized *as beliefs*; they are taken instead to be matters of fact, resolved issues, mathematical certainties. This is the naïveté of all science, and it is thoroughly overcome in theology's recognition that everything theology is about rests on faith and faith alone. To practitioners of theology I would say here: congratulations! How lucid, how honest, modest, and true!

This has led one of my teachers, Josef Simon (a philosopher), to declare that theology, insofar as it acknowledges resting on faith, is perhaps the most reflective, thought-out, and indeed the most advanced science there is, while the other sciences, including philosophy (but not all philosophy), have forgotten it.[1] With Gianni Vattimo, one could add that theology is the only discipline that knows it rests on hearsay—on what the New Testament calls *fides ex auditu*, "faith by hearing"—while all the other sciences deny such a dependence even though it is equally true of them.[2]

This leads me to my last point (not the eighth, because the number seven has a nice ring in this context). Theology is also a most exemplary discipline in that it posits a higher reality beyond its avowedly feeble doctrines. An honest theology will recognize that God is ineffable and far beyond our discourse.[3] At the same time this reality is the acknowledged purpose of all the stammering discourse of theology: there is a God, a One, a higher Being, whom we do not really comprehend, but who gives meaning to everything we know, do, and say.

In this, theology appears to me to be far more coherent than philosophy. It is more coherent because philosophy *also* posits a higher wisdom, even if it often stubbornly fails to acknowledge it. There is, to be sure, no authoritative definition of philosophy (philosophers are not strong either on that sort of thing), but if its name retains anything of its original meaning, philosophy is the "love of wisdom." Philosophers strive for something that can be called "wisdom" (*sophia*), yet most philosophers seem to be content with merely "striving" and seem to relinquish the notion that there is any wisdom to be attained. Such an attitude might seem better suited to human finitude, but what is the point of seeking wisdom if wisdom does not exist? Philosophy thus risks being a pointless exercise. Again, theology appears to be superior and more coherent in this regard: the discourse of theologians is a *logos theou*, a discourse about God or about some wisdom they necessarily recognize as existing beyond their quest and giving purpose to it. To

---

1. Simon, "Philosophischen Ortsbestimmung," 204–7.
2. Vattimo, "Age of Interpretation," 28.
3. On this point I agree with Gary Madison ("Philosophy/Theology/Religion") when he invokes the testimony of St. Thomas Aquinas, who said: "*Tunc enim solum Deum vere cognoscimus quando ipsum esse credimus supra omne id quo de Deo cogitari ab homine possibile est.*" ("For then only do we know God truly, when we believe him to be above every thing that it is possible for man to think about him.")

conclude, then, my admiring message to theologians would be: keep up the good work—or return to it.

BIBLIOGRAPHY

Madison, Gary. "Philosophy/Theology/Religion." In *Irreconcilable Differences*. Edited by David Peck. Eugene, OR: Pickwick Publications, 2015.

Simon, J. "Zur philosophischen Ortsbestimmung theologischer Wissenschaft von ihrem Gegenstand her." *Tübinger Theologische Quartalschrift* 157 (1977).

Vattimo, G. "The Age of Interpretation." In *Between The Human and The Divine: Philosophical and Theological Hermeneutics*. Edited by A. Wiercinski. Toronto: Hermeneutic Press, 2002.

2

Philosophy/Theology/Religion

Gary B. Madison

We are gathered together here today to discuss the dialogue, or lack thereof, between philosophy and theology. Actually, there has never been any lack of "dialogue" between philosophy and theology, and this for the simple reason that theology itself is nothing other than natural reasoning—i.e., philosophy—applied to the content of religious faith. I am not referring here merely to what goes under the heading of "natural theology," i.e., the attempt to demonstrate or "prove" the existence of God (as the necessary First Cause, Final Cause, etc. of everything that is) by means of natural reason alone. Natural theology is nothing other and nothing more than one of the many branches of philosophy (*metaphysica specialis*). It is, moreover, one of those branches of philosophy which, like metaphysics in general, has no cognitive or scientific value whatsoever; as a good postmodern phenomenologist I have no hesitation in saying that, although it may appear in the eyes of some to be a rather scandalous thing to say. I have no objection to anyone dabbling in natural theology, or metaphysics, so long as they don't delude themselves by thinking that they're engaged in anything other than an interesting, albeit inconsequential, pastime or parlor game for intellectuals. As a philosopher I do not believe that anyone can ever hope to know—*know*, in the proper sense of the term—anything about God, when the word "God" is taken ontotheologically to mean some kind of *ontas on* or *ens realissimum*, some kind of ultimate metaphysical entity lurking behind the "realm of appearances." That is, I do not believe anyone can ever hope to know either that God exists or, *nota bene,* that he doesn't ("Only the fool says in his heart, 'There is no God.'"—Psalm 14:1). I am in this regard in complete agreement with St. Thomas Aquinas, who said: "*Tunc enim solum Deum vere cognoscimus quando ipsum esse credimus supra omne id quo de Deo cogitari ab homine possibile est* / For then only do we know God truly when we believe Him to be above every thing that it is possible for man to think about Him."[1]

So much for natural theology. But what about that other form of theology that Aquinas referred to as *sacra doctrina,* "sacred" theology? This is much more interesting. Sacred theology is not philosophy as such; it is, rather, philosophical or natural reasoning *applied* to the "revealed truths" of religion in an attempt to make religious dogma (e.g., the Incarnation, the Trinity, or the resurrection of the dead) intelligible. Theology in this sense comes under the rubric of what St. Augustine called *fides quaerens intellectum,* faith in search of intellectual explication, or understanding. In sacred theology one does not seek to "prove," in the manner appropriate to science, the existence of what an article of faith is purportedly a faith in; rather, one seeks by means of intelligent discourse and argumentation to show that one's adherence to various "revealed truths" is not nonsensical or irrational, such that one can then say that it makes "good sense" or is "meaningful" to believe what one believes ("*Intellego ut credam*")—and that on the basis of faith alone ("*Credo ut intellegam*").[2] We all have faith commitments of one sort or another, and there is nothing more befitting what it means to be human than to attempt to spell out our fundamental, lived experiences of meaningfulness, of what makes life worth living. We are, after all, beings that are endowed, as no other animal species is, with the *logos.* As Pope John Paul II has said, "the human being is by nature a philosopher."[3]

When theology is viewed in this Augustinian manner—or as what today we would call "systematic theology"—there are no limits to a productive dialogue between philosophy and theology. There is nothing very original or exciting about my saying that, so let me go on to say something more, something that is liable to be a bit more provocative. Let me first of all draw your attention to yet another of the basic characteristics of human being. Human beings are by nature prone to what Sextus Empiricus called "dogmatic rashness"; that is, they inevitably tend to identify, surreptitiously and

---

1. Aquinas, *Summa contra Gentiles,* I, 2, 30.
2. See in this regard Aquinas, *Summa theologiae,* I, 1 ("De sacra Doctrina, quails sit, et ad quae se extendat").
3. John Paul II, *Faith and Reason (Fides et ratio),* 95.

in an underhanded manner, their own subjective beliefs with reality itself. That is not only naïve; it can also be very dangerous. It is an especially great danger when it comes to theology. How so?

If you believe, as I do, that the imperative of compassion, of peace and good will, lies at the heart and soul of all the great world religions, then the "dogmatizing" (absolutizing) of the particular dogmas of any one particular religion is a recipe not for compassion but for *intolerance*. When religion is dogmatized, it ceases to be, as the word implies, a "binding together" (*religare*) and becomes instead a means for setting people at odds with one another. (Think of the early disputes over the nature of the Trinity—an arcane issue if ever there was one—which fractured the unity of Christianity, or the different theological interpretations that Catholics and Lutherans attach to the sacrament of the Eucharist—a matter of no import as far as religious praxis is concerned, but one over which religious believers were nonetheless for a long time prepared to fight to the death).

It goes without saying that dogmatism is an especially great danger for those religions, like Christianity and Islam, which lay claim to *universal* validity. To believe that any particular culturally and historically relative theological doctrine expresses the transcendent truth of religious faith and is, so to speak, literally true (i.e., not just merely one theory among others) is a recipe not for compassion but for mutual insurmountable hostility. It should therefore come as no surprise that, given the dogmatizing proclivities of humans, religion has always been a prime source of human discord and war. Here, then, is a provocative thesis for you: Theology is the enemy of religion. Maybe I should water that down a bit by saying that theology can be—and usually has been—the enemy of religion.

Do not misunderstand. In saying what I just said, I do not in any way mean to endorse any form of antitheological anti-intellectualism, like that which is so pervasive in Russian Orthodoxy. Those of you who have read Tolstoy or Dostoevsky should understand what I'm talking about. These and other Slavophile writers extolled the deep, dark "Russian soul," the humble, ignorant Russian peasant, and, in a paroxysm of ethnocentric Occidentalism (i.e., Orientalism turned upside down), lambasted Western theology for its reliance on reason and intellect. No, I do not subscribe to any such sort of know-nothing mysticism. On the contrary, I would maintain that what we need, what theology needs, is not less reason and less intellect but a better and more sophisticated form of reasoning and thinking. By that I mean a form of reasoning that has managed to surmount the natural tendency of humans to dogmatize, i.e., to universalize their own culturally relative theories about what it means to believe in any particular article of religious faith. This form of reasoning ("reasonableness"), which seeks to overcome the metaphysical opposition between universality and particularity (the one and the many) and which privileges unrestrained communication and the open-ended search for truth, is one that has been defended by hermeneutical philosophy. A theology attuned to the need to foster tolerance and dialogue would find in hermeneutics, the science of interpretation, a ready and willing dialogical partner.

In this connection, one of the great tasks confronting theology today, as I see it, is that of confronting the spread of religious "fundamentalism," a worrisome phenomenon as much in evidence in Christianity as in Islam, as well as in some other religions.[4] Fundamentalists equate religious faith with a particular, literal, and absolutist interpretation of the words of Scripture—which leads them to treat as infidels or *kafirun* all those who do not share their own literalist (and usually extremely naïve) interpretations of holy writ ("born again" Christians think that only they are genuine Christians, and have no compunction about consigning all others to Hell). The trouble with fundamentalism is that, given the way human misunderstanding functions, it has a built-in tendency to degenerate into dogmatic intolerance and fanaticism. And from fanaticism it is a short step to terrorism, the attempt to eradicate the other simply because the other is other, i.e., different—a step that is all too easy for superficial literalists to take. (And make no mistake: any "evangelicalism" hell-bent on converting the other by hook or by crook to one's own particular world view is an attempt to eradicate the other as other. People in disaster-torn Muslim countries visited by over-zealous Christian humanitarian workers know this all too well.) As Voltaire pertinently remarked, religious fanaticism is an "epidemic illness." "Religion," he said, "far from being a beneficial food in such cases, turns into a poison in infected brains." How, he asked—and it is as if he were speaking today—can you talk with a man who is "sure to deserve heaven in cutting your throat?"[5] Christian proselytizers may be less inclined to cut other people's throats than Muslim fanatics, but it is all a matter of degree.

Voltaire, I grant you, was not all that well disposed to (organized) religion in the first place, but he did have a point. Theology and philosophy can and should work together to combat the scourge of fundamentalism by making it clear that religion and science are two quite different modes of human understanding and that, accordingly, religion is not to be confused with science. As regards a topic that is currently hotly debated in some circles, the scientific notion of evolution is indeed a *theory*, in the proper, scientific sense of the term (and is thus not a "fact"), but "creation theory" is

---

4. See, for instance, Armstrong, *Battle for God*.
5. Voltaire, "Fanaticism."

"theory" only in the crackpot sense of the term. It is simply not the case, as asserted by the somewhat more sophisticated and devious advocates of Intelligent Design, that religion is or ever could be an alternative to science. (If these people understood what modern science is, they would never think it was a case of Darwin vs. God.) Religion is not (presumptive, proto-, primitive, pseudo-, quasi-, ersatz, or otherwise) science. Religion is *myth*—again, in the proper, non-pejorative sense of the term, as Karen Armstrong has attempted to make clear in her various writings on religion.[6]

Religious myth is a way (the only way?) of giving expression to certain transcendent truths; it is a way of expressing our awareness of or encounter with the Transcendent. And it does so in the only way possible: by expressing these truths in symbolic guise—in, as St. Dionysius the Areopagite said, a "veiled" manner.[7] As the famous phenomenologist of religion Gerardus Van der Leeuw said, the definition of religion is that it is "the lived experience of the limit which withdraws from our gaze; . . . a revelation which, by its very essence, is and remains hidden."[8] The task of a hermeneutically-informed theology should be to rescue the truths of religious myth from the vulgarizations and, as St. Augustine would call it,[9] the "foolishness" of literalist fundamentalists, heeding the admonition of St. Matthew: "Do not throw pearls to swine" (Matt 16:25).

We live today in what Hans-Georg Gadamer called the "Age of Science," and the task of both philosophy and theology should accordingly be that of not letting our understanding of things be dominated by an idolizing of science—which is unfortunately the case with the fundamentalists (for them, religion is nothing if it cannot claim to be science). Or, as Karl Jaspers has said, "We should seek not to destroy, but to restore the language of myth."[10] The task of theology today should be that of combating the fetish of science with the goal, as Gadamer would say, "of letting myth speak more clearly than before."[11]

In this vein, I think it could be useful to make a distinction between *faith* and *belief* (or *pistis* and *gnosis*[12]). Religious faith is often taken to be a kind of knowledge—or, at least, a particular sort of knowledge-claim, a

---

6. See in particular Armstrong, *History of God*.
7. See Dionysius the Areopagite, *De coelesti hierarchia*, I.
8. Van der Leeuw, *La religion*, 665.
9. See Augustine, *Confessions*, XII, 25.
10. Jaspers, "Myth and Religion," 17.
11. See Gadamer, "Foreword," x.
12. Cf., for instance, Bultmann, *Primitive Christianity*, 202: "[T]he Christian religion is not knowledge (*gnosis*), but faith (*pistis*)."

kind of quasi-theoretical belief that an entity called "God" exists. There is, however, in accordance with what I've said, nothing cognitive or "epistemological" about religious faith. True faith, faith in the proper sense of the term, I would be inclined to say, is an existential, *practical orientation* or disposition, not a theoretical-propositional belief. Religious faith is not a belief *that* God exists (as one might believe in the existence of UFOs), but a deep-seated confidence—trust—*in* or reliance *upon* "God," "Divine Providence," or some such ultimate, all-encompassing reality, call it what you will.

Where does this leave theological dogma in the traditional, "dogmatic" sense of the term, all the various "credos" that have been spelled out in black and white over the centuries? A good question, but one that I cannot go into here, given the time constraints we are under today. So let me simply allude to something that well-known theologian Harvey Cox, of the Harvard Divinity School, has said. Like me, Cox is unhappy with the way Christianity has for so very long been obsessed with finely formulated *doctrine*, with what's supposed to count as orthodox belief (and what, conversely, is damnable heresy). The effect of this, as I suggested a moment ago and as Cox also observes, has been to set the various Christian denominations at insurmountable odds with one another. Since (as hermeneutics has demonstrated—and as St. Augustine fully realized) there is no end to the ways in which one can interpret Scripture (or anything else), literalist absolutism is necessarily a divisive force in human affairs, pitting one sect against another in a never-ending *bellum omina contra omnes*. "What we need now," Cox has said, "is not a new credo but a wholly different way of thinking about what it means to be a Christian." "Creeds," he says, "are meant to divide, to create insiders from outsiders." Cox doesn't recommend that we simply junk all our traditional creeds (theological theories), but he is personally convinced, he says, "that the best thing to do is to sing them." Why is this? Because, as he says, "that reminds us they are more like poetry than prose."[13] As someone who in his youth developed a great appreciation for Gregorian chant and a festive and sacramental ritual designed to celebrate the great Mysteries of faith—the "hidden Mysteries," as St. Dionysius referred to them[14]—I couldn't agree more.

To wrap things up, let me remind you that we are living today in a rapidly globalizing world. In this situation, the overriding task confronting theology, as I see it, is that of bringing all available philosophical and hermeneutical resources to bear on facilitating a global conversation among the world's great religions—so as to avert what could otherwise turn out to

---

13. See Cox's remarks in Franck et al., *What Does It Mean to Be Human?*, 279–80.
14. Dionysius the Areopagite, "Celestial Hierarchy," last line.

be a global and very bloody "clash of civilizations." This would require all the philosophical ingenuity that theology is capable of, for it would necessitate a radical and, in many ways, unprecedented transformation in the religious consciousness (going well beyond ordinary ecumenism). It would require the rejection of one historically tenacious belief of the customary religious mindset: namely, that there can be only *one* true religion or, as some Christians used to say, that "there is no salvation outside the church." There can be no genuine tolerance where this mindset prevails.

In the West, this was a lesson that took the various warring Christian factions a long time to absorb. The Catholic Church, for instance, has only fairly recently (since the Second Vatican Council) capitulated to the forces of the Enlightenment and embraced (at least in theory) the civic and democratic virtue of tolerance. The Muslim world, which is riddled with at least as many disparate factions as Christendom ever was, faces a like challenge. In the case of Islam, which is bedeviled by the literalist absolutism of some very vocal and intolerant Muslim sects (Salafism, Wahhabism, and so on), it is imperative that the old, pre-fourteenth-century notion of *ijtihad*—independent reasoning or interpretation—be revived and everywhere put into practice.

All the great world religions make a claim, in one way or another, to universal validity, and rightly so. Universality, however, should not be equated with uniformity and homogeneity; properly (i.e., hermeneutically) understood, universality (or what, in a related fashion, Muslims call *tawhid*, "making one") is not at all incompatible with difference and diversity. Religious pluralism, the plurality of religious traditions, is a basic and ineradicable *fact* that religious believers in an age of globalization must come to terms with, abandoning in the process all forms of religious imperialism. It calls for a profound change in the self-consciousness that Christians, Muslims, and others have—a change in their sense of identity, in the way the self views itself in its relations with the other. In a globalizing world, no religion can claim to be true to itself—that is, to the imperatives of tolerance, compassion, and peace on earth—that does not undertake this task. More so than ever before, theology has its work cut out for it. As Muslim scholar Abdulaziz Sachedina has remarked in this connection, "By offering the community of believers an interreligious hermeneutic based on the inherently pluralistic nature of the divine revelation, there is hope that we shall learn to understand and respect the other for what he or she is rather than for what [we think] he or she ought to be." The "pressing task," as Sachedina points out, is that of "recognizing religious pluralism as a cornerstone of interhuman relations."[15]

By way of conclusion, let me remind you of something Heidegger once said: There exists between the thinker and the poet a vital communication, even though each inhabits a separate mountaintop. One could perhaps say the same of the philosopher and the religious believer (even when these two personages happen to inhabit the same individual). The noblest calling of a rational, nondogmatic theology is to act as a hermeneut, a go-between, an *interprète* or *mujtahid*, between *homo philosophicus* and *homo religiosus*, bringing the two into productive dialogue with one another and so helping to bridge the cultural divide that separates the two—that separates, as it always has and always will by the nature of things, Athens from Jerusalem.

BIBLIOGRAPHY

Armstrong, Karen. *The Battle for God*. New York: Ballantine, 2000.

———. *A History of God: The 4,000-Year Quest of Judaism, Christianity and Islam*. New York: Knopf, 1993.

Augustine, Saint. *Confessions*. Translated by R. S. Pine-Coffin. London: Penguin, 1961.

Bultmann, Rudolph. *Primitive Christianity in Its Contemporary Setting*. Translated by R. H. Fuller. New York: World, 1956.

Dionysius, the Areopagite, Saint. "The Celestial Hierarchy." In *Pseudo-Dionysius: The Complete Works*. Translated by Paul Rorem. Mahwah, NJ: Paulist, 1988.

Franck, Frederick, et al. *What Does It Mean to Be Human?* New York: St. Martin's Griffin, 2000.

Gadamer, Hans-Georg. "Foreword." In *Introduction to Philosophical Hermeneutics*, by Jean Grondin. Translated by Joel Weinsheimer. New Haven: Yale University Press, 1994.

Jaspers, Karl. "Myth and Religion." In *Myth and Christianity: An Inquiry into the Possibility of Religion Without Myth*, by Karl Jaspers and Rudolph Bultmann. Translated by Norbert Guterman. New York: Farrar, Straus & Giroux, 1958.

John Paul II, Pope. *Faith and Reason (Fides et ratio)*. Montréal: Médiaspaul, 1998.

Leeuw, Gerardus van der. *La religion dans son essence et ses manifestations*. Paris: Payot, 1970.

Sachedina, Abdulaziz. *The Islamic Roots of Democratic Pluralism*. Oxford: Oxford University Press, 2001.

Thomas Aquinas, Saint. *Summa contra Gentiles: Book One: God*. Translated by Anton Charles Pegis. Notre Dame: University of Notre Dame Press, 1991.

———. *Summa theologiae*. Translated by Thomas Gilby. Cambridge: Cambridge University Press, 2006.

Voltaire. "Fanaticism." In *Philosophical Dictionary*. Translated by Theodore Besterman. London: Penguin, 1984.

15. Sachedina, *Islamic Roots*, 40, 49.

3

Philosophy and Faith

Henry Pietersma

The topic is an old one with a long history. It began as an attempt on the part of early Christian scholars to justify their faith to the philosophers of the day. Until very recently it was an essential discipline, under the name of apologetics, in every theological seminary. I shall not try to follow that example in any of its historical forms. I want to speak to you more personally—that is, from my own point of view and mainly as a philosopher, not as a theologian or anything else. I taught philosophy at the University of Toronto for nearly forty years. To be sure, I know some theology and something about other topics of human inquiry, but my perspective today will be mainly philosophical, given that most of my experience is in this discipline.

Now, what is a specifically philosophical perspective? What distinguishes it from theology, for example? Over the years I have asked myself that question several times, but I haven't always come up with the same answer, and still find it difficult to answer. There has always seemed to me to be such a thing as a Christian philosophy, but if so, precisely how is it related to a Christian theology? I wish I could tell you clearly and definitively, but I fear I cannot. Setting aside that problem, however, and assuming for now that we are clear about that distinction, I should perhaps tell you at the outset that although I have written a fair bit about what is commonly called continental (i.e., European) philosophy and taught many courses in that area, I would not call myself a continental philosopher. I am not a Husserlian or a Heideggerian, or an admirer of Derrida. If I were, I could be brief and say that the specifically philosophical perspective is transcendental, although I might want to (and presumably should) further specify that denomination. However, I am not a transcendentalist in philosophy.

If I were, that would make things easy, in a way. I could then simply say that I am of course not a theologian, not primarily because I do not know any theology, but especially because, in traditional transcendentalist terms, a theological stance is not transcendental and therefore not philosophical. Theology, Heidegger put it once, is a positive science, a position that a transcendental philosophy considers to be in need of philosophical critique. From the point of view of transcendental philosophy, such a science is dogmatic, naïve, abstract, one-sided, and positive. Each of these terms is intended as an expression of critical disapproval. A philosopher of the transcendental school will acknowledge the existence of positive sciences, likely including theology, but she will not accept any of them as a viable philosophical position. Her position with respect to them all, again including theology, is critical; that is to say, she is convinced that they need to be examined or evaluated by philosophy.

When I talk here of a theological stance, I am thinking of Christian theologians like Augustine, Aquinas, Luther, Calvin, and Barth. None of them, it is safe to say, adopted anything like a transcendental attitude in their work. I am far less familiar with Jewish or Islamic theologians, but I think that the same could be said about them. They were not transcendentalist (in the broadly Kantian sense) for the simple reason that they based themselves on a divine revelation and were therefore (again in a Kantian sense) dogmatic. I think they all held, in one way or another, the view that God, a being independent and different from us, has "come across" and presented himself to us so that we have knowledge of him. According to a Kantian philosopher, such a claim to revelation must be subjected to a transcendental critique, which is meant to show how it is possible. A philosopher cannot begin, as a theologian does, with the actuality or factuality of a specific revelation. He can appeal to it only if it has previously been demonstrated in a cogent philosophical manner—or, depending on the particular philosophy in play, if it has been interpreted in a philosophically acceptable way. Hegel went so far as to hold that philosophy is the *only* genuine science.

What, then, is philosophy? As a colleague of mine used to say, it is a many-splendored thing. Let me first say something fairly vague. I would be inclined to say that in a certain sense, philosophy is an effort to continue the enterprise of human thinking beyond that of common sense and the natural and social sciences, and to press it as far as our finite human capacities will allow. In ancient Greece almost everything beyond common sense was called philosophy. Nowadays it is a distinct discipline. One can put it this way: philosophy is a matter of articulating and developing, possibly deepening, *all* our opinions or convictions, scientific as well as others. It is generally distinguished from the sciences, or considered a distinct science.

When one distinguishes philosophy emphatically from the social and natural sciences, one is tempted to rank them and hold that philosophy is cognitively superior to science (as Hegel certainly did) or the latter to the former (a very common view today). When I said a moment ago that philosophy has something to do with *all* of our reputed knowledge, I did not mean by that to put philosophy above all of our other convictions and opinions. I do not subscribe to scientism, the view that particularly the natural sciences are in a position to evaluate all our beliefs. And I already indicated that I also dissent from transcendental philosophy, which holds that all other beliefs must be subjected to transcendental critique because they embody theories or opinions that are dogmatic, naïve, abstract, one-sided, or "positive." Without examining in detail what is meant by each of these terms, which are often used interchangeably, suffice it to say that they are supposed to single out a defect inherent in all objective knowledge. This defect attaches to all claims to knowledge of mind-independent entities, including knowledge of God by faith. I already mentioned that the acceptance of a divine revelation is held to be dogmatic. My own characterization of the philosophical enterprise wants to steer clear, however, of any suggestion that philosophy is in a position cognitively superior to forms of religious faith. I do not share the broadly Kantian view that there is anything inferior in a cognition directed upon an entity such as God—even when we acknowledge, as Christians certainly do, the divine initiative in revelation: it is a matter of God's revelation of himself to us, rather than our discovery of him.

For it is precisely my intention to raise the question about the relation between philosophy and non-philosophical convictions or commitments, in particular religious faith. I am going to argue that to develop or articulate such convictions in philosophical vocabulary does not require that we consider ourselves in a position to evaluate or criticize them. The question I want to put before you is this: when becoming a philosopher, do I have to break with all my religious beliefs? Can none of those beliefs become part of my philosophy, when I enter upon a career in philosophy? The answer often given is that we should indeed keep faith and philosophy apart. In philosophy (and wherever one adopts a so-called theoretical stance), it is said, one cannot allow such a conviction to influence one's theoretical or scientific work.

Let me mention as an example something most of us are familiar with. If I become a biblical scholar, I may continue to adopt a Jewish or Christian attitude to the Bible and adhere to the practices of the religion in question, but in my scholarly work, it is said, I cannot continue to accept the Bible as God's word. For me as a scholar, it is simply a collection of ancient texts that I have to decipher in the company of my fellow scholars. I cannot approach them with an interpretation already in hand, one supposedly originating with the Holy Spirit or the church. In the social and natural sciences the same attitude is displayed. Similarly, as a philosopher I may continue my church membership, but in my practice of philosophy (it is suggested) I cannot continue to simply accept the proposition that God exists, or (to put it in a way that is a little closer to life) that he loves us in Jesus Christ and that my sins are forgiven. I put it in these terms because I am a Christian; I am not speaking like a philosopher. If I were a Muslim, of course, I would put it differently, but I would still express my faith in a divine revelation that is basic and decisive in my life. And I would also see myself as a member in a religious community, which in my own case is the Christian church. But we are told that I have then ceased to be a philosopher and become a theologian.

Now if in philosophy I have to set aside my faith in God, an important question immediately arises: can God's existence be demonstrated? Can we come up with an argument showing that it is rational to believe that he does? There are many philosophers who think that God's existence can be demonstrated by rational considerations. The five "proofs" offered by Thomas Aquinas are well-known and widely discussed, but by no means universally accepted. And what they prove, if anything, is rather minimal in terms of theological content, so that faith in a divine revelation must come in as a supplement: for Aquinas, God is more than a First Cause and a Highest Good. So we get the traditional duality of reason and faith. This duality amounts to something like this: a human being is assumed to be endowed with rationality, i.e., the ability to reason from one proposition to another.

But there are also many philosophers who hold the proofs to be insufficient or hold that in fact upon purely rational consideration it is uncertain or improbable that there is a God. In one of his recent books, *The God Delusion*, the scientist-philosopher Richard Dawkins roundly declares that there almost certainly is no God. In terms characteristic of his scientific background he refers to religion as "the God hypothesis." In other words, a religion such as Christianity is considered and evaluated as an explanatory hypothesis of the kind we find in the natural and social sciences. Dawkins' attitude is a characteristic form of scientism, although he himself does not seem to be aware of that. He does not engage in epistemological discussion.

The scientific stance is simply his implicit point of departure; it is like a religious faith for him, whether he admits it or not.

Is an adherent of one or another of the theistic religions who enters upon a career in philosophy obliged to limit herself to what can be concluded by reason or rationality? Does she have to be able to offer a proof of the existence of God or an argument to the effect that the balance of evidence is in favor of the existence of a God? If I remain a Christian, am I as a philosopher limited to reason or argument? Is my religious faith to be kept out of philosophical considerations? Do I have to justify what I believe as a religious person before the tribunal of reason? Or is there, or could there be, for example, a philosophy based on faith? If what I said about Dawkins a moment ago is true, an affirmative answer to these questions would seem to be at hand.

Before we can go further with questions like these, and particularly the last one, we have to ask ourselves what is at issue. Suppose I hold that faith does have a role in philosophy. And suppose I elaborate on the idea of a Christian (or for that matter a Jewish or Muslim) philosophy. I say that I hold that there exists a God, but I do not go much beyond that. In my philosophical practice my views are pretty much in line with those of the philosophers who dominate the major departments of philosophy in North America and do not believe there is a God. I subscribe for the most part, with some misgivings, to their naturalism, determinism, and evolutionism. Yes, I do differ with them on the question of God's existence, but in most philosophical matters I agree with them. I labor on the body-mind problem, the problem of freedom and determinism, and the epistemological questions that are current. What are we to say about this attitude of the Christian in philosophy?

The first thing to note is that it lacks coherence and unity, that it is a conglomeration of heterogeneous elements. I have a belief in God, but at the same time I have all kinds of belief rather hostile to that religious belief. I believe in God, but in the initial sketch I gave of it just now, I took this rather minimally. There is this religious belief, but it stands in isolation from other beliefs. I also have beliefs about the world as a whole, its origin and future, the place of human beings within it, etc. But is there no relation between my belief in God and those other beliefs? How does it fit into the general epistemology and metaphysics that make up my philosophy as a whole? The God we concretely believe in is the creator of heaven and earth, including human beings, whom he created in his own image. He was incarnate in Jesus Christ, forgives sins, and wants to restore the world. In short, Christianity is a life and world view. Therefore, if I hold my religious belief in its fullest extent, it cannot fail to be relevant to philosophical questions on many issues, and when that happens, it will often conflict with non-Christian philosophy. Take, for example, philosophical anthropology, which so frequently has a naturalist tone. In my Christian anthropology, however, the human being has been created in the image of God. This means, among other things, that he or she has been created as a person capable of knowing God and knowing all kinds of other things divinely created. Think of the issues of determinism and free will. If a human being is a person, there cannot be any doubt that he or she is capable of free action. In short, my belief in God in its full sweep is nothing short of a life and world view. It comes with its own metaphysics and epistemology.

My thesis so far developed is that philosophy is, at least partially, based on faith. By faith I understand a form of religious belief in God. It is knowledge, though it is more than that (trust, assurance, confidence, affection). It is knowledge inasmuch as there is a personal being who is independent of us and indeed of the world, and whom we call God, who reveals himself to us. Philosophy is, on the other hand, a theoretical and rational discipline; but this does not mean that it does not have a faith component. Philosophy does not require of us that we give up a deep-rooted commitment such as our religious belief. The non-Christian philosopher, too, has something like a religious belief—that is to say, something that is as basic for that philosopher as belief in God is for the Christian philosopher. Call it a faith in reason or in human autonomy and self-sufficiency.

The important thing to note here is that one does not argue for what is basic. It is called basic, because it is where you start from as opposed to where you arrive at from somewhere else. For a Christian it is the Word of God as it is heard in the Bible, in particular in the gospels about Jesus Christ. That is where Christians start from, even in interpreting the part of the Bible they call the Old Testament. What is crucial here is that the Bible is taken as interpreted. Earlier in this paper I noted a different approach, namely the so-called scholarly approach. According to this, the Bible is a collection of Near Eastern writings whose various contents must be determined by scholars applying the same literary-historical methods used for such texts in general. As we know, the result of such study is a multiplicity of very different interpretations. From a Christian point of view, on the other hand, the Bible is a unity that, as a whole, has a specific message. This unity can of course be formulated in a number of ways—for example, as the history of God's covenant and his activity of redeeming the world from sin through Jesus Christ. While there is plurality and variety in God's historical acts, Christians understand them as acts of the same God throughout, constituting a history that still goes on.

If at a point such as this you ask about the distinction between Christian philosophy and theology, you can appreciate how difficult it is to make that distinction. It is clear that both proceed from faith in the unity of the Bible. That the triune God reveals himself is basic for both the theologian and the philosopher. I do think, however, that we can distinguish them by way of noting their different focus. If we follow in the footsteps of Karl Barth's theology, we would view theology as closely associated with the practices of the church, especially preaching. Theology is principally concerned with whether that preaching is faithful to what is supposed to be its source, namely, the Bible. Barth's main work is called *Church Dogmatics*; to be sure, it includes a great deal of what one might well call philosophy, but the focus of the theological criticism in it is the preaching of God's Word. As I see it, the Christian philosopher's focus is different. Although he or she is also taking what the Bible says seriously, the philosopher is not directly concerned with the purity of preaching. She draws from the Bible but uses it for different ends.

Let me give an example. Philosophy comprises several disciplines, including epistemology, which is a consideration of human knowledge in general. For a long time, an especially urgent question has been whether we know anything at all. This is called the problem of skepticism, but in my discussion I shall not elaborate or discuss it. The problem I want to discuss is that of rationality. Earlier I noted that a Christian philosophy is based on faith in revelation, but that the view of someone like Dawkins is likewise based on a kind of faith. This raises the question whether either position is rational. I admitted that the Christian view is not one for which the philosopher has a proof or evidence. Christian faith takes itself to be based on divine revelation, that is to say that God presents himself and that the initiative for this revelation lies with him rather than with human beings. The question a Christian philosopher will have to address has to do with the rationality of what the Christian faith comprises. A well-known example is the so-called problem of evil, to which the Christian philosopher Alvin Plantinga has devoted a great deal of his work, showing that the idea of a powerful and loving God does not constitute a logical contradiction with the existence of evil as alleged by non-Christian philosophers. What we see here is the confrontation of Christian and non-Christian philosophy in the domain of rational discussion. What I claimed earlier remains valid: the Christian's basic epistemological starting point is faith in God's revelation. But faith is confident of the fact that it is rational and that it can be defended as intellectually acceptable, as Anselm of Canterbury saw it in the Middle Ages and as Plantinga has forcefully argued in recent times.

Theory of knowledge is of course not the only subject matter that concerns the Christian philosopher. Traditionally, philosophy has also comprised metaphysics, ethics, and political philosophy. In all these cases, the Christian philosopher will undertake to show the relevance of her biblical starting point and to present, in discussion with non-Christian philosophers, a rationally respectable theory with respect to these domains of philosophy.

Here I conclude my discussion of faith and philosophy.

4

The Understanding of Being
The Case of St. Anselm

Graeme Nicholson

A philosopher who looks into religious life will often be able to recognize there a fellow philosopher looking back. This is true across the board, I think, but it is particularly true wherever a religion has developed a theology. A religion contains an understanding of the world, which always has some philosophical aspect, but a theology augments this understanding and moves it still more in the direction of philosophy. Whereas a religion contains an understanding of the world, its theology, we may say, undertakes an interpretation of the world. But since the religious understanding is directed not only to the objective world but also to the self and to the God with whom that self lives, the theological interpretation of that understanding will be at one and the same time an interpretation of the world, of the self, and of God. In speaking here as a philosopher, looking at a religion and a theology, my remarks will have the character of a meta-interpretation that brings into focus both a religious understanding and the theological interpretation thereof. The philosopher who looks at a theology with the intent of interpreting it will have some fellow feeling for this philosophical aspect of religion, yet may also discern in the theology some things that seem alien to philosophy as such, and that spring from the religion. The present study is an exercise of philosophical hermeneutics directed towards theological hermeneutics.

One point is crucial to the method of hermeneutics: it is from the theologian that the philosopher takes a picture of religion or an interpretation of religion. Such philosophy does not try to "peer around the corner" with a philosophy of religion of its own that seeks to thematize the religious life in its original forms, i.e., free of theology. This is because philosophy must acknowledge the very tendency in religion to bring forth a theology. It is rude and counter-productive for intellectuals to dismiss the theological elaborations whereby the religion has come to understand itself, for this cuts out a key aspect of the religion itself.

UNDERSTANDING AND INTERPRETATION IN HEIDEGGER

When I speak of "understanding" and "interpretation" here, I am inspired primarily by Heidegger's account of *Verstehen* and *Auslegung* (understanding and interpretation) in *Being and Time*,[1] and I shall pick out a few points from Sections 31, 32, and 33.

First of all, we are dealing here with elements of human *being*, not merely of cognition. According to Heidegger, we are always directed to what is *possible*, striving beyond the present moment. As I reach for a hammer to drive some nails into a wall, this undertaking has its sense because of the projected end: the possible bookshelf on the wall. Putting the hammer to work demonstrates my understanding of it and also of myself as a handyman: I am able to be a handyman. The competence that shows up in this example is a human ontological character, and it brings about a fuller understanding of the environment, e. g., this wall, these nails, these boards, in terms of their possible functions. We "understand" them; we know how to use them.

Now a religion is also a way to *be*, an ability to live in a certain way in the world. It too has the character of an "understanding" of what is significant in the world.

Heidegger says that when you understand yourself and your world, this always develops further into an interpretation (*Auslegung*). Projection of possibilities will become an interpretation when every item in your room and in your world is assigned its explicit function, so that this thing is seen *as* a hammer, and a hammer is taken *as* a nail-driver. The projection was forward-driving towards the possible, and now the interpretation is the

---

1. Heidegger, *Sein und Zeit*.

"*As*-structure" that sprang from it. It is the interpreted world that has meaning, and thus the world and its contents are revealed or disclosed; for the projection-interpretation structure is not a mere power of the self, but an endowment of our *being* as disclosive being-in-the-world. Now the furthest ramifications of interpretation become possible, and the full meaning of a handyman's activity is revealed through the theory and practice of architecture, though its primordial roots were in the very practice of building and renovation.

Likewise, theology is the interpretation that arises out of the understanding that is religion. It expresses the connections among the soul, the sacraments or rites, and the divinities, but it is aware that these explicit connections arose out of a primordial and unarticulated way of being: the ability to be religious.

At this point we need to see that philosophy is, like architecture and theology, a system of interpretation. It does not spring from being a handyman or being religious, but according to Heidegger it does spring from an ability or capacity that is also an understanding. Heidegger postulates that everyone has the ability to *be* (*Seinkönnen*) that is an understanding of how to be. He calls this the "understanding of being" (*Seinsverständnis*). He does not pretend that his theory is self-evident, for one of the goals of his phenomenology is to display how this understanding of being is at work in various phenomena of everyday life—for instance, in construction work, community life, emotional experiences (especially fear and anxiety), the awareness of time, and our projection of our death. It is also deeply intertwined with language and discourse. Philosophy is able to reveal our perpetual understanding of being because it springs from that very understanding of being. It is the *interpretation* of being. Philosophy asks what it means to understand being *as* existence or *as* substance, actuality, essence, identity, and so on.

Just how the antecedent understanding of being is intertwined with being a handyman was treated in one of Heidegger's most famous chapters (Sec. 14–18), but that will not concern me in this paper, and I won't be concerned with architecture. But I do want to look further into religious existence with the following question in mind: What sort of "understanding of being" is involved in being religious? And in particular, I want to apply a philosophical interpretation to theology. Here one kind of interpretation is coming to grips with another kind. Philosophy interprets the religious life through the theological interpretation of religious life. Above all the question of principle is whether religious existence (and its theological elaboration) is disclosive. That is, does it reveal truth?

I must lay stress on the fact that a religion brings an understanding of the *world*. We are at times too inclined to restrict religion to its views about God, separating this "God" from everything else, and this is especially common among philosophers writing about religion. Religion and theology do not concern themselves exclusively with God, or with the stories about divine deeds and interactions—they also have their views of animals and plants, of the earth in relation to the heavens and the celestial bodies, and of the human community with its divisions by sex, by the "ages of man," by nation, by calling, or by rank. Religions contain views about labor and production, wealth and poverty, the body in its states of sickness and health—all these elaborated in a visual setting of forest and field, mountain and sea. We do not assume that every religion incorporates the same understanding of the world, but every religion does communicate some understanding of this world-totality or cosmos, and the God or gods of a religion are set into certain positive relations with this cosmos. The understanding of the world is no doubt different from religion to religion, and each religion is no doubt capable of being interpreted in many different ways, just like a literary tradition. But because the picture is in every case comprehensive, it can be set off against other ways of understanding the world. Just as one religion can be contrasted with another on this score, so a religious world-picture can be set off against a poetic, literary one, for instance, or a scientific, political, or military one, or a pragmatic one—a handyman's picture of the world, or that of a modern businessman.

I have been stressing the comprehensive world-picture offered by a religion, stating that divinities stand within the totality of these relations. Certainly the divinities do belong to the religious understanding of the world, so that one should never separate them from the cosmos. But that would be the effect if one inserted the divine figures at the summit of some other picture or understanding of the world—if, for instance, one located them at the summit of a scientific understanding of the world, operating as a cause within a body of physical theorems. One cannot assume some other world picture, such as the scientific, and then shove in the figure of God at the top, thus separating God from the totality of the religious understanding. We recognize that there are many pictures that undertake to represent the totality of things, but we assign the figure of God to the totality of the *religious* picture. Hermeneutics instructs us in how to elicit a world-picture from one religion or another, or from science, literature, business, and so on.

The understanding of being manifests itself primarily in two forms, as I argued in *Illustrations of Being*.² (a) There is a *linguistic* understanding expressed in the ontological vocabulary, words like "is" and "be" that are far more widespread in all human languages than most scholars suspect.³ The relation of language (terms, statements, and discourse) to our understanding is a major topic there, and in this form of understanding we put terms like "is" and "being" in quotation marks. (b) Far more prominent in *Being and Time* is the connection of our existing to our understanding, our self-projection into the future, which involves an *existential* understanding of being.⁴ What is understood thereby is not merely a word, so we do not use quotation marks. I shall adduce both forms of the understanding of being (*Seinsverständnis*) in the remainder of this paper.

In applying this point to religion I am following the maxim, expressed in *Being and Time*, that all understanding—including both devotional and theological—incorporates from the start an understanding of being; moreover, that this latter includes as a principal part an understanding or sense of *our own being*, or our existence as humans. On the other hand, because it is an understanding of being in general, it includes a sense of world and others and things and God, with some unitary meaning of being (*Sinn von Sein*) that orders all these elements to one another in a continuity. The question of being is central for any discourse concerning God, but whenever we discuss the being or existence of God, it is necessary to consider our *own* being or existence first: we are to investigate how God may be present to us by virtue of our own being, by virtue of our existing.

ANSELM: FIDES QUAERENS INTELLECTUM

These introductory reflections can now be put to work in a particular case. What understanding of being can we find in Anselm of Canterbury, especially in his *Proslogion*? We can look in two places. First, Anselm as theologian gave expression to a pre-theological religious consciousness in the first chapter, "A Rousing of the Mind to the Contemplation of God," so we shall look there for a religious understanding of being. Then, in Chapter 2, the theology as such makes its entrance, and here we shall look for several things: (a) Can we see it as adding interpretation (*Auslegung*) to the antecedent understanding? (b) Is there an interpretation of God here? If so, in what way does it preserve the antecedent understanding of God expressed

---

2. Nicholson, *Illustrations of Being*.
3. Ibid., 7–14, 93–96.
4. Ibid., 94–106.

in Chapter 1, and in what way does it go beyond the latter? (c) Anselm himself expressed their relation in the phrase *fides quaerens intellectum*, "faith seeking understanding." Can that be assimilated to the Heideggerian relation of understanding to interpretation? (Notably we must never confuse Anselm's *intellectus* with Heidegger's *Verstehen*.) (d) And, central for us, is there an interpretation of *being* evident in Chapter 2 and later? If so, in what way is it continuous with the antecedent understanding of being found in Chapter 1, and in what way might it go beyond the latter? The exceptional interest of this topic is connected with the later receptions of Anselm's thought. Anselm is concerned with the existence of God. But just how does he conceive this "existence" or "being"? It has become common since the days of Kant to reproach him and his followers for assuming that "being" is a real predicate. We must ask whether that is the case here. In a related reading, some scholars have reproached Anselm for regarding existence or being as a perfection. But is that actually true of Anselm's discourse?

Anselm was, like many of the great medieval philosophers, an expert logician, and thus it is not surprising that early modern and recent readings of his text have been informed by logic. The commentators have probed again and again into the "ontological argument," searching for evidence of its soundness or unsoundness. We have a penetrating study of these logical aspects, and of the varying readings of the logic, in a short book by Schufreider,[5] which has now been extended into a much more complete study, *Confessions of a Rational Mystic*,[6] whose title betrays its integrated mode of reading Anselm. Here I would draw attention to a general truth: almost none of the great treatises in the history of philosophy can claim to have been demonstrated with the cut-and-dried norms of purely *logical* validity. Elements of experience, scientific information, memory and tradition, psychology, suggestions of language, religious intimations, and other sources have entered into them all from Parmenides to Quine. Anselm certainly invited logical scrutiny, but that does not exclude religious and psychological elements from being premises of the argument; a logical appraisal cannot stand alone. The imputation that being works here as a "real predicate" has certainly pre-interpreted the text in terms of logic, and leads to the erroneous view that logic alone is guiding the reasoning. While I shall acknowledge the strong rational component of Anselm's text, my effort will be to display it first of all within the discourse of religion. This runs against the Kantian way of treating it, and is indebted to Hegel's profound exegesis.

---

5. Schufreider, *Anselm's Argument*. On pp. 41–42, the author summarizes his case against the usual readings about the "real predicate" and "existence as a perfection."

6. Schufreider, *Confessions*.

All the proofs for God's existence were a constant provocation for Hegel's logical thought.[7] They exemplify a unique and profound fusion of logical motifs with spiritual activity. Unlike Kant, Hegel does not want to abandon the arguments but to give them a new interpretation. In their traditional articulation, springing from the intellect (*Verstand*), they were the wooden utterance of something else, something that is essential to the life of spirit and needs another mode of expression. The proofs are just the copies of an original movement of spirit itself whose original home is in the religious life of human beings. Though they acquired an intellectual form, their original content is an activity of spirit that Hegel calls the "elevation of the human spirit to God" or the "self-elevation of the finite spirit to the infinite spirit."[8] For even the spiritual self-elevation is an activity of the *thinking* spirit. The ontological argument was, traditionally, just one of a number of arguments, but both Kant and Hegel brought them together into a systematic outline. Kant showed that there could be only three—the ontological, the cosmological, and the "physico-theological" one, which we now call teleological—but Hegel improved on this by reducing them to two. Since all such arguments aim to show that God has being, you can either take the path from God to being (and that is the ontological argument that infers God's being from an account of what we mean by God) or the path from being to God, which shows from the study of what is—the world—that God must be included within what is.

For Hegel, the proofs represent a truth that must be re-asserted in the post-Kantian situation, where many voices were renewing the call for faith, intuition, immediate knowledge: where we achieve knowledge of God, we are raising ourselves up to him, because knowledge is not a mere relation but a spiritual activity. The ontological argument is the most daring and profound exercise of our cognitive spirit, for it begins with God, the infinite spirit, and passes over to the being of God. Hegel understands this meditation as the profoundest liberation of the spirit, turning away from the world and making its start with God himself.

---

7. Hegel was led to go back again and again to the proofs for the existence of God. He treats them in all four series of lectures in the *Philosophy of Religion*: 1821, 1824, 1827, and 1831. See *Lectures on the Philosophy of Religion*, three volumes, edited by Peter C. Hodgson. The one-volume paperback edition brings the 1827 version of the lectures; the original text appears in *Vorlesungen über die Philosophie der Religion*, ed. Walter Jaeschke. Hegel brings the proofs into his *Encyclopedia*, and they also constitute the subject of the very last book he completed: *Lectures on the Proofs for God's Existence* (*Vorlesungen über die Beweise vom Dasein Gottes*), finished 1831 but based on lectures given in 1829 in connection with his lectures on Logic.

8. Hegel, *Lectures (1827)*, 162–89.

Nevertheless, our Heideggerian approach will allow us to differentiate, more than Hegel did, the contemplative understanding of the being of God (chapter 1 of Anselm's *Proslogion*) from the articulating interpretation of God and his being (chapter 2ff.). In this discourse faith and revelation are fused together with intellect and reason. I am indebted to Hegel for interpreting Anselm's proof and other proofs as the elevation of thought to God, but Hegel does not pause very long over the letter of Anselm's text and its logical articulation. So I'll try to accomplish that while allowing the logic to appear in its fusion with the spiritual activity, and without concealing any logical gaps that may appear in the argument so long as it is regarded only from the viewpoint of intellect or reason. The fitting together or joining of the parts is a fusion that guides the reading and interpreting: chapter 1 is indeed a spiritual exercise, the "elevation of the mind to the contemplation of God," but chapter 2 is an exercise of intellect and reason. The relationship between the two exercises is described first, in the Preface, as *ratio fidei* (the "reason of faith"), and then, in chapter 1, in two phrases: *fides quaerens intellectum* ("faith seeking understanding") and *credo ut intelligam* ("I believe in order that I may understand").

My study of the understanding and interpretation of "being" in Anselm's text does not move to a definite conclusion regarding the validity of Anselm's argument, because it does not devote the needed attention to chapters 3 and 4; nevertheless, an account of how he treats "being" prepares the ground for reckoning with the argument. I review the Preface, chapter 1, and chapter 2 in order; none of the later chapters, in my view, would conflict with this understanding-and-interpretation (*Verstehen-und-Auslegung*) line of reading.

As I stated at the end of the introductory remarks, our understanding of being includes an understanding of our *own* being, and that will appear very clearly in Anselm's chapter 1. Thereafter, the text indicates in many distinct ways how Anselm thinks of being when he is considering the being of God. As philosophy has taught since antiquity, "being" is said in many ways: the title of chapter 2 shows an intimate link of being to *truth*. The body of chapter 2 offers an interpretation of God, introducing a distinction between being and the subject to which being is ascribed. That will pose the question whether greatness is to be ascribed to God or to the being of God. Then, in connection with the so-called "fool," the *insipiens*, we are led to question whether God, and the being of God, can enter into human thought. One crucial thread within being is the principle of identity, and this will be invoked (in two forms) in connection with the analogy of the painter. At the end of chapter 2, Anselm is obliged to introduce for the first time the term *existit* ("exists") instead of *est* ("is"), and we shall see that this takes on a complex relation to reality.

PROSLOGION, PREFACE: DEVOTION AND ITS DISCOURSE: MONASTIC EXISTENCE

Anselm has chosen to exist as a monk, to engage his whole self in the exercises of monastic devotion. Many others keep away from abbeys of that kind and even scoff at them, never entering them, maintaining a hostile distance. The Preface situates the work within such a monastic community, reporting the great interest that the work found there, and focuses mostly on the single *argumentum* that would express the *ratio* of the *fides*. Then chapter 2 will begin with the hope of finding an argument that contributes *intellectum* or *ratio* to that which we believe, *credimus*—that you, God, are, and that you are what we believe you to be. The appropriate title for that which adds *ratio* or *intellectum* to *fides* is *fides quaerens intellectum*.

The monastery is one prominent locale where a life of devotion can be led, and the meditations and exercises undertaken there are one form of spiritual practice. Moreover, where they are given expression in texts, these can be our clue to the devotional life. Written devotionals that also incorporate philosophical reasoning will be valuable for an inquiry like ours that is philosophical in character. The monastery is by no means the only locale in which devotion is practised and expressed, but a study of such monasticism can well ask the question whether such writings exemplify something found also in other situations.

The *Proslogion* is a devout discourse, imbued with anxiety and guilt, yet somehow these are interwoven with questioning, argumentation, philosophy; this relation of philosophy to devotion can, I think, be comprehended as the interpretation (*Auslegung*) added to an antecedent understanding (*Verstehen*). It is a hopeless misunderstanding to think that devotion must have ceased wherever questioning or philosophizing has begun. There is a rigorous kind of thought, indeed, that *depends* on devotion!

These monks, formed into a community, are thereby also elevated to the infinite, seeking God. "Finding God" is just the hope and project of the inquiry. But why do they seek? Why is there questioning in the abbey? Anselm and the community still want to ask whether there is truly a God (*quod vere sit deus*), even though as believers they have already devoted their lives to God. Why is that? What is lacking to Anselm and his fellow monks? There is a representation, a word, "God," circulating in this community and central to it, but Anselm is not content with that; it is not enough. The tip-off here is *vere* ("truly"): something must now confirm itself. And that will be the point at which the transition is accomplished from *Verstehen* to *Auslegung*. So as we ponder the question of their mode of life, i.e., the question why they join the community, we have the further question: While they are there in the midst of the devotional community, why do they continue to seek God? What can be lacking now?

Chapter 1: A Rousing of the Mind to the Contemplation of God

In the Latin text in the standard edition,[9] chapter 1 is divided into six paragraphs, a format repeated in the most common bilingual edition[10] and in all reliable translations. In the first paragraph the monk addresses himself, appealing to himself to turn away from all distracting business and enter into the inner chamber of his mind (*mentis*). He demands of himself that he be receptive to God, and although God cannot be shut out like everything else, even here the monk does not readily find God: he asks his whole heart (*totum cor meum*) to utter forth its urgent inquiry or search: "I seek (*quaero*) your countenance, O Lord." He is still dissatisfied.

In the second paragraph the monk calls out to God—but God is at a great distance or remove. The monk implores God to teach his heart where and how to seek: of itself, the heart lacks direction. Perhaps, he says to God, "you are not present (*hic non es*)"—but where then can one seek you when you are absent? Or perhaps "you are everywhere (*ubique es*)"—why then do I not see you as present (*non video presentem*)? God, distant and removed, dwells in inaccessible light, yet what the monk wants is to approach precisely that light which is inaccessible (*accedam ad lucem inaccessibilem*). The monk is exiled and cast off "far from your face," yet desires to see God's face even though it is too far away. Filled with desire and yearning, the monk begs for direction from God, with some claim of right: "I was made in order to see you, and I have not accomplished what I was made for." In Exodus 33, Moses was on the mountain of the Lord and yearned to see the Lord's face, and the glory of the Lord, even though this was what the Lord had forever forbidden: "You cannot see my face, for man shall not see me and live." And yet the Lord did yield—up to a point: "Behold there is a place by me where you shall stand upon the rock, and while my glory passes by I will put you in a cleft of the rock, and I will cover you with my hand until I have passed by; then I will take away my hand . . . "

9. Anselm, *Opera Omnia*, vol. 1.
10. Charlesworth, *St. Anselm's Proslogion*.

In the third paragraph the monk meditates on the melancholy history of the sin of Adam and its grievous consequences for the human race. It is all expressed in contrasts: "He lost the blessedness for which he was made and found the misery for which he was not made . . . alas the universal lamentation of the children of Adam! He groaned with fullness; we sigh with hunger. He was prosperous; we go begging . . . Why did he deprive us of light and surround us with darkness?" And the relation to God was broken: we fell "from the vision of God into our present blindness."

Next, this macro-historical meditation is brought back home in the fourth paragraph to the monk himself as an individual, his cry of distress springing from the terrible fate of all human beings: "I hoped for gladness and, lo, my sighs come thick and fast."

The fifth paragraph renews the call out to God: "How long, Lord, will you be unmindful of us?" For God has all the treasures in which we are so terribly lacking: enlightenment, power, consolation, riches. "I came to you as one famished; do not let me go without food. Poor, I have come to one who is rich." And after the recitation of need, the monk returns to the theme of his opening, the way to seek God: "Teach me to seek you, and reveal yourself to me as I seek . . . Let me seek you in desiring you, let me desire you in seeking you. Let me find you in loving you, let me love you in finding you."

In the sixth and concluding paragraph the monk reminds himself that he has within him the image of God that may be renewed and reformed. And his final address is: "I do desire to understand your truth a little, the truth that my heart believes and loves. For I do not seek to understand so that I may believe; but I believe so that I may understand. For I believe this also, that 'unless I believe, I shall not understand.'"

To conclude the account of chapter 1, we have discovered the division within the monk: the believing heart and also the inquiring mind. We discover also the solitary monk, who yet prays for all the children of Adam and for his monastic community. As for God, we discover the hiddenness, the remoteness and self-sufficiency of God, and yet also a prayer that he may show himself. We have seen in chapter 1 that man stretches out to God and hopes for some inclination of God, some bending towards the petitioner. This distance is the principal feature of the world-picture of religious faith: the monk's thought moves with desire and yearning into that great separation, with the hope of inducing God to move downwards. The understanding of being is dominated by that separation between the ecstatic movement of the monk upwards and the grandeur and self-possession of God. The human being stands in that relation, and even what we conceive here as the remoteness of God is nevertheless also a relation.

On Truth and Being: What We Seek

First we ask: In the overall structure, what is the relation of chapter 1 to the following chapters? In the "rousing of the mind . . . " every aspect dwelt on the relationship between God and the individual monk, or the monastic community, or the vast history of humankind. God was at all points in these relations. When we now proceed to interpretation (*Auslegung*), this element of relatedness will not be entirely forgotten, but the discourse will be inquiring into God himself, thinking him as he is in himself or, as we shall say, absolutely rather than relatively.

Still the sense of greatness is certainly carried forward from chapter 1. We pick up first the theme of the greatness of God in relation to human (and monastic) self-abasement. The second chapter starts from "what we believe" (*credimus*). It establishes a characterization of God that is owing to the contemplative spirit. *Maius* ("greater") has here a spiritual sense. We know from chapter 1 that God's greatness is his power to save us, to give us everything good that we in our wretchedness lack: to teach us, to make and remake us, while we ourselves lie in hunger, darkness, and loneliness. God is wealthy and compassionate and able to raise us up. This differs from the idealist notion of God that reason has formulated, and that Kant was later to express, for the present meditation expresses the spirit's own care or need while it is seeking what is great. The monk will proceed to the inference of real being or existence, which we assign to the *Auslegung*, and we will come to that in a moment.

Above we asked what might still be lacking to these monks even after they are numbered among the devout. What does the faith lack while it is still seeking? What does it intend to have? What understanding of being (*Seinsverständnis*) characterizes this seeking? Why is it so stretched out? For what? It seeks a true being (*vere esse*). This is a risky venture that might fail. The seeking faith sets out on its path with an anticipated completion in the correspondent action of God, as in words from chapter 1: *Ostende te quaerenti* ("show yourself in my seeking")—that is, the event of the divine self-showing is to occur in the midst of the monk's seeking. He anticipates a confirmation. *Inveniam amando* ("let me find you by loving")—that is, while the loving occurs, there can be the further event, the finding, *in* the loving. He sets out with an intention, anticipating what can fulfill the intention: that would be the being that is true (*vere esse*), that excludes countless falsehoods.

In the words of the monk, we have found in You the foundation for our being—now we have to ask about Yours, questioning both *that* You are and *what* You are. The monk begins his inquiry with the hope that You will be in accord with what we believe, i.e., believe in advance. But the experience of seeking, even while believing, is one of being separated from the truth (You are hidden in inaccessible light). That true being is apprehended by faith in advance, though we are removed from it. Such heavy, doubt-laden awareness is quite lacking to those who will not seek, who will not enter the abbey.

Chapter 2: The Subject: Something Than Which Nothing Greater Can Be Thought

We are concerned with the interpretation of being that is at work in chapter 2. A key condition for this is that there has to be something that *is*; there must be a subject of being. And certainly the author's interest, and our own, is in the subject God. But we now discover a new terminology, for the monk says that "We believe that you are something than which nothing greater can be thought" (*credimus te esse aliquid quo nihil maius cogitari possit*). That is not what is to be demonstrated in chapter 2: it is the starting point for the demonstration. This line expresses the ascent itself: the intention of the spiritual exercise that has preceded and introduced the argument. It brings before our reason and intellect the One to whom we have been directing our spirit. The intellect and reason have already participated in this spiritual exercise; they did not resist it, for there was no reason to do so. Anselm has thrown his whole self into the meditations and exercises.

We may be tempted to call this Anselm's predicate, as if it were something he is predicating of God. But in view of my overall interest, I am recognizing that here he is launching an interpretation, *Auslegung*, and so I'll avoid the logical category "predicate," and call it his characterization of God. We have to regard this characterization as an interpretation of God—an *Auslegung* that makes explicit something inchoately understood in the contemplation. The monk thinks God *as* something than which nothing greater can be thought (*aliquid quo nihil maius cogitari possit*). What relation does that have to the antecedent understanding of God? Someone is divine if he or she or it is marvellous and great by a special measure that puts it beyond everything we normally experience. We used to use the term "supernatural" for this, yet my sense is that this word has become shopworn. I would prefer St. Anselm's phrase. We are now entitled to derive the force and substance of the "something than which nothing greater can be thought" from the contemplations of chapter 1. The greatness follows from what we have experienced as poor, weak, and needy creatures in relation or confrontation with God—the move of *Auslegung* is the step to absolutizing what was first relative. Commentators have been able to show that this formula "*aliquid*

..." can be found in previous authors, especially Augustine[11] and Seneca,[12] and I do not dispute this; however, an immanent explication of the formula that finds it prepared in the preceding contemplation is more satisfactory.

Our Capacity to Think This Subject

The monk's claim here is that while we are able to think many truly great subjects—x, y, z—we are also able to think the subject God, than which no other subject could be greater. God is unique: nothing greater could be thought; and yet we *are* able to think that unique subject, and also think that character by which God is unique. We attribute this power to our thought, knowing of this ability in us. We are able to surpass any x, y, or z presented to thought—such is our vast freedom of thought—and *besides that* we are aware of a still further power of ours: we are able to identify a subject that does *not* permit such a surpassing—something than which nothing greater can be thought. Here our thought encompasses something that sets a limit to thought. But for Anselm this discovery only augments the power of thought. A thought that is able to think (encompass) that which it cannot surpass is manifesting a fuller and greater freedom of thought than a thought that does not encompass such a (limiting) subject. A thought that was conscious of an ability to surpass any subject would be more limited than a thought that was able to surpass many subjects but also to identify that which it could not surpass. Later Anselm will add that God is greater than can be thought (chapter 15)—yet, putting that statement in the *Proslogion*, he says we must think *that*.

The assertion not only invites agreement with this characterization of God; besides that Anselm puts forward a reflection upon the mind, asserting that this subject (God) is in the intellect. The positive fact that the intellect contains (in its own intellectual, representational way) this unsurpassable subject is a further fact in addition to the interpretation of God in terms of unsurpassibility. Here we may put the question: Could someone say, "I cannot think this"? Might it not be too large an item, a mountain too high to be contained in our poor intellect? No; Anselm is confident that we can all think this, including the "fool" he is about to introduce. In what way, then, is this in the intellect? We'll discuss that below with reference to the painter.

---

11. Anselm, *De Libero Arbitrio*, II, ii, Sec 5. In Charlesworth, *St. Anselm's Proslogion*, 55.

12. Anselm, *Naturales quaestiones*, I, Praef. In *Opera Omnia*, 102.

Whose Greatness?

First we pose a preliminary question: what is the subject, actually, of this greatness we are predicating? It would seem at first glance that it is God whose greatness is so unsurpassable. But there are indications that, strictly speaking, the greatness pertains to the *being* of God.

For after the example of the painter (which we shall treat further below), the monk contrasts two states of affairs: one in which something (greater than which nothing can be thought) is present in the mind, but thought not to exist; and one in which we have this something in the mind and also understand that it exists in reality. In his words, "For if it exists solely in the mind even, it can be thought to exist in reality also, which is greater" (*Si enim vel in solo intellectu est, potest cogitari esse et in re, quod maius est*). It is greater to be in both ways (i.e., in the intellect and in reality) than just to be in one way (in the intellect); here the subject of greatness is *being*.

Again, the argument of chapter 3 (which we cannot survey in further detail here) is that some things that are can be thought not to exist, while other things that are cannot be thought not to exist: contingent being versus necessary being. The monk seems to say that only God's being is necessary, so that he is greater than any creature, yet the text has no personal pronouns; it reads, "*quod maius est quam quod non esse cogitari potest*," which can be translated, "to be such that [it] cannot be thought not to be is greater than to be such that [it] can be thought not to be," so that, again, being is the subject of "greater" (*maius*).

One possible way forward with our question might be to say that, in the case of God, there can be no difference between the subject and the being of the subject—to say, in other words, that God *is* his being. This will be the teaching of Thomas Aquinas, and there are some Anselm texts that point in that direction, e.g., *Proslogion*, chapter 12; see also *Monologium*, chapters 4–6. However, I do not think this solution is explicitly stated by Anselm.

The Challenge of the "Fool"

The main argument begins with the recognition that, perhaps, there may be no such subject as we have supposed, a subject greater than which nothing can be thought. For "the fool has said in his heart, 'There is no God.'" (Psalm 14:1) The meditating monk knows that the spiritual community of the brotherhood is not all-embracing, and that there is opposition to it.

However, this meditative argument is not a missionary proclamation made on the street to convert naysayers; rather, it proceeds inside the abbey. This shows that the monk, the spiritual one, interiorizes this "fool": he has an eye for the human world that stays away from the community, and thereby finds the fool or naysayer inside himself. It is for this reason, above all, that the question needs to be answered; only later can there be proclamation. The contemplative is in a position like that of Moses hidden in the cleft of the mountain, eager to see the face of God, or like that of Jesus in the wilderness, tempted by Satan before beginning his mission to the multitude.

This "fool," then, is supposed to understand that God is "something greater than which . . . " while denying that God exists. The thesis the monk is considering here, the fool's thesis, is that God is impossible—not merely that God is not actual. His thesis is that God *cannot* be. The idea that there is a lack of empirical *evidence* for God is a modern, even contemporary, form of argument—expressed in Dawkins' slogan, which has moved onto the city streets: "There's *probably* no God." (Just why the second half of the slogan, "so relax and enjoy your life," is supposed to follow from the first half needs study sometime, but not here.) The atheism Anselm confronts, by contrast, is based on reason.

Anselm's fool considers the possibility that there might be no such thing as this "something greater than which nothing can be thought," for two different reasons that can only involve the relation of the thinking mind to this subject. (A) The thinking might go on forever: so strong and mighty is it that it would never encounter any subject serving to set a limit for it. The unending scope of intellect shows that it suffers from no fault or failure; its infinite extent proves its triumph. (B) The opposite might be true: the mind might be sufficiently weak that, if there were something than which nothing greater could be thought, the mind would be completely unable even to apprehend or entertain that thing, whatever it might be. (Alternatively, our "fool" may wish to assert both A and B—but that would be mendacious indeed.)

When the "fool" says in his heart, "There is no God," he may apprehend this heart of his as his intellect, signifying that he himself exists only intellectually. But if we exist spiritually, we can identify the heart of the fool as his spirit, one hardened into the narrowness of mere intellect. The spiritual employment of intellect invites an infinite stretching, such that the finite intellect is to contain something infinite. The formula or character ("something greater. . . ") enters into the fool's intellect: he understands what he hears and thinks it. That is the condition for an *esse in intellectu*, an existence in intellect. The "fool" is initially able to understand and think, even contemplate, this subject, all the while not yet understanding it to be. So too the painter who hasn't started to execute the work.

The Analogy of the Painter: On Identity

The analogy is that when the "fool" entertains the subject (something greater than which nothing can be thought, *aliquid quo nihil maius cogitari possit*) in his intellect while denying its existence, he is like a painter who has the subject of his painting in his intellect but knows that the picture is not (yet) painted. This intended painting is supposed to *be* in the painter's intellect in the same way that our subject is in the fool's intellect. When the painter completes his execution of the painting, the latter now has, in addition to its existence in intellect (*esse in intellectu*), a real existence, an *esse in re*—which, the monk now adds, is greater. In this analogy, it is evident that the subject of greatness is the *being* of the painting rather than the painting itself: what is greater is for the painting to *be* both *in re* and *in intellectu*. It is not that the executed picture itself is greater; when it is executed, it does not increase in size, from 2 square feet to 6 square feet. We are reminded here of Kant's insistence that 100 real dollars do not contain a penny more than 100 imagined dollars. Moreover, we are not comparing a painting *in intellectu* with some other subject, like a mountain existing *in re*. There would be no grounds to argue that this latter is greater than the picture *in intellectu*, nor even for arguing that the *being* of this mountain was greater than that of the picture *in intellectu*. Central to the argument is that it is one and the same picture that can be either in the intellect alone, or both in the intellect and in reality: it is this "both-and" that lets us call the being of the painting greater when the painting has been executed. And we are not concerned with the case in which the painting ceased to be in the intellect after it achieved existence in reality, a painting both forgotten and unseen. Moreover, it is a necessary condition here that the painting be one and the same, identical, in the intellect and in reality.

What is the meaning of this *esse* qua identity? To find an identity here, we are obliged to say that the artist's conception is not a separate item, thing, or event from the completed work, but one and the same thing, at an elementary stage of its being. This can be analogized, perhaps, to clear cases of identity, in which the fetus of 1960 is declared to be identical with the child of 1965 and the adult of 1990. This analogy is hardly unproblematic, but neither is it outrageous. In making this analogy, we are avoiding a doctrine of *kinds* of being, e.g., "mental" being and "physical" being. If we postulate an identity between the picture *in intellectu* and the picture *in re*, we shall need to find an even higher-level sort of identity, an identity within being itself. That is to say, the being manifested by the picture requires an identity of that subject *in intellectu* and *in re*, but in addition, the very being invoked here is marked by an identity of a higher order, not only of the being of that subject but of the being of all subjects. Being is radically one and the same with itself. But that, surely, must be Anselm's hypothesis, whereby he is able to find the comparison of greatness.

How do these reflections apply to the case under discussion, the being of the subject "than which nothing greater can be thought" that might, hypothetically, be in the intellect alone or both in the intellect and in reality? If our account of the painting example is right, it seems the monk has made his case: it is greater to have being both in the intellect and in reality, provided the subject's identity holds. But in the case of our subject "than which nothing greater can be thought" (*aliquid* . . .) we are seeking to *defend* its being in reality through the comparison. We have no empirical presentation of the subject as we do in the case of the picture. Rather, we are saying that *if* the subject existed in reality and not only in the intellect, its being would be greater. So we argue by adopting the hypothesis that this "something than which nothing greater can be thought" (*aliquid* . . .) does *not* exist in reality, and then we make a supposition: "Suppose that there were another subject of this very same nature, *aliquid 2*, that *did* exist in reality. It would be equivalent in all respects to our original subject, but have in addition a being in reality." We conclude that, by virtue of being in reality, this subject would be greater than our original one. But in that case, the original subject could not have satisfied the description we started from: something than which nothing greater could be thought. By this reasoning, then, we conclude that our original subject does exist, not only in the intellect but in reality as well.

But our theme in these studies is the existence of God, and we may find some difficulty in discerning the relevant identity in this case. If we are concerned with finding out whether God exists, and make use of Anselm's argument to that end, do we have any assurance that the original interpretation of the subject was true? That is, is it true to say that God *is* this "something than which nothing greater can be thought"? Someone might doubt this. And yet it was, after all, postulated in the first place by the contemplation, so who would deny with any confidence that such greatness is in the idea of God? This reply does require assigning greatness to God rather than just to the being of God.

Existence and Reality

The argument contrasts existence in the intellect with existence in reality—*in re*, as the Latin puts it more simply in the concluding sentence of chapter 2. It is only in this sentence as well that the monk uses the word "exists," *existit*; hitherto he has used forms of *esse* in that context. The switch to *existit* is because of a further complexity that he has noted and that we too must note. What is the reader to understand by "being *in re*," or "existing in reality"? If we understand this phrase at all, it is because it stands in contrast to "being *in intellectu*" (and we have already seen why it is greater than the latter taken by itself). Were it not for this contrast, we might suppose that there is no more contained in "being in reality" than in just plain "being." What does reality add to being? Both Latin and English use this as an emphatic term. But both languages exhibit a further puzzle at just this point. Anselm has also earlier used the word *res* (of which *re* is a form) in quite another way, in accordance with standard Latin usage, to refer neutrally to any thing, any object or subject, at all. It can stand either for a subject that is in the intellect alone or for one that is comprehended as truly being, even beyond the intellect: "*Aliud enim est rem esse in intellectu, aliud intelligere rem esse.* (For it is one thing for an object to exist in the mind, and another thing to understand that an object actually exists.)" We note that here the translator introduced the term "actually" to render the same thought that in the concluding sentence is rendered "in reality." This neutral term *res*, "thing/object/subject," is not the same as the *res* ("reality") mentioned in the concluding sentence. But since in the earlier context *esse* had been used for both levels of "being" under discussion, it is evidently preferable to introduce the term *existit* to distinguish them in the concluding sentence. Both the English "exists in reality" and the Latin equivalents express a widespread and deep-seated feature of our understanding of being (*Seinsverständnis*): the use of "reality" at times to express "being" and at other times to have a more neutral or restricted sense. This is a deep-seated feature of Western ontology.[13] For present purposes, we cannot explore the history of the Latin expressions; we need only articulate the contrast that Anselm himself intends in this chapter.

The God who "is in the intellect" only is a God far away, an indefinite ideal floating above the heavens. But the God who "exists in reality" is one who engages himself with us. Anyone, says Anselm, who hears the words "something than which . . . " (*aliquid . . .*) can understand them, and so can

---

13. Nicholson, *Illustrations of Being*, chapter 7, "Reality," shows by an examination of Kant's concept of "reality" that there are two different conceptions at play, similar to the two uses of *res* (*re*) by Anselm.

think of or imagine what sort of thing might exemplify or instantiate this intention. But it is an empty intention at this point. The intellect may begin by imagining something or other, projecting a possible something—a possible God, therefore—somewhere out beyond the world. Such a being "out there" is merely a thing posed for and by the intellect. We can think of this as the intellectual imagination. Anselm says that the subject is in your intellect if you have understood the words, just as the painting-to-be inhabits the painter's intellect. But if God *is* the *aliquid quo nihil maius cogitari possit*, the "something than which nothing greater can be thought," then by virtue of his being in reality he approaches and enters our own heart. The real being of God is his real being in the heart. That is required by his infinity, the power of overreaching all that is, not only far but also near. Such an *aliquid* cannot be merely in the intellect, says Anselm. Such a "something" must exist, for the reason he gives: if it didn't, we could always suppose an equivalent that did, so that our "something" that lacked existence would by no means be the greatest we could think.

BIBLIOGRAPHY

Anselm. *Opera Omnia*. Vol. 1. Edited by F. S. Schmitt. Edinburgh: Nelson, 1946.
Charlesworth, M. J., ed. and trans. *St. Anselm's Proslogion*. Oxford: Clarendon, 1965.
Hegel, Georg Wilhelm Friedrich. *Lectures on the Philosophy of Religion (1927)*. Edited and translated by Peter C. Hodgson. Berkeley: University of California Press, 1985.
———. *Vorlesungen über die Beweise vom Dasein Gottes*. Hamburg: Meiner, 1966.
Heidegger, Martin. *Sein und Zeit*. Translated by Joan Stambaugh. Albany: State University of New York Press, 1996.
Nicholson, Graeme. *Illustrations of Being: Drawing on Heidegger and on Metaphysics*. Atlantic Highlands: Humanities, 1992.
Schufreider, Gregory. *An Introduction to Anselm's Argument*. Philadelphia: Temple University Press, 1978.
———. *Confessions of a Rational Mystic: Anselm's Early Writings*. West Lafayette, IL: Purdue University Press, 1994.

5

Reformers, Philosophers, Kierkegaard, and the *Akedah Yitzakh*

VICTOR A. SHEPHERD

Whether or not philosophy and theology are deemed irreconcilable appears to depend on where one stands in the theological spectrum. The papal encyclical *Fides et Ratio*, promulgated by the late John Paul II on September 14, 1998, stated unambiguously the relationship between philosophy and theology that John Paul himself upheld and expected others in his denomination to uphold. As a student of the Magisterial Reformation, on the other hand, I am aware that the Reformers regarded philosophy—by which they frequently meant medieval scholasticism—as an encroachment upon theology that denied the gospel's inherent integrity, militancy, and efficacy.

Martin Luther, for instance, voiced this notion as nascent Reformer. In early autumn of 1517 (perhaps even before his putative nailing of the *Ninety-Five Theses* to the door of the *Schlosskirche* in Wittenberg on October 31) he published the ninety-seven theses of his *Disputation Against Scholastic Theology*. Its anti-scholastic, anti-philosophic tone is unmistakable. Discussing the understanding of the human will typically advanced by medieval philosophers, Luther writes, "We are not masters of our actions, from beginning to end, but servants. This in opposition to the philosophers."[1]

---

1. Luther, "Disputation," 15. Luther's point is that humans can never be more than

The *Disputation* is replete with similar references. Consider the following: "Virtually the entire *Ethics* of Aristotle is the worst enemy of grace. This in opposition to the scholastics."[2] "It is an error to say that no man can become a theologian without Aristotle. This in opposition to common opinion."[3] "The whole Aristotle is to theology as darkness is to light. This in opposition to the scholastics."[4] Lest we think that Luther has targeted Aristotle only, we should hear Luther on someone in the tradition of Plato: "It would have been far better for the church if Porphyry (233–303) . . . had not been born for the use of theologians."[5] ("Better . . . if [he] . . . had not been born" is an unambiguous allusion to the biblical statement about Judas, implying that Porphyry, with his philosophically compromised theology, is no less spiritually treacherous than the arch-traitor. Philosophy, in other words, is no little threat to faith in the gospel.) Luther concludes his *Disputation*, "In these statements we wanted to say and believe we have said nothing that is not in agreement with the Catholic church and the teachers of the church."[6]

Soon Luther rendered more specific his objection to philosophy as he developed his *theologia crucis* or "theology of the cross" in the years that remained to him. Since Luther wrote no systematic theology, his *theologia crucis* is found in no single place but rather recrudesces in fragments throughout his work.[7]

Luther developed his *theologia crucis* in opposition to a *theologia gloriae* ("theology of glory") in its many forms. One form of it was the attempt to read the truth and nature of God off the face of world occurrence, off the face of history. Another form was the attempt to argue for the truth and nature of God from nature. Another form, perhaps more subtle, was the church's triumphalistic self-promotion (which is to say, the church's persecution of others) inasmuch as the church confused its triumphalism with the triumph or victory of the crucified One: the church had forgotten that the crucified One is raised crucified, with wounds still gaping. When the church confuses its triumphalism with the victory of its still-suffering Lord,

mere servants of their will, since their will, *coram Deo*, is governed either by sin or by Christ-in-his-righteousness.

2. Ibid., 16.

3. Ibid.

4. Ibid. By "whole Aristotle" Luther means not only Aristotle's metaphysical writings but also his scientific writings, newly uncovered in the burgeoning scientific exploration of the sixteenth century, and just as newly exposed as false by telescope-aided astronomers.

5. Ibid., 17.

6. Ibid., 20.

7. See, e.g., von Loewenich, *Luther's Theology of the Cross*.

the resurrection ceases to be the effectiveness of the cross, becoming instead the supersession of the cross, and is matched by the church's imagined superiority to its own divinely-appointed crossbearing. While this distortion was a matter of ecclesiology, Luther insisted that ecclesiology is a predicate of Christology, and that a distorted ecclesiology could therefore be traced to a Christology warped by philosophy.

All of which brings us to the last form of *theologia gloriae*, the identification of God with metaphysical speculation. Here Luther has two principal objections in mind.

One objection is his insistence that the Holy One of Israel is qualitatively distinct from the "God" of the philosophers—that is, from Being, Being-itself, "ground of being," etc. The living God is to be understood not as the *ens realissimum* of the philosophers, the static "that which is," but rather in terms of the dynamic personalism of the Hebrew Bible: God is *he who acts*. (The Reformers' reading of Exodus 3:14, where Moses asks for God's "name" and God replies, "I shall be who I shall be," was quite different from that of Aquinas; Aquinas' reading of the text as declaring God's self-existence the Reformers found utterly wide of the mark and an instance of corruption by philosophy.)

The second objection is Luther's insistence that the God who acts is not the only actor; Satan acts too. God, however, defines himself at the cross, and supremely at the cross. For this reason Luther maintained that apart from the cross God is indistinguishable from the devil.[8]

On account of its espousal of metaphysics, philosophy remains wedded to the *theologia gloriae*. Metaphysical speculation never terminates in the God who humbles himself in the manger and humiliates himself at the cross. Philosophy forever remains an aspect of that "wisdom of the world" that the Gospel inverts.

Consider the discussion of power, including omnipotence. At the cross God not only acts most characteristically (he loves to the uttermost, love exhausting his nature); at the cross God also acts most effectively (he reconciles a wayward world to himself). To say that the cross, therefore, is God's mightiest work is to say that the cross alone determines the meaning of "almighty" or "omnipotent." Since power is the capacity to achieve purpose, God acts "almightily" when he overcomes all impediments to the fulfillment of his purpose, and does so precisely where, from a human standpoint, he cannot do anything. God's power can never be understood by means of an argument that begins with finite, creaturely power and concludes with infinite, divine power. No philosophical argument for God—let alone for

---

8. cf. Forde, *Captivation of the Will*, 45.

God's omnipotence—terminates in the God-forsakenness of a bedraggled Jew (someone the world loves to hate) executed at a city garbage dump. Luther has spoken.

What about John Calvin? Calvin, to say the least, is cautious concerning the theologian's deployment of philosophy. In the course of expounding the doctrine of the Trinity he writes laconically, "Here, indeed, if anywhere in the secret mysteries of Scripture, we ought to play the philosopher soberly and with great moderation . . . For how can the human mind measure off the measureless essence of God according to its own little measure . . . Indeed, how can the mind by its own leading come to search out God's essence . . . ?"[9] More characteristically, however, Calvin speaks critically of the "Sophists," scholastic writers whose hybrid theology has accommodated philosophy so as to distort the biblical message. In this regard, when Calvin discusses the will of God (which for him is the will of God made manifest in Jesus Christ), he contrasts it with "that absolute will of which the Sophists babble."[10]

Not every philosophical predecessor is equally evil, however. Calvin thought more highly of the "Schoolmen," the older, more notable medieval thinkers, than he did of theological opponents temporally proximate to him. In his assessment of the distinction between operative grace and cooperative grace, for instance, Calvin writes, "How far I disagree with the sounder Schoolmen [note that regardless of how 'sound' these thinkers may be, Calvin still finds ample scope for disagreement], I differ with the more recent Sophists to an even greater extent, as they are farther removed from antiquity."[11] He has in mind here principally Ockham and Biel.

Regardless of Calvin's approach to philosophy, and particularly to Aristotle, the fact is that Scholastic theology never disappeared in the Reformation era. Alongside the Humanist flowering, which had no little effect on most of the Magisterial Reformers (here we need only recall that Calvin's first published work was a commentary on Seneca's *De Misericordia*), Scholastic theology thrived in the "old church" even as Reformers denounced it. It was soon to thrive in the "new church" too, as both Lutheran and Reformed theologians began to write in a scholastic mode, and triumphed in the work of Jacob Arminius, the Remonstrant in whom philosophy looms much larger than his followers appear to appreciate. Indeed it is no exaggeration to say that Arminius is chiefly a philosopher whose Thomistic theology (Aquinas is the most frequently quoted thinker in Arminius' work) happens

---

9. Calvin, *Institutes*, 1.13.21.
10. Ibid., 1.16.7.
11. Ibid., 2.2.6.

to use a Protestant vocabulary. And of course the English Puritans returned to a use of philosophy that was more than merely illustrative: Jonathan Edwards, New-World Puritan theologian, remained the ablest philosopher in America until the advent of Charles Sanders Peirce.

Over the centuries the relationship between philosophy and theology has varied in the details of the respective disciplines, even as the disciplines appeared sometimes to wed each other, at other times to act as necessary foil to each other (and therefore still to need each other). If theology announced itself divorced from philosophy, the divorce appeared not to last.

HEGEL

In Hegel there occurred what may be regarded as one of philosophy's larger-scale "takeover bids" of theology; namely, Hegel's notion of the Absolute or Mind or Spirit. Ultimate reality is Spirit, but such Spirit is not an exclusive or monistic claim to reality. Neither is Hegel's postulated "Spirit" that God of Scripture whose Being is ontically utterly distinct from the being of the world, linked to it only by God's grace. "Spirit" is not that God whose infinite self-transcendence is categorically distinct from the self-transcendence of philosophical thought.

Hegel maintains that it is possible by means of philosophical thought to rise to the Absolute Standpoint, where the distinction between subject and object is overcome and the thinker becomes one with cosmic Mind, this "Mind" being nothing other than self-thinking thought, or Mind thinking itself. Note that Hegel does not mean by this a flight into solipsism or fantasy, let alone the self-referential world of the deranged. Mind thinking itself is the philosopher's ascent to that standpoint, that of the Absolute or the Idea or God, in which all the dichotomies of the universe are acknowledged and yet are overcome in a higher synthesis. Since philosophy aims at a comprehensive rational apprehension of reality (and in Hegel's opinion his own philosophy succeeded at this), sin and evil must be seen as aspects of, or stages on the way towards, the mediation that overcomes the ontic distance between God and humankind. In other words, evil is denatured as evil by Hegel's philosophy; radical evil—evil for the sake of evil, evil subserving no good whatsoever—is not acknowledged.

Moreover, the God of biblical faith who utterly transcends the creation is reduced to a manifestly penultimate "God," since such a deity is necessarily "limited" by what it is not. According to Hegel, God is that which gathers up into a higher ontic unity what was hitherto regarded as ontically distinct. In connection with this notion Hegel speaks of two forms of the infinite, one adequate and the other inadequate. The inadequate infinite is simply the non-finite. If the infinite is defined as the non-finite, however, then the infinite is limited by what it is not, and to this extent is not infinite at all. Then the adequate infinite must be the infinite that *includes both* the finite *and* the infinite, overcoming the distinction between them.

Where has this development been illustrated, according to Hegel? (Note that the question is not "Where has this occurred?") It has been "illustrated" in the Incarnation, where the God who up to that time had been viewed as transcendent only—albeit infinite—is now acknowledged to include precisely what it had previously excluded. The infinite, in short, is the sum of infinite plus finite. The Incarnation, says Hegel, is a symbol or illustration of this.

Who needs the illustration? Inferior or immature philosophers. Hegel maintains that Christianity is a pictorial representation of truth helpful for those who cannot, or to date have not, risen philosophically to the Absolute Standpoint. In saying so, Hegel intends no disparagement. At the same time, what is substantive according to biblical faith or theology—Incarnation, atonement, resurrection, Spirit-suffusion—are regarded philosophically as penultimate and illustrative only. They remain pictorial representations of a reality that has moved beyond them even as it includes them.

KIERKEGAARD

Kierkegaard objects. He denies that there can ever be mediation of Hegel's sort between God and humankind. He denies that the Absolute's knowledge of itself and humankind's knowledge of the Absolute are two aspects of the same reality. He denies that the creature (if such a word is still appropriate) can rise by means of philosophical thought to the standpoint of the Absolute so as to render human self-consciousness ultimately the same as God's self-consciousness. He insists that there is an "infinite qualitative distinction" between God and humankind that cannot be overcome. The God of Abraham, Isaac, and Jacob is never to be confused with Hegel's Spirit or Absolute. We may encounter the God who forever remains GOD, but we are never ontically "one with" that God.

Whereas Hegel insists that "The Truth is the Whole," Kierkegaard maintains that "Truth is subjectivity." This assertion, of course, has nothing to do with subjectiv*ism* or make-believe or even postmodernism's denial of truth. "Truth is subjectivity" means that the real is the relational. Whereas Hegel insists that "the Real is the rational and the rational is the real" (presupposing his own carefully delineated sense of "rational"), Kierkegaard anticipates Martin Buber's notion that the real is the "between"; the real is the existent's encounter and engagement with the God who infinitely transcends us yet accommodates himself to us so that we may meet and know him. The real is the engagement of subject with Subject—hence his dictum "Truth is subjectivity."

To exist, insists Kierkegaard, is qualitatively different from to think—however pregnant Hegel's notion of thinking may be and regardless of what it may include. For this reason, Kierkegaard does not hesitate to say "Existence cannot be thought." Rejecting the "thought experiments" of metaphysicians as the approach to truth, Kierkegaard insists that the real is apprehended only by means of a commitment that forsakes all earthly securities and "leaps," at incalculable risk, in faith that issues in action.

The paradigm of such commitment is Abraham of old, Kierkegaard's "knight of faith." The story that overwhelms Kierkegaard is the *Akedah*, the "binding" of Isaac as Abraham offers up his only son in obedience to God's command.

ABRAHAM AND ISAAC

Abraham, the prototype of the person of faith, has been promised spiritual descendants as numerous as the sand on the seashore. If the promise is to be fulfilled, two conditions must be met: Abraham must *persevere in faith* (or else he cannot be the foreparent of descendants-in-*faith*), and Isaac must *survive* (or else there will be no *descendants*-in-faith.) The dilemma is plain. If Abraham obeys God and offers up his son, then God's promise is null and void, since Isaac has not survived; on the other hand, if Abraham second-guesses (i.e., disobeys) God and preserves Isaac, then God's promise is also null and void, since Abraham's disobedience is unfaith. In short, Abraham's obedience and his disobedience alike nullify the promise. What is he to do? Abraham decides to stake everything on obeying God's *command*, trusting God to fulfill God's *promise* in ways that Abraham cannot foresee or even imagine. He will obey God even though such obedience, from a human perspective, ensures the non-fulfillment of the promise.

Precisely at the moment of the knife's descent God forbids the dreaded act. God's unaffected awareness and candid acknowledgment, "*Now* I know that you fear God" (Gen 22:12), dovetails exactly with Abraham's utter surprise at the provision of the ram. Abraham's surprise is no more feigned than his intent to obey God at any cost. Both dimensions must be underscored: it is true simultaneously both that Abraham never doubts that "God will provide" (otherwise he has abandoned faith in the promise-fulfilling God) *and* that he is genuinely astounded at the appearance of the ram (otherwise the trial of faith was no trial at all.)

KIERKEGAARD AND HEGEL

Kierkegaard's *Fear and Trembling* targets Hegel unambiguously. Hegel's understanding of religion, of course, includes his understanding of faith. And according to him, since philosophy "goes further" than religion, philosophy necessarily goes further than faith—only, says Kierkegaard, to turn wine into water.[12]

Philosophy, meanwhile, is not aware that it denatures faith, insisting that philosophy comprehends faith in superseding it. In all of this, says Kierkegaard, theology is seemingly unaware that its mandate is *theos*, God. The result is that theology, or what's left of it, "sits all rouged and powdered in the window and courts its favours, offers its charms to philosophy."[13] In other words, theology has prostituted itself to philosophy while preening itself on an intellectual sophistication it considers superior to the crudeness of Abraham and Isaac. After all, says Kierkegaard with mordant irony, "it is supposed to be difficult to understand Hegel, but to understand Abraham is a small matter."[14] Turning the vocabulary of "going further" back upon his opponent, Kierkegaard glories in the fact that in 130 years Abraham "got no further than faith."[15] Kierkegaard, overwhelmed by the story of the patriarch, knows that Abraham had in fact moved ahead to *existence*, and it was the philosophical speculators who were stalled; existence cannot be gained or entered upon by means of the "thought experiments" of the metaphysicians, but only as the detachment of "worldly understanding" is left behind in favour of radical commitment.[16]

This radical commitment is to God—not the "God" of philosophical constructs, but the One who summons every would-be believer to trial like that endured by Abraham. Such trial consists in enduring, in utter anguish, the contradiction between promise and command. This contradiction is nothing less than "absurd." As faith paradoxically embraces the absurd (and here we must keep in mind the "*this*-worldliness" of Isaac and the blessing to come through him), that faith is vindicated and confirmed, not in an

12. Kierkegaard, *Fear and Trembling*, 37.
13. Ibid., 32.
14. Ibid.
15. Ibid., 23.
16. When Kierkegaard speaks of faith's leaving worldly understanding behind, he is not advocating irrationality as such. See Evans, *Faith Beyond Reason*, chapters 6 and 7.

ethereal eternal but in the temporal: it is in *this* life that Abraham trusts God to fulfill the promise even as God's command is obeyed. By way of reminder of this link between the absurd and the temporal Kierkegaard adds, "Only he who draws the knife gets Isaac."[17]

The loneliness of Abraham (and of every believer) is his inability to make any of this understandable to even one other human being. Since no one can foster the understanding requisite for faith, no believer can help someone else *into* faith: "either the single individual himself becomes the knight of faith by accepting the paradox, or he never becomes one."[18]

In light of philosophy's non-comprehension of all this, together with the human horror that surrounds the particular absurdity pertaining to Isaac, Kierkegaard does not hesitate to say that Abraham's life is not only the most paradoxical that can be thought; it is so paradoxical that it *cannot* be thought.[19] Still, the foregoing must never be regarded as unique to Abraham. As the prototype of faith he is to be imitated by all those who have never settled for the cheap edition of him that the church is forever trying to sell. He remains the "guiding star that saves the anguished."[20]

Kierkegaard's point is that Hegel's category of self-consciousness, even a self-consciousness that is one with an eternal self-consciousness, is still only *consciousness*; it is not yet *existence*. Faith alone embraces existence, and does so only by means of a radical commitment, a "leap": a qualitative transition that nothing can precipitate and that cannot be effected incrementally. The single individual knows that we can be saved only as faith, itself a paradox, grasps the absurd. Such faith is the antithesis of the detachment of philosophy, and the antithesis of the heart's spontaneous inclination.[21] Such faith is always the paradox of *existence*.

In light of all that has been said concerning the absurd, paradox, leap, existence—together with the fact that the single individual can be neither understood nor admired—Kierkegaard is correct when he contends that the believer is finally a witness, not a teacher.[22] A teacher, after all, teaches what others who have the requisite philosophical equipment can understand. A witness, on the other hand, attests reality outside the categories comprehended by philosophy. Existence, *contra* Hegel, is indeed "beyond" all philosophical thought-experiments.

17. Kierkegaard, *Fear and Trembling*, 27.
18. Ibid., 71.
19. Ibid., 56.
20. Ibid., 53, 21.
21. Ibid., 47.
22. Ibid., 80.

A REPRISE

And yet it appears philosophy will always be necessary—at least if theological impasses are to be dealt with. One such impasse was the Christological dispute between Arius and Athanasius in the fourth century. In his understanding of Jesus Christ Arius had managed to combine the worst of two heresies, Ebionitism and Docetism. While he never hesitated to speak of Jesus as the Son of God, Arius' "Son of God" was a *tertium quid*, something neither divine nor human. For if the Son of God is less than God in any sense, then the Son is not God. And if the Son of God is more than human, then neither is the Son human.

When Athanasius attempted to rebut Arius he realized that both he and Arius were using the same biblical expression, "Son of God," but were ascribing antithetical meanings to it. While Arius maintained that the Son was *homoiousios* with the Father—of similar substance—Athanasius insisted that Son and Father were *homoousios*—of the same or identical substance. The difference between *homoousios* and *homoiousios* is an iota, the smallest letter of the Greek alphabet (in Greek it lacks even a dot), and subscript as well. (How much hangs on such a distinction is indicated in English by the difference between asking someone to run your business and asking her to ruin it.) Athanasius understood that nothing less than the gospel was at stake here, and that if the crucial difference between him and Arius was to be identified, he would have to resort to non-biblical, philosophical language. *Homoousios* is not a biblical word. Athanasius defended his use of it by insisting that it exuded the spirit of Scripture; in other words, *homoousios* locates the meanings of biblical words and the realities to which they point.[23]

What did Athanasius do for the church through his deployment of a non-biblical, philosophical expression? No less a figure than Karl Barth maintained that the Athanasian *homoousios* was the most significant theological statement since the apostles.

It is not difficult to multiply instances where philosophical concepts and vocabulary are crucial in theological articulation. Despite Calvin's protests against the divagations of schoolmen and sophists whose Aristotelian encroachment upon theology he finds objectionable, Calvin resorts to Aristotle's vocabulary in expounding the doctrine of justification.[24] Concerning

---

23. See Torrance, *Trinitarian Faith*, 128, 129.

24. We might note that Calvin published his *Commentary on Romans* in 1540. Between 1532 and 1542 at least 35 commentaries on Romans were published, including many by Roman Catholic exegetes who disagreed with the Reformers' reading of that epistle which Protestants cherish above all others.

Romans 3:24, "[All who believe] . . . are justified by his [God's] grace as a gift, through the redemption that is in Christ Jesus," (RSV) Calvin regards it as "perhaps the most remarkable place in the whole of Scripture for explaining and magnifying the force of this righteousness."[25] Here Calvin writes, "He [Paul] shows that the mercy of God is the efficient cause; that Christ, with his blood, is the material; that the formal, or instrumental, is faith conceived from the Word; and the final is the glory of the divine righteousness and goodness."[26] Elsewhere Calvin readily acknowledges philosophy as the servant of Christian understanding: " . . . we see that there was good ground for the distinction which the schoolmen made between necessity, *secundum quid*, and necessity absolute, also between the necessity of consequent and of consequence."[27]

None of the above suggests that the substance of philosophy determines the substance of theology. It is to say, however, that theology appears to need—or at least, to find highly useful—the deployment of philosophical concepts in theological exposition.

Karl Barth makes the same point in his exposition of the doctrine of the Trinity. Barth regards as short-sighted those who are impatient with the doctrine on the grounds that it appears to rely for its articulation on the categories of the philosophy current at the time of the Council of Nicea (ca. 325). Barth acknowledges the indisputable connection of the dogma [of the Trinity] with the philosophy of the age. However, the knife cuts both ways: by proving philosophical involvement we can reject the confessions and theology of *any* age and school, and can do so more effectively the less we see the beam in our own eye. Linguistically theologians have always depended on some philosophy, and linguistically they always will. But instead of getting pharisaically indignant about this and consigning whole periods to the limbo of a philosophy that is supposed to deny the gospel simply because it differs from our own, it is better to ask what the theologians of the earlier period were really trying to say in the vocabulary of their philosophy.[28]

Theology cannot be articulated apart from some philosophical concepts and vocabulary. At the same time, the content of philosophy and theology are not the same. If theology fails to adapt its proper content to the forms of discourse in its immediate environment, it speaks to no one, however rich its content may be. On the other hand, if in seeking to adapt, theology adopts the substance advanced by those forms of discourse in its

---

25. Parker, *Commentaries on Romans: 1532–1542*, 198.
26. Ibid., 197.
27. Calvin, *Institutes*.
28. Barth, *Church Dogmatics*, I/1, 378.

immediate environment, it will find that it has nothing to say, since it can do no more than reflect the world back to the world.

The line between "adapt" and "adopt" is finer than a hair and harder than diamond. In truth, most of the time Christian witness finds itself now on one side of the line and then on the other, trusting that on balance it tiptoes down the boundary. The option that theology never has is to "play it safe" by making no effort to adapt for fear of adopting: "playing it safe" guarantees the disappearance of witness.

Kierkegaard knew as much. While remaining an unrelenting foe of philosophy's disdain for Abraham, who "got no further than faith," Kierkegaard concludes his criticism of Hegel and of Hegel's "Absolute" by conscripting Hegel's vocabulary: he tells the reader that Abraham—the prototype of philosophy-defying faith—is lost unless "the single individual as the single individual stands in an absolute relation to the absolute."[29]

Since it appears philosophy will always be essential to theology, is the difference between philosophy and theology an irreconcilable one? In some respects there may continue to be an irreconcilable difference. Years ago my chief philosophical mentor, Emil Fackenheim, commented to me that radical evil, evil enacted for no other reason than perverse delight in evil, is precisely that surd over which metaphysics finally stumbles—"surd," in mathematical parlance, being that which can never be made to fit an expression that is mathematically elegant.

At the same time, *within* the realm of truth or reality that theology acknowledges, might there be room for philosophy in the form of a reformulated natural theology? *Within* this realm cannot philosophy argue from the creaturely order to its "silent cry" for a sufficient reason? This is not a philosophical attempt at supplanting, for instance, redemption as the content of revelation. But it is to argue, from within the realm established by revelation, that the truth of theology is not inherently philosophically impossible.[30]

Hans Urs von Balthasar, in discussing the relation between philosophy and faith, appears to grasp the challenge that has convened this colloquium when he writes, "Ought one not . . . to say that the Christian, as proclaimer of God's glory . . . takes upon himself—whether he wants to or not—the burden of metaphysics?"[31]

---

29. Kierkegaard, *Fear and Trembling*, 120.
30. See Torrance, *Karl Barth*, chapter 5.
31. Von Balthasar, *My Work in Retrospect*, 85.

BIBLIOGRAPHY

Balthasar, Hans Urs von. *My Work: In Retrospect*. San Francisco: Communio, 1993.
Barth, Karl. *Church Dogmatics* I/1. Translated by Geoffrey W. Bromiley. Edinburgh: T. & T. Clark, 1975.
Calvin, John. *Institutes of the Christian Religion*. Translated by Henry Beveridge. Grand Rapids: Eerdmans, 1953.
———. *Institutes of the Christian Religion*. Translated by Ford Lewis Battles. Edited by J. T. McNeill. Philadelphia: Westminster, 1960.
Evans, C. Stephen. *Faith Beyond Reason: A Kierkegaardian Account*. Grand Rapids: Eerdmans, 1998.
Forde, Gerhard O. *The Captivation of the Will*. Grand Rapids: Eerdmans, 2005.
Kierkegaard, Søren. *Fear and Trembling*. Translated and edited by Howard V. Hong and Edna H. Hong. Princeton: Princeton University Press, 1983.
Loewenich, Walter von. *Luther's Theology of the Cross*. Translated by Herbert J. A. Bouman. Minneapolis: Fortress, 1976.
Luther, Martin. "Disputation Against Scholastic Theology." In *Martin Luther's Basic Theological Writings*, edited by Timothy Lull. Minneapolis: Fortress, 1989.
———. "The Ninety-Five Theses." In *Martin Luther's Basic Theological Writings*, edited by Timothy Lull. Minneapolis: Fortress, 1989.
Parker, T. H. L. *Commentaries on Romans: 1532–1542*. Edinburgh: T. & T. Clark, 1986.
Torrance, Thomas F. *Karl Barth: Biblical and Evangelical Theologian*. Edinburgh: T. & T. Clark, 1990.
———. *The Trinitarian Faith*. Edinburgh: T. & T. Clark, 1988.

6

A Phenomenological Analysis of Basic Concepts Shared by Evolutionary Theory and Intelligent Design

Jeff Mitscherling

INTRODUCTION

Theologians and philosophers have been debating among themselves about the being and nature of God ever since they started talking, and one of their favorite topics has always been what we have come to call "the argument from design." As Xenophon recounts, Socrates defended a version of this argument,[1] and we find it being offered in various forms from Plato up to the present day. Over the past century the argument from design has been at the center of a controversy that has increasingly involved religion and science more than religion and philosophy. This is the "creationism vs. evolutionism" controversy, which has also taken the form of a controversy between what is called "intelligent design" and evolutionary theory. When philosophers have entered this debate, they have most often done so in defense of either the religious or the scientific (aka "secular") contingent, and those defending the latter position have tended to argue as Darwinians, or

---

1. Xenophon, *Xenophon*, vol. IV, I:iv, 5–6.

"Neo-Darwinians."[2] In other words, the debate has now come to be between "the theists" and "the scientists."

It is interesting to note, from a sociological point of view, that most philosophers who have entered the fray have done so in support of the scientists—or more precisely, in support of evolutionary biology—and that they have been extremely vocal in their commitment to the very sort of materialist metaphysics that Newton himself, a famous champion of the argument from design, found so abhorrent. Be that as it may, philosophy can usually contribute to a debate without announcing its allegiance to one side or the other. Philosophy is often at its best when it steps into a debate in just such a non-committal manner: not to moderate—or at least not only to moderate—but to clarify the concepts, analyze the arguments, and perhaps suggest new ways of approaching the matter at hand. In this paper I shall be attempting to do just that: I shall be examining a few of the central concepts in the debate, drawing from the sort of realist phenomenology that was pursued by some of Husserl's students and colleagues and is currently being revived by several researchers in the area.[3] I emphasize at the outset that I am not attempting to offer support for either of the two camps, and I certainly do not presume to be offering anything even vaguely resembling a solution to the problem that inspires this debate. In fact I consider the problem, as currently formulated, to be insoluble. I do hope, however, that the perspective of realist phenomenology might at least contribute a slightly different way of regarding some of the central issues.

While the general lines of argumentation pursued by the two opposed camps are no doubt familiar to all, it will nevertheless be helpful to begin with a brief discussion of the argument from design and some of the most trenchant criticisms of it. I shall focus on statements of the arguments and criticisms that rely most heavily on the concepts to be examined.[4]

---

2. Darwinism is sometimes distinguished from "Neo-Darwinism," the latter being described as Darwinism (as characterized by its novel interpretation of natural selection) combined with Mendelian genetics. Current "philosophy of biology" consists largely of an extended defense of the Neo-Darwinian position.

3. Most notable among those of Husserl's students who argued against their master's idealism and in support of some realist version of phenomenology were Roman Ingarden, Edith Stein, and Adolf Reinach. There is currently renewed interest in early phenomenology, particularly of "the Göttingen period."

4. I shall be considering only the argument from design and well-known criticisms of it. I shall not be examining the arguments that evolutionary theorists have directed against the position of the creationists. For a provocative response to some of these arguments and to the theory of evolution more generally from the point of view of intelligent design theorists, see the controversial textbook *Of Pandas and People* by Davis and Kenyon.

THE ARGUMENT FROM DESIGN AND MAJOR CRITICISMS THEREOF

One of the earliest formulations of the argument that has been preserved is the above-mentioned version attributed to Socrates by Xenophon in his *Memorabilia*. In a passage that clearly anticipates later, more familiar versions of the argument, Socrates asks "Aristodemus the dwarf, as he was called":

> Do you not think then that he who created man from the beginning had some useful end in view when he endowed him with his several senses, giving eyes to see visible objects, ears to hear sounds? Would odours again be of any use to us had we not been endowed with nostrils? What perception should we have of sweet and bitter and all things pleasant to the palate had we no tongue in our mouth to discriminate between them? Besides these, are there not other contrivances that look like the results of forethought? Thus the eyeballs, being weak, are set behind eyelids, that open like doors when we want to see, and close when we sleep: on the lids grow lashes through which the very winds filter harmlessly: above the eyes is a coping of brows that lets no drop of sweat from the head hurt them. The ears catch all sounds, but are never choked with them. Again, the incisors of all creatures are adapted for cutting, the molars for receiving food from them and grinding it. And again, the mouth, through which the food they want goes in, is set near the eyes and nostrils; but since what goes out is unpleasant, the ducts through which it passes are turned away and removed as far as possible from the organs of sense. With such signs of forethought in these arrangements, can you doubt whether they are the works of chance or design?

It is not a little ironic, given the current state of affairs, that the argument from design became most popular, and its formulations more sophisticated, with the birth of modern science. One of its most powerful modern statements is indeed to be found in the famous "General Scholium" published by Newton as an appendix to Book Three, "The System of the World," in the second edition of his *Principia Mathematica* in 1713:[5]

> This most beautiful System of the Sun, Planets, and Comets, could only proceed from the counsel and dominion of an

---

5. Newton, "General Scholium." This work was first published as an appendix to the second (1713) edition of the *Principia*; he revised it for the third (1726) edition. I have quoted only two of the passages from his much longer argument.

> intelligent and powerful being. And if the fixed Stars are the centers of other like systems, these, being form'd by the like wise counsel, must be all subject to the dominion of the One... And lest the systems of the fixed Stars should, by their gravity, fall on each other mutually, he hath placed those systems at immense distances from one another.
>
> ... We know him [God] only by his most wise and excellent contrivances of things, and final causes; we admire him for his perfections; but we revere and adore him on account of his dominion. For we adore him as his servants; and a God without dominion, providence, and final causes, is nothing else but Fate and Nature. Blind metaphysical necessity, which is certainly the same always and every where, could produce no variety of things. All that diversity of natural things which we find, suited to different times and places, could arise from nothing but the ideas and will of a Being necessarily existing.

In 1748, some thirty-five years after the publication of Newton's "General Scholium," Hume published his influential *Enquiry Concerning Human Understanding*, in which he briefly presents several criticisms of the argument from design. A few years after this, between 1751 and 1755, Hume completed an early draft of his *Dialogues Concerning Natural Religion*,[6] in which he elaborated these criticisms at length. The criticisms that later authors have tended to find most incisive include the following: (i) that the analogy between the universe and objects designed and produced by humans is too weak to support the (analogical) reasoning of the argument; (ii) that the totality of the universe is beyond human comprehension, and the rational and ordered portion of it that we experience may well be not at all representative of the larger whole; (iii) that the design we think we see in the universe might equally well provide evidence not of one God, but of many gods; (iv) that since the world bears more resemblance to an animal than a machine, its origin might be ascribed more properly to generation or vegetation than to reason or design; and (v) that "uniformity of appearance" might simply arise after many ages of chaos and disorder in "the eternal revolutions of unguided matter," and the parts of organisms might arise through precisely such adjustment, with regularity of form characterizing them.[7] Most relevant for our present purpose is a passage, appearing to-

---

6. Hume extensively revised this early draft in or prior to 1761, and again in 1776, the year of his death. The final version of *Dialogues* was edited by Hume's nephew and published in London in 1779.

7. These criticisms are most fully developed in Parts VII and VIII; see Hume, *Dialogues Concerning Natural Religion*, 176, 182–83, and 184–86.

ward the end of Part VIII, in which Philo sums up his immediately preceding discussion with Cleanthes of the manner in which matter, when it has been corrupted, "tries some new form":

> At least, you may safely infer, said PHILO, that the foregoing hypothesis is so far incomplete and imperfect; which I shall not scruple to allow. But can we ever reasonably expect greater success in any attempts of this nature? Or can we ever hope to erect a system of cosmogony, that will be liable to no exceptions, and will contain no circumstance repugnant to our limited and imperfect experience of the analogy of nature? Your theory itself cannot surely pretend to any such advantage; even though you have run into *anthropomorphism*, the better to preserve a conformity to common experience. Let us once more put it to trial. In all instances which we have ever seen, thought has no influence upon matter, except where that matter is so conjoined with it, as to have an equal reciprocal influence upon it. No animal can move immediately any thing but the members of its own body; and indeed, the equality of action and re-action seems to be an universal law of nature: But your theory implies a contradiction to this experience.

The theory of Cleanthes to which Hume here refers is, quite simply, the argument from design—namely, that numerous examples drawn from nature provide "sufficient proof of design, and of a benevolent design, which gave rise to the order and arrangement of the universe."

SHARED PRESUPPOSITIONS OF THE ARGUMENT AND CRITICISMS

In his *Prolegomena to Any Future Metaphysics* Kant famously announced that he was indebted to Hume for his inspiration in writing the *Critique of Pure Reason*. He proclaimed that the skeptical empiricist had awakened him from his "dogmatic slumber" and set him on the critical path that enabled him to establish a firm foundation for the sciences in the wake of the skeptic's assessment of their possibility. While Kant chiefly has in mind Hume's critique of the concept of causality, it is clear that he recognized the implications of this critique not only for science but also for metaphysics—which, according to Kant, revolves first and foremost around questions concerning God, freedom, and immortality. As he explains in his Introduction to the *Prolegomena*:[8]

---

8. Kant, *Prolegomena*, 8.

> I openly confess my recollection of David Hume was the very thing which many years ago first interrupted my dogmatic slumber and gave my investigations in the field of speculative philosophy a quite new direction . . . I therefore first tried whether Hume's objection could not be put into a general form, and soon found that the concept of the connection of cause and effect was by no means the only concept by which the understanding thinks the connection of things *a priori*, but rather that metaphysics consists altogether of such concepts.

Kant had probably read Hume's *Enquiry* at least ten years before conceiving the basic line of critical argument in the first *Critique*; however, it cannot be denied that the "Copernican hypothesis" grounding and guiding Kant's entire critical philosophy clearly echoes the fundamental assumption of the most powerful of Hume's criticisms of the argument from design, an assumption that underlies also his criticism of the concept of causality; namely, that the order we find in nature—"the connection of things" that the understanding thinks—and interpret as evidence of plan or design is in fact the product of our own psychological projection. For Hume, this projection is largely a matter of habit inculcated through experience; for Kant it originates in the *a priori* nature and structure of our cognitive faculties. According to both Hume and Kant, however, we tend to think in terms of particular sorts of ordered relations, so that in regarding the world we naturally tend to make sense of it in those terms. In short, whatever design we might be able to see in the world is precisely that which we inject into it. This is essentially the theoretical starting point of the central lines of argumentation of both the *Critique of Pure Reason* and the *Critique of the Power of Judgment*: that the most fundamental features of the world as we experience it derive from the contributions of our cognitive faculties.

In the third Critique, Kant agrees that organisms are rightly to be regarded as natural ends, and that the purposiveness in and of organisms can be acknowledged with certainty. The design we see in the world as a whole, however, is a reflection of our natural tendency to take what we can establish with certainty and, by the same line of reasoning, to extrapolate from it in an attempt to make sense of what we ought to recognize as beyond our cognitive grasp. It is this tendency that leads us to interpret natural events, actions, and processes as purposive.[9]

---

9. Kant had already devoted a short section of his *Critique of Pure Reason* to criticism of the argument from design, which he referred to as "the physicotheological proof"; see "Transcendental doctrine of elements," Division Two; "Transcendental dialectic," Book II; "The dialectical inferences of pure reason," Chapter III; "The ideal of pure reason," Section VI: "On the impossibility of the physicotheological proof." While

That this view of purposiveness in nature has such a decidedly Humean ring to it might suggest that it was the religious and theological concern with design—the *metaphysical* concern—far more than the strictly epistemological issue of the origin of the concept of causality, which Kant found so troubling as to awaken him from his dogmatic slumber. More important for our present purpose, however, is the observation that Hume's and Kant's various criticisms of the argument from design all rest on metaphysical and epistemological presuppositions that are in fact shared by the very argument against which they are directed. The most fundamental of these is the assumption that the natural world and the human mind are ontologically distinct—or, more precisely, that the formal ontology of the world is essentially different from the formal ontology of the mind. This distinction is basic to modern philosophy and science, and it is to be found in modern Christian theology as well.[10]

---

purposiveness, conceived primarily as directedness toward an end, is central to the version of the argument as he examines it in his third *Critique*, in his first *Critique* Kant's formulation of the argument from design revolves around the concept of causality: "The present world discloses to us such an immeasurable showplace of manifoldness, order, purposiveness, and beauty; whether one pursues these in the infinity of space or in the unlimited division of it, that in accordance with even the knowledge about it that our weak understanding can acquire, all speech concerning so many and such unfathomable wonders must lose its power to express, all numbers their power to measure, and even our thoughts lack boundaries, so that our judgment upon the whole must resolve itself into a speechless, but nonetheless eloquent, astonishment. Everywhere we see a chain of effects and causes, of ends and means, regularity in coming to be and perishing, and because nothing has entered by itself into the state in which it finds itself, this state always refers further to another thing as its cause, which makes necessary just the same further inquiry, so that in such a way the entire whole would have to sink into the abyss of nothingness if one did not assume something subsisting for itself originally and independently outside this infinite contingency, which supports it and at the same time, as the cause of its existence, secures its continuation. This highest cause (in regard to all things of the world)—how great should one think it is? We are not acquainted with the world in its whole content, still less do we know how to estimate its magnitude by comparison with everything possible. But since in respect to causality we need an ultimate and supreme being, what hinders us from at same time positing in it a degree of perfection exceeding everything else that is possible? This we can easily effect, though to be sure only through the fragile outline of an abstract concept, if we represent all possible perfection united in it as a single substance—which concept is favorable to our reason in its parsimony of principles, not subject to any contradictions, and even salutary for the extension of the use of our reason within experience, through the guidance such an idea gives to order and purposiveness, but is nowhere contrary to experience in any decisive way." Kant, *Critique of Pure Reason*, 579.

10. In Christian theology prior to the advent of the modern era—that is, before the emergence in the Renaissance of new directions and methods of inquiry and new criteria for truth and certainty—the human mind was not always as clearly distinguished from the rest of God's creation as it has since come to be. This bears on the reflection

This assumed distinction seems not only reasonable, but unavoidable and even self-evidently true, for we see it reflected in the structure of our everyday experience. When I glance at the clock on the wall to see what time it is, the distinction between the clock and myself is a given: It's a physical object hanging on the wall, and I'm the perceiving subject sitting here looking at it and interpreting what it "says." Further, it's just a physical, mechanical thing, whereas I'm a thinking organism. (We'll postpone for the moment questions regarding whether and in what ways an organism's mental operations may be distinct from or identical with its bodily functions—in other words, whether the mind is reducible to the body.) This subject/object (or mind/world) distinction has been a *necessary* assumption for modern science, which its earliest proponents advanced as the sole means whereby we might obtain certain knowledge of our world. All considerations finding their origin in the subject—individual or cultural preferences, tastes, opinions, prejudices, and so on—are to be taken out of the equation in modern scientific investigation, whose ideal goal has traditionally been certain, objective knowledge. Thus the very conception of science has demanded an ontological difference between the knowing subject and the known object.

This distinction has been increasingly called into question over the past century, and from different quarters. It has already been almost a hundred years since Heisenberg first published his principle of indeterminacy, and the nature and extent of the relatedness of the scientific observer and the object under observation have been a matter of debate (sometimes quite heated) among physicists and philosophers of science ever since. At this point in the debate, both the scientific and the philosophical communities seem to be polarized, each consisting of one camp that tends toward retaining the objectivist ideal and another that tends toward subjectivity; representatives of the former are generally wedded to some variety of materialist, mechanist metaphysics, while representatives of the latter tend to find varieties of idealist metaphysics most compatible. Already by the last decades of the nineteenth century, in the wake of the remarkable successes of the materialist-oriented natural sciences, materialism had firmly entrenched itself as the metaphysical foundation for the philosophy of science. To the present day, the overwhelming majority of philosophers of science remain committed to materialism of one sort or another. This is perhaps most clear in the case of philosophers of biology, the most vocal of whom proclaim Darwin's theory of natural selection as the supreme triumph of modern

---

concerning the "location" of the person in God's creation, which became problematic in a new way after the heliocentric view of Copernicus replaced the geocentric view that had held sway since before the beginning of the Christian era.

materialist science.[11] Following the lead of this approach to the study of biology, current research in cognitive science seems committed to the view that the mind is identical with, or in one way or another "reducible to," the brain or central nervous system. This view extends the "brain-mind" of the biological subject to its objective, physical environment, thereby overcoming in an exclusively materialist manner the distinction between subject and object.

The opposed "idealist" view has few philosophical champions today, and I doubt that any are philosophers of science. This approach to overcoming the subject-object distinction more or less died with the British Neo-Hegelians of the late nineteenth and early twentieth centuries, their young students finding the materialist orientation of utilitarianism more down-to-earth and commonsensical than the Neo-Hegelians' peculiar brand of idealism.[12] Those speaking in support of an anti-materialist position nowadays are generally those who are at the same time speaking as apologists for a particular religious view, and who usually regard contemporary science as atheistic and the enemy of religion.

This might appear to be an exaggerated caricature and a gross oversimplification of the situation, but it is surprisingly accurate. Only these two opposed extremes are commonly maintained as legitimate positions with regard to the various epistemological and metaphysical problems in the traditional distinction between the subject and the object. Yet each of these diametrically opposed positions suffers from so many serious difficulties—all of which have been so well rehearsed that they warrant no repetition here—that the only thing truly surprising in this situation is its continued perseverance. Our thinking appears to have hit a wall when it comes to the subject/object relation in modern science, and this suggests that we ought to reconsider the basic concepts at work here. Current realist phenomenology has been doing just that. Many of its investigations have immediate bearing not only on the subject/object relation, but also on the concept of purposiveness remaining at the heart of the controversy over evolution regarded as *contra* intelligent design.

---

11. Richard Dawkins is perhaps the best known of these authors. See, for example, Dawkins, *The Selfish Gene* (1976) and *The Extended Phenotype* (1982).

12. As represented chiefly by T. H. Green, F. H. Bradley, and Edward Caird, British Neo-Hegelianism in fact arose in large part precisely as a response to the materialism of utilitarianism and to the threat that the increasingly materialist tendencies of science were posing to religion. Among those students who were alienated by the idealist teachings of the Neo-Hegelians were Bertrand Russell and G. E. Moore.

Part 1: Philosophy and Theology

THE PHENOMENOLOGICAL APPROACH

While its origins may be located in various thinkers throughout the history of philosophy, phenomenology as an actual philosophical movement began shortly after the turn of the twentieth century, with Husserl's development of a unique method by which to approach the study of human consciousness. Husserl's investigations quickly led him to conceive of and articulate this method as committed to a type of idealism which, following Kant, he called "transcendental," anxious to distinguish it from the sort of "metaphysical" idealism that both he and Kant identified with Berkeley. Yet Husserl himself never managed to clarify to anyone's satisfaction just how his form of idealism was different from Berkeley's, a failure that became all the more urgent as Husserl increasingly stressed the extent to which consciousness "constitutes" the objects towards which it is directed. The fear of relapsing into older varieties of idealism prompted some of Husserl's earliest and most devoted students to formulate "realist" phenomenological alternatives to what they perceived as Husserlian idealism, all the while remaining true to their master's original vision of the goals and methods of phenomenological research. Two of these early students and critics of Husserl were Edith Stein and Roman Ingarden, who offered two different conceptions of realist phenomenology.

Basically, any phenomenology is to be called "realist" if it denies that subjectivity is the sole origin and exclusive ground of the objects constituted by consciousness. The two main schools of realist phenomenology disagree about the nature and origin of the elements essential to these objects and not originating in the subject. What we might call the "theological" or, more precisely, Christian school of realist phenomenology maintains that God is the ground and origin of these elements, which function as transcendental conditions of various sorts of cognition—most importantly, those sorts having to do with the moral and spiritual dimensions of human existence. Edith Stein was the earliest major proponent of Christian realist phenomenology, which was further developed after her death and continues to flourish today.[13]

13. Dietrich von Hildebrand, who moved from Munich to Göttingen in the summer semester of 1909 to study with Husserl, was another early representative of Christian realist phenomenology; Josef Seifert, founder of the International Academy of Philosophy, has continued this tradition. John F. Crosby explains in his Introduction to Volume V of *Aletheia*, a special issue of the journal devoted to "The Philosophy of Dietrich von Hildebrand": "I think it is true to say that no one has done more than the present rector of the Academy, Josef Seifert, to explain, defend, develop, and also to test critically and to correct, the philosophical legacy of von Hildebrand. Now that the Academy is in possession of a complete copy of the literary remains of von Hildebrand, it has established

The non-theological school of realist phenomenology originated with Adolf Reinach and Roman Ingarden, two of Stein's friends and fellow students of Husserl at Göttingen. Reinach died in World War I, leaving instructions that his unpublished works be destroyed; some of them nevertheless survived, but what was clearly to have been a huge program of research now remains tragically incomplete and fragmentary. Ingarden's published work, on the other hand, is quite extensive, and it is this body of work that supplies the foundation for current research in non-theological realist phenomenology.

The revision of the Husserlian concept of intentionality is central to the development of realist phenomenology I have suggested,[14] a revision that leads to a new model of the mind and, accordingly, to a new way of viewing the relation of mind and world—that is, a new way to overcome what Merleau-Ponty referred to as "the subject/object dichotomy." The doctrine of the intentionality of consciousness remains at the basis of all phenomenology; as traditionally stated, it is that "consciousness is always consciousness of . . ." This version of intentionality sees it as a feature of consciousness. In my own development of realist phenomenology I have suggested reversing the relation so as to regard consciousness as a feature of intentionality. In other words, we should think of consciousness arising as a product of intentionality, or "directedness." As directedness characterizes all of creation, from the simplest and most basic constituents of what we call "inorganic matter" to the most complex organic systems of nature, some degree of intentionality is to be acknowledged at every level of creation.

This view of the relation between consciousness and intentionality has profound implications for any discussion of design in the world, and also for the analysis of any possible relation between such design and what we might want to call "intelligence." If intelligence is regarded as belonging to consciousness, and consciousness arises as the product of a "directedness" that characterizes all of creation, there must persist an essential affinity between intelligence and its origin in nature. In other words, while there most certainly exists a material distinction between mind and world, there persists a shared formal ontological identity.[15] According to this view, intelligence

---

itself as *the* main center of von Hildebrand studies in the world, and thereby also as one of the main centers of the realist phenomenology, as well as of the particular kind of Christian philosophy, represented by von Hildebrand." Crosby, "Introduction," 2.

14. I have discussed the program of realist phenomenology at length in *Aesthetic Genesis*; and DiTommaso, Nayed, and I examine the concept of intentionality in depth in *Author's Intention*. For an extensive treatment of Ingarden, see my *Roman Ingarden's Ontology and Aesthetics*.

15. The arguments I state too briefly in this paragraph and the next demand far

did not "cause" the design—intelligence *is* the design. The assumption on the part of both those supporting and those opposing the argument from design is that no such formal ontological identity persists—in other words, that there is a formal ontological distinction between mind and world, between intelligence and creation. Intelligent design theorists proceed from an anthropomorphist analogy, maintaining that there must be some intelligent agent or being that has imposed order on creation by injecting form into matter and thereby "designing" the world. Darwinians opposing the argument from design claim that whatever "design" exists in the world has arisen through a long series of natural accidents, and that the order we see in nature, inorganic and organic alike, is not only incomplete (in that it does not characterize all of creation) but inessential to creation and entirely transitory (as the very word "evolution" seems to suggest to some). Both approaches to the question of design in the world fail to see the identity of design and intelligence, and thereby fail to see this "natural intelligence" as necessarily informing every moment of material creation.

My use of the term "informing" in that last sentence was technical and an allusion to Aristotle. Aristotelian philosophy provides realist phenomenology with many of its key concepts, with "form" being perhaps the most important. The Aristotelian description of the relation between form and matter is crucial here, and has significant implications for our discussion of design. To state it most simply, all matter has form, and all form endures only in matter; there is no matter than is not "informed," and no form can persist without a material substrate. Aristotelian philosophy stands in opposition to the account of creation we find in *Genesis*—or at least, to the sort of literal interpretation of that account that inspires the creationist formulation of the argument from design. For the Aristotelian, it is inconceivable that there could first exist formless matter that a separate intelligence subsequently imbued with form. Matter *always* has form, and no material entity can exist without its form. Indeed, it is the form of a thing that is, to a great extent, responsible for that thing's coming into being in the first place. Without entering too deeply into the complexities of the Aristotelian view of the relation between formal and final causality in nature, we may briefly say that the form of a natural entity—for simplicity, we'll speak now of "organisms"—dictates the manner in which the matter of the organism will be ordered in such a way as to enable the organism to live. The most basic condition to be fulfilled in this ordering is supplied by *purposiveness*: the organism's individual organs must be ordered in such a

---

more support than I can provide in the space of the present paper. For the full arguments, see "The Negative Lexicon," chapter 2 in *Aesthetic Genesis*.

way that they fulfill their respective purposes, and the organism as a whole must behave purposively in order to continue in existence. This purposiveness is part of the very *form* of the organism and, again, this form is always embodied in matter. In short, purposiveness belongs to the very nature of matter (most clearly in the case of organisms, but a similar account may be given of "inorganic" nature), and when we regard natural entities or nature as a whole as "acting with some purpose," it is not only unnecessary but indeed illegitimate to infer that this purpose must have been bestowed by some separate intelligence. Indeed, our very perception (or cognition) of this purposiveness is an instance of our participating in the same form as the object that we are perceiving (or cognizing). This very brief presentation of the Aristotelian position, while painfully incomplete, suffices for the task at hand: realist phenomenology, adopting many of the insights of Aristotelian metaphysics and the Aristotelian account of cognition, regards all of creation as informed and purposive, and human consciousness and intelligence as simply more complex developments of features that are to be found at every level of nature.

CONCLUSION

As I stated in the Introduction, it has not been my intention in this paper to argue for or against either the intelligent design theorists or the evolutionary theorists. My critical look at some of the concepts shared by both sides in the debate does call into question certain features of the arguments of both sides, but these criticisms are offered merely as a means to a different end. As I also stated in the Introduction, I regard the problem motivating the debate between intelligent design theorists and evolutionary theorists to be insoluble as currently formulated. My brief presentation of the approach of realist phenomenology will hopefully encourage a somewhat different manner of reflecting on the problem of design in nature, and with such further reflection we may even be able to formulate the problem in such a way as to move beyond the current stalemate. It may well be that realist phenomenological analysis will lead us to regard purposiveness in nature—and the "final Causes" that Newton spoke of in his "General Scholium"—as nothing more than natural. We may conclude, in other words, that it simply belongs to the essence of nature that it consist of informed matter ordered purposively. The acknowledged presence of design in nature may then not of itself imply the necessary existence of a Creator, although it could well lead us to identify previously neglected conditions of this design and thence to a more compelling formulation of the argument from design. Further reflection along these lines may also call into question—or, alternatively, buttress—other assumptions of evolutionary theorists that become explicit in their argument against intelligent design. In any event, further phenomenological examination of the issue will at the very least provide us with a fresh way to engage in the current debate over this ancient argument.

BIBLIOGRAPHY

Crosby, John F. "Introduction." *Aletheia* V (1992).

Davis, Percival, and Dean H. Kenyon. *Of Pandas and People*. 2nd ed. Dallas: Haughton, 1993.

Dawkins, Richard. *The Extended Phenotype: The Long Reach of the Gene*. Oxford: Oxford University Press, 1982.

———. *The Selfish Gene*. Oxford: Oxford University Press, 1976.

Hume, David. *Dialogues Concerning Natural Religion*. Edited by Norman Kemp Smith. Indianapolis: Bobbs-Merrill, 1947.

———. *Enquiries Concerning Human Understanding and Concerning the Principles of Morals*. 2nd ed. Edited by L. A. Selby-Bigge. London: Oxford University Press, 1902.

Kant, Immanuel. *Critique of the Power of Judgment*. Translated by Paul Guyer and Eric Matthews. Cambridge: Cambridge University Press, 2000.

———. *Critique of Pure Reason*. Translated by Paul Guyer and Allen W. Wood. Cambridge: Cambridge University Press, 1998.

———. *Prolegomena to Any Future Metaphysics*. Translated by Lewis White Beck. Upper Saddle River, NJ: Prentice-Hall, 1997.

Mitscherling, Jeff. *Aesthetic Genesis: The Origin of Consciousness in the Intentional Being of Nature*. Lanham, MD: University Press of America, 2010.

———. *Roman Ingarden's Ontology and Aesthetics*. Ottawa: University of Ottawa Press, 1997.

Mitscherling, Jeff, Tanya DiTommaso, and Aref Nayed. *The Author's Intention*. Lanham, MD: Lexington, 2004.

Newton, Isaac. "General Scholium." In *Principia Mathematica*. 3rd ed. Translated by Andrew Motte, 1729. Online: The Newton Project Canada: www.isaacnewton.ca/gen_scholium/.

Xenophon. *Xenophon*, vol. IV: *Memorabilia and Oeconomicus*. Translated by E. C. Marchant. Loeb Classical Library. Cambridge: Harvard University Press, 1948.

7

Faith in Reason and Faithful Reasoning

Polanyi's Fiduciary Program as Common Ground between Philosophy and Theology

MARTIN X. MOLESKI, SJ

We have but one instrument for the investigation of any kind of question whatsoever: the human mind. All humans who think in any way at all think just like all other humans. Philosophy uses the resources of the human mind to determine what can be discovered by relying solely on the resources of human reason. Theology directs the same mental resources toward the question of understanding a religious tradition. Although the focus of theology differs from that of philosophy, in the background the very same power of human reason is at work; apart from the premises supplied by the religious tradition, theology has no other tools to use to explore religious questions than any other human discipline.

The thesis I have just stated in the first paragraph is a personal philosophical commitment that I propose as a universal truth. It is a sweeping, but, I hope, not a hasty or unwarranted generalization. In my view, it is the job of philosophy to address the whole of reality, which includes all possible religious interpretations of reality along with every other existing or conceivable branch of study. The philosopher surveys all things under the aspect of what is or can be known just from thinking about thinking or reasoning about reasoning.[1]

A good theory of all possible theories should be self-referentially consistent. The standards that I apply to all possible ideas about ideas have to apply to themselves, too; otherwise, I would be guilty of using a double standard: one set of guidelines to judge everybody else and a different set for myself. That would not be fair. My theories must account for my own theorizing—both when my theories succeed and when they fail.

POLANYI'S FIDUCIARY PROGRAM: A CONSCIOUSLY POST-CRITICAL PHILOSOPHY

Michael Polanyi (1891–1976) was, in turn, a medical doctor (1914), a physical chemist (PhD, 1917), a lecturer in Economics (1948), and a mostly self-taught social analyst, philosopher, and theologian (1940–76). Born into a non-practicing Jewish family, he was baptized Catholic (1919) but lived, practiced, and wrote as a non-denominational Christian.[2] Polanyi's success as a physical chemist gave him a wealth of personal experience and a set of convictions from which he developed his own philosophy of science, epistemology, and religious views. "We have . . . begun to live in a new intellectual period, which I would call *the post-critical age of Western civilization*. Liberalism to-day is becoming conscious of its own *fiduciary foundations* and is forming an alliance with other beliefs, kindred to its own."[3]

The objectivist critical philosophies of the Enlightenment strove to make a clear distinction between knowledge and belief, with the natural science and scientists holding pride of place when contrasted with the untestable, subjective opinions of religious believers. Polanyi realized that the knowledge gained by scientists is itself derived from and inextricably linked to a kind of faith in reason that is structurally and epistemically indistinguishable from the religious act of faith. The denial of faith as a way to know reality undercuts not just religion but science as well; to vindicate the role of faith in reasoning about the universe accessible to our senses also upholds the potential of faith to disclose metaphysical realities. Polanyi expected that

---

1. This slogan is derived from Bernard J. F. Lonergan's *Insight*: "A unification and organization of other departments of knowledge is a philosophy. But every insight unifies and organizes. Insight into insight, then, will unify and organize the insights of mathematicians, scientists, and men of common sense. It seems to follow that insight into insight will yield a philosophy." Lonergan, *Insight*, x.

2. For full details of Polanyi's life, see Scott and Moleski, *Michael Polanyi*.

3. Polanyi, *The Logic of Liberty*; emphasis added.

a correct understanding of the fiduciary dimension of science would also revitalize religion: "Men need a purpose which bears on eternity. Truth does that; our ideals do it; and this might be enough, if we could ever be satisfied with our manifest moral shortcomings and with a society which has such shortcomings fatally involved in its workings. Perhaps this problem cannot be resolved on secular grounds alone. But its religious solution should become more feasible once religious faith is released from pressure by an absurd vision of the universe, and so there will open up instead a meaningful world which could resound to religion."[4]

In my view, Polanyi should also be understood as a realist. Olive Davies preserved an excerpt from a letter that Polanyi wrote to a logical positivist, most likely during the 1950s when he was working on *Personal Knowledge*:[5]

> It is necessary for me, and others of my kind of convictions, to believe that *science possesses reality*; that it is discovered by man but not made by man; that it is not 'artificial' but possesses an ungovernable life of its own. *Unless such a reality, external to man's action, is recognized, science—and truth in general, and the whole realm of intellectual and moral statements—inevitably becomes subordinate to man's material needs.* There is no sense of this inevitability in people who, in T. S. Eliot's phrase, live near the Bank and the Police Station (i.e., can rely on a steady flow of tradition, for the time being)—but to me this theoretical subordination appears as a catastrophic reality. I know the phrases in which it was formulated to persecute our fellow scientists in Soviet Russia, I recall the almost identical form of words on Hitler's and Himmler's lips when they settled on the fate of German scholars resisting their historical and anthropological theories.
>
> I cannot rely on the mercies of common sense against logic in these matters. Your conception of reality has been recently elaborated to its final conclusion on academic grounds in Logical Positivism. This is a complete denial of validity in any theoretical statement. It reduces all moral, aesthetic, and religious conceptions to "ways of talking."
>
> There seems only one way to fight, however hopelessly perhaps, for the rehabilitation of civilized thought: *to secure by an act of faith the reality of our ideals.* Unless we accept that position, we open, as Logical Positivism has clearly demonstrated it, the central citadel of all human convictions to the rule of nihilism. We lay down our arms and abandon any ground on which

---

4. These are the closing sentences of Polanyi's *Tacit Dimension*, 92.
5. Polanyi, *Personal Knowledge*.

Hitler and Himmler (in their million shapes all over the world) can be resisted.[6]

By showing that science depends upon the faith (personal commitment) of scientists in the power of reason to make contact with reality, Polanyi intended to affirm a philosophy that had room for the notions of "truth in general, and the whole realm of intellectual and moral statements," including the domain of religious thought. The "act of faith" that could secure "the reality of our ideals" was an act of faith in the natural powers of mind, not a religious act of faith directed toward some kind of supernatural order.

For Polanyi, science is a body of knowledge because scientists make contact with reality through their theoretical constructs. *Believing* that a theory will be supported by future developments in the field is an essential ingredient of scientific activity.

> What Copernicus believed of this system was what we all mean by saying that a thing is real and not a mere figment of the mind. What we mean is that the thing will not dissolve like a dream, but that, in some ways *it will yet manifest its existence, inexhaustibly, in the future.* For it is there, whether we believe it or not, independently of us, and hence never fully predictable in its consequences. The anticipatory powers which Kepler, Galileo and Newton revealed in the heliocentric system were as many particulars of the general anticipations that are intrinsic to any belief in reality.
>
> *This defines reality and truth.* If anything is believed to be capable of a largely indeterminate range of future manifestations, it is thus believed to be real. A statement about nature is believed to be true if it is believed to disclose an aspect of something real in nature. A true physical theory is therefore believed to be no mere mathematical relation between observed data, but to represent an aspect of reality, which may yet manifest itself inexhaustibly in the future.[7]

---

6. Davies served as Polanyi's personal secretary from 1941 to 1958, the period during which Polanyi worked out his philosophy of personal knowledge. "The note on science and reality is an extract I made from a letter which Michael wrote to someone (I regret that I now cannot remember to whom it was written). (I wonder if it might have been written to Karl Popper?). At any rate it interested me so much that I kept an extract for myself" (Davies to Scott, December 10, 1978). The whole extract made by Davies is reproduced here with emphasis added.

7. Polanyi, "Science and Reality," 190.

The act of faith in the value of scientific reasoning is not an object of science; it is not a sensible reality apprehended by seeing, hearing, tasting, touching, or smelling, nor are there any laboratory instruments that can be used to observe or quantify the contribution that faith in reason makes to the scientific enterprise. Faith in reason is a metaphysical action; scientists may or may not notice that they are making such personal commitments when the focus of their attention is on the proper objects of natural science found in the sensible universe.

Polanyi presented his theory of the role of faith in science as a consciously a-critical statement: "I pointed out how everywhere the mind follows its own self-set standards, and I gave my tacit or explicit endorsement to this manner of establishing the truth. Such an endorsement is an action of the same kind as that which it accredits and is to be classed therefore as a consciously a-critical statement."[8] Before we can formulate critical questions, we are already embedded in and committed to the belief that we can recognize the proper answers to the questions. It is a vital, not a vicious, circle to recognize and affirm our reasoning powers as a given. To call them into question is to *use* them to formulate the questions and seek the answers. Anyone who denies our powers-of-reason view can do so only by using those very same powers of reasoning and is therefore self-referentially inconsistent: contradicting what they say by what they do, the skeptics are intellectual hypocrites. In one branch of the Jesuit Thomist (Aristotelian) tradition, the act of pointing out such inescapable self-referential inconsistencies is called "retortion" (or, in Europe, "retorsion").[9] Polanyi employs this kind of argument to secure the foundations of his epistemology without pinning any particular label on it.[10]

KEY FEATURES OF PERSONAL KNOWLEDGE: POST-CRITICAL EPISTEMOLOGY

In this section I want to present some of Polanyi's insights in a summary fashion for those unfamiliar with his thought. I have selected these features for my own purposes; it is by no means a complete catalog of Polanyi's thought.

---

8. Polanyi, *Personal Knowledge*, 268.
9. See Moleski, "Retortion."
10. See Moleski, "The Role of Retortion in Lonergan and Polanyi," 218–38.

1. **"All knowledge is tacit or is rooted in tacit knowing."**[11] There is no strict proof that "all knowledge is tacit or rooted in tacit knowing." This is an insight that you must see for yourself, that you can personally verify by paying some attention to how you know what you know. No one else can force you to endorse this view by mere logical argument. Polanyi offers many examples of tacit knowing as clues to support this fundamental insight: riding a bike, swimming, solving puzzles, speaking and listening, recognizing faces, musical performance, the physical skills employed in sports and in laboratory work, applying maps to terrain, the skillful use of tools, and interpreting texts.

2. **"We know more than we can tell."**[12] We can see more than we can say. Therefore, our words always *mean* more than we can tell. Speaking is linear and fragmentary; understanding is holistic.

3. **Knowing consists of the skillful integration of** subsidiaries **to a focus.**[13] The *subsidiaries* function tacitly in the background; the *focus* is associated with attention and articulation. When we focus on the *parts*, we lose sight of the *whole*.[14] The more complex the whole under consideration, the more complex the integration of subsidiaries required for understanding. Understanding is predominantly synthetic (putting pieces together) rather than analytic (taking things apart). An airplane taken apart and reduced to pieces is not a real airplane; no part of it can fly by itself. "All thought contains components of which we are subsidiarily aware in the focal content of our thinking, and . . . all thought dwells in its subsidiaries, as if they were parts of our body. Hence thinking is not only necessarily intentional, as Brentano has taught: it is also necessarily fraught with the roots it embodies. It has a from-to structure."[15]

4. **Comprehensive (synthetic) views [i.e., interpretive frameworks] direct and interpret analysis.**[16] Polanyi's theory of interpretive frameworks precedes and resembles Thomas Kuhn's notion of paradigm in some respects.[17] It is radically different because Polanyi appeals to an

---

11. Polanyi, *Meaning*, 61; Polanyi, *Knowing and Being*, 195; Polanyi, *Science, Faith and Society*, 10.

12. Polanyi, *Tacit Dimension*, 4.

13. Polanyi, *Personal Knowledge*, 343, 347, 363, 373–74, 381.

14. Ibid., 199.

15. Polanyi, *Tacit Dimension*, x.

16. Polanyi, *Personal Knowledge*, 60.

17. See Moleski, "Polanyi vs. Kuhn: Worldviews Apart" and Jacobs, "Michael Polanyi and Thomas Kuhn: Priority and Credit."

unspecifiable *vision of reality* as the ultimate interpretive framework by which we judge all other frameworks. "Yet personal knowledge in science is not made but discovered, and as such it claims to establish *contact with reality* beyond the clues on which it relies. It commits us, passionately and far beyond our comprehension, to a *vision of reality*. Of this responsibility we cannot divest ourselves by setting up objective criteria of verifiability—or falsifiability, or testability, or what you will. For we live in it as in the garment of our own skin."[18]

5. **There is a subjective and objective pole in all knowing**. The knower is a person, a subject, and the known is an object. "Comprehension is neither an arbitrary act nor a passive experience, but a responsible act claiming universal validity. Such knowing is indeed objective in the sense of establishing contact with a hidden reality; a contact that is defined as the condition for anticipating an indeterminate range of yet unknown (and perhaps yet inconceivable) true implications. It seems reasonable to describe this fusion of the personal and the objective as *personal knowledge*."[19]

6. **All efforts to depersonalize knowing are self-defeating**. "I start by rejecting the ideal of scientific detachment. In the exact sciences, this false ideal is perhaps harmless, for it is in fact disregarded there by scientists. But we shall see that it exercises a destructive influence in biology, psychology, and sociology, and falsifies our whole outlook far beyond the domain of science. I want to establish an alternative ideal of knowledge, quite generally."[20]

7. **Although I know I may conceivably be wrong, I must make commitments in order to know**. The fiduciary program is *self-referentially consistent*: "I have shown that into every act of knowing there enters a passionate contribution of the person knowing what is being known, and that this coefficient is no mere imperfection but a vital component of his knowledge. And around this central fact I have tried to construct *a system of correlative beliefs which I can sincerely hold*, and to which I can see no acceptable alternatives. But ultimately, it is my own allegiance that upholds these convictions, and it is on such warrant alone that they can lay claim to the reader's attention."[21]

---

18. Polanyi, *Personal Knowledge*, 64; emphasis added. Cf. 135, 144, 150, 159, 164–65, 335, 380, 396.
19. Ibid., vii–viii; emphasis added.
20. Ibid., vii.
21. Ibid., viii; emphasis added; cf. 267.

8. **We must first dwell within a tradition before we can break out of it.**[22] Scientists learn the art of thinking like scientists from masters of the tradition.[23] The articulate elements of the scientific interpretive framework are embedded in the tacit dimension.

9. **All of our thinking is guided by intellectual passions.** "Science can no longer hope to survive on an island of positive facts around which the rest of man's intellectual heritage sinks to the status of subjective emotionalism. It must claim that certain emotions are right; and if it can make good such a claim, it will not only save itself but sustain by its example the whole system of cultural life of which it forms part."[24]

10. **"Scientific knowing consists in discerning Gestalten that are aspects of reality.** I have here called this 'intuition'; in later writings I have described it as the tacit coefficient of a scientific theory, by which it bears on experience, as a token of reality. Thus it foresees yet indeterminate manifestations of the experience on which it bears."[25]

CONFLICTING IDEAS ABOUT IDEAS

In the following chart I try to show how Polanyi's post-critical philosophy of personal knowledge differs from the critical, objectivist philosophies derived from the successes of science in the Enlightenment.

Enlightenment: Cartesian, formal, positivist, mathematical	**Post-Critical Philosophy**: personal, tacit, fuzzy, informal
Clear	unclear, vague
Distinct	related, intertwined, dependent
sharply bounded	bright center, shadowy edges
Formal	informal
manipulated by strict logic	drawn out by analogies (*models*)

---

22. Ibid., 196.
23. Ibid., 53.
24. Ibid., 134.
25. Polanyi, *Science, Faith and Society*, 10. Optical illusions and the Magic Eye puzzles demonstrate the difference between *sensation* and *perception*. There is only one sensation, but there are *competing perceptions* (*Gestalten*, interpretations) of the sensory data. Polanyi uses this insight from Gestalt psychology as a general model for how scientists make discoveries that then may call for a revision of their previous interpretative frameworks. See Moleski, "Self-Emptying Knowledge."

rigid links in a chain of reasoning	strands woven into a rope or cable of thought
Unchanging	evolutionary, developmental
Objective	both objective and subjective
Impersonal	personal
atomic (smallest indivisible units of thought)	compounded, like molecules
Simple	complex
monovalent (just one meaning)	multivalent (many connected meanings)
exhaustively and completely defined	understood in context
completely communicable	cannot be put fully into words (known *tacitly*)
has the qualities of a part	has the qualities of a whole
grasped by analysis, i.e., taking things apart	developed by synthesis, i.e., seeing things as wholes (*Gestalt switch*)
self-evident or proven from self-evident axioms	recognized by insight and sound judgment
Deductive	intuitive, creative
Infallible	conceivably false
true or false	more or less adequate; more or less important
We know only what we can prove.	We know more than we can prove.
If we know something, we can put it into words.	The greater the reality, the less completely we can define it.
Pure reason compels people to accept ideas.	Knowing depends on being willing to know.
Feelings are irrelevant; we are thinking machines.	Feelings (*intellectual passions*) help us to reason rightly.
All knowledge can be systematized.	Systems are rooted in and upheld by personal knowledge.

I am sure that some of these attributes are synonymous—we could probably reduce "objective" and "impersonal" to the same concept, as we could "clear," "distinct," "simple," and "atomic." But the chart was created by someone who strives to think post-critically, if at all possible, and so I favor elaboration over compression.

The chart is also misleading because there is room *within* the post-critical idea of an idea for formal reasoning: "*All knowledge is tacit or rooted in tacit knowledge.*" Polanyi's fiduciary program was not intended to diminish the accomplishments of science in any way at all. He was not opposed to science; his concern was false philosophies of science that overlooked the personal commitments of scientists that guided them to contact with reality. The Cartesian claim that "all knowledge is based on clear and distinct ideas" is not clear and distinct, not self-evident, and not established from experience. Based on his personal experience of being a scientist, working with scientists, and teaching scientists, Polanyi testified that there is much more to science than appears in the reductionist philosophies of science developed in the critical era.

When a materialist like Carl Sagan finds vagueness in religion, he upholds the Enlightenment model of ideal ideas and uses it to mock the realities that religious thinkers find hard to discuss.[26] When he finds vagueness in science, he trots out the unproven, unclear, vague, impalpable, unquantifiable, unscientific theory that humans are incapable of making anything other than approximations to the truth: "All that can be hoped for is a set of successive approximations."[27] (Note that Sagan's view that "all knowledge is approximate" is *not* an approximation, but an absolute; it is not self-referentially consistent.) He claims that only those who have studied mathematics for 15 years can understand quantum electrodynamics and is comfortable with the obscurities imposed by the authorities of such experts on the general public: "It's no good, Richard Feynman once said, asking why it *is* that way. No one knows why it is that way. That's just the way it is."[28] If a believer took a similar stance concerning the mysteries of religious faith, Sagan would dismiss their views as "baloney."[29]

Polanyi knew—and hoped—that his broader view of science would break down the artificial dichotomy between science as authentic knowledge and religion as mere wishful thinking. Both scientists and religious thinkers necessarily operate on a vision of reality that cannot be fully articulated or reduced to a series of self-evident axioms.

---

26. See Sagan, *Demon-Haunted World*, 213.
27. Ibid., 245.
28. Ibid., 249.
29. Ibid., 213.

SOMETHING LIKE A CONCLUSION

I have argued here that Polanyi's understanding of the fiduciary foundation of scientific knowing creates common ground between science and religion. The personal act of commitment in religion is structurally similar to that required of scientists. Any philosophy that discredits the act of commitment in religion also undercuts the foundations of personal knowledge in science. Polanyi's philosophy of tacit, personal knowledge makes room for the religious act of faith. It is reasonable to believe in the power of reason to make contact with reality. Faith in reason is the bedrock of progress in science. Scientists, like all other human beings, live by faith. They do not possess a privileged, faith-free, impersonal, universal method that grinds out results automatically.

Scientists—like philosophers and theologians—have a moral obligation to seek the truth and to say what they see, even if they may conceivably be wrong. We are all Lutherans when we have done the best we can to check our insights against our own vision of reality. We all must say, "Here I stand; I can no other."

Polanyi's observations do not form a Cartesian system. In my view, he is right about some things and wrong about others. In my bachelor studies, when I first read *Personal Knowledge*, I had thought that it provided a complete natural theology that would provide a firm philosophical foundation for my Catholic worldview. I was wrong. There is no seamless transition from Polanyi's philosophy to any particular theology. Polanyi provides constructive tools—wise insights—that can be employed in virtually any theology (even atheology[30]).

We do not deduce a house from a hammer nor an omelet from eggs. Acceptance of the testimony of the apostles is an act consistent with Polanyi's understanding of the role of tradition and authority in establishing an interpretive framework—a vision of reality. *It is a free choice to do so, not something required by Polanyi's own worldview.* I choose to trust the testimony of the apostles because I judge that they are reliable witnesses to an event that cannot be repeated nor observed under laboratory conditions—the resurrection of Jesus from the dead.

The fact that philosophy can never dictate theology resembles the axiom of choice in mathematics. As in the Euclidean and non-Euclidean geometries, one may add axioms to a system that cannot be *formally* derived from the previous axioms. The Catholic axioms that lead me far from Polanyi's own Christian commitments deal with sin, freedom, the Trinity,

---

30. I am thinking of atheists like Marjorie Grene and Norman Wetherick, who found much to like in Polanyi's epistemology and much to dislike in his theology.

Incarnation, atonement, apostolic succession, the "deposit of faith," and the much vexed questions about the relationship between tradition and the Scriptures.

In my view, Polanyi's God is too small. He saw God as an object of inquiry on par with mathematics or a work of art. That is why his philosophy is congenial both to theism and to atheism.

> Religion, considered as an act of worship, is an indwelling rather than an affirmation. God cannot be observed, any more than truth or beauty can be observed. *He exists in the sense that He is to be worshipped and obeyed, but not otherwise; not as a fact—any more than truth, beauty or justice exist as facts.* All these, like God, are things which can be apprehended only in serving them. The words 'God exists' are not, therefore, a statement of fact, such as 'snow is white,' but an accreditive statement, such as "'snow is white" is true,' and this determines the kind of doubt to which the statement 'God exists' can be subjected."[31]

Because of my vision of reality, I cannot say that God's existence is no different from the existence of truth and beauty. God is unquestionably not an empirically observable reality. His existence does not fall within the scope of scientific methods; natural science, in and of itself, can neither affirm nor deny God's existence. For me, if I exist, then God exists. If the universe is meaningful, there must be One who meant it.

Faith in the power of reason to disclose the existence of God is a dogma in the Roman Catholic tradition (Vatican I). No particular argument was endorsed or specified by the council. The conciliar teaching echoes Paul: "Ever since the creation of the world, his invisible attributes of eternal power and divinity have been able to be understood and perceived in what he has made" (Romans 1:20).

I use Polanyi's epistemology to help me understand and appreciate the difficulties of saying what I see about religious realities. As Lao-Tzu said, "The Tao that can be put into words is not the real Tao."[32] The me that can be put into words is not the real me. The God that can be put into words is not the real God. The dogma that can be put into words is not the real dogma. For me, we dwell in what is given in the Church's tradition in order to *break into* its meaning, not *break out of* it. The faith proposes a vision of reality that goes beyond all telling. In Polanyi's account, this is not a perplexity unique to religion. It is a feature of all comprehensive worldviews, including that of science.

---

31. Polanyi, *Personal Knowledge*, 279–80; emphasis added.
32. This is one possible translation of the first verse of the *Tao Te Ching*.

BIBLIOGRAPHY

Jacobs, Struan. "Michael Polanyi and Thomas Kuhn: Priority and Credit." *Tradition and Discovery* 33:2 (2006–2007) 25–36.

Lonergan, Bernard J. F. *Insight: A Study of Human Understanding*. New York: Harper & Row, 1978.

Moleski, Martin X. "Polanyi vs. Kuhn: Worldviews Apart." *Tradition and Discovery* 33:2 (2006–2007) 8–24.

———. "Retortion: The Method and Metaphysics of Gaston Isaye." *International Philosophical Quarterly* 27 (1977) 59–83.

———. "The Role of Retortion in the Cognitional Analyses of Lonergan and Polanyi." In *Self-Reference: Reflections on Reflexivity*, edited by Steven J. Bartlett and Peter Suber. Dordrecht: Nijhoff, 1987.

———. "Self-Emptying Knowledge: The Tacit Apprehension of Mysteries in Science and Religion." In *From Polanyi to the Twenty-First Century*, edited by Richard Gelwick. Biddeford, Maine: Polanyi Society, 1997; revised and republished as "Self-Emptying Knowledge: Michael Polanyi's Vision of the Moral Foundations of Scientific Revolutions." *Appraisal* (Supplementary Issue, 1997, Part I) 22–29.

Polanyi, Michael. *Knowing and Being: Essays by Michael Polanyi*. Edited by Marjorie Grene. Chicago: University of Chicago Press, 1969.

———. *The Logic of Liberty: Reflections and Rejoinders*. London: Routledge & Kegan Paul, 1951.

———. *Personal Knowledge: Towards a Post-Critical Philosophy*. Chicago: University of Chicago Press, 1962.

———. *Science, Faith and Society*. Chicago: University of Chicago Press, 1963.

———. "Science and Reality." *British Journal for the Philosophy of Science* 18 (Nov. 1967).

———. *The Tacit Dimension*. New York: Doubleday, 1966.

———. *The Tacit Dimension*. Garden City: Anchor, 1967.

Polanyi, Michael, and Harry Prosch. *Meaning*. Chicago: University of Chicago Press, 1975.

Sagan, Carl. *The Demon-Haunted World: Science as a Candle in the Dark*. New York: Ballantine, 1997.

Scott, William T., and Martin X. Moleski. *Michael Polanyi: Scientist and Philosopher*. Oxford: Oxford University Press, 2005.

8

Religion and Philosophy
Same Content, Different Form—What Does Hegel Mean?

Jay Lampert

In *Phenomenology of Mind*, Hegel says that "the content of this picture-thinking [i.e., religion] is absolute spirit; and all that now remains to be done is to supersede this mere form."[1] And in *Lectures on the Philosophy of Religion*: "The content of philosophy, its need and interest, is wholly in common with that of religion. The object of religion [content here equals object[2]], like that of philosophy, is the eternal truth, God and nothing but God and the explication of God . . . Thus religion and philosophy coincide in one . . . But each of them is in the service of God in a way peculiar to it."[3] Quentin Lauer concludes that religion and philosophy are two expressions of the same worldview.[4] The Christian notions of Trinity, of creation,

---

1. Hegel, *Phenomenology*, 788.

2. George Kline has a refreshingly careful examination of Hegel's uses of "content," "object," and related terms in his texts on religion. See "Hegel and the Marxist-Leninist Critique of Religion."

3. Hegel, *Philosophy of Religion*, 78–79.

4. Lauer has many texts to this effect, for example *A Reading of Hegel's Phenomenology of Spirit*, 262–63. Hodgson, has a similar view of philosophy's equivalence to theology; see his *Hegel and Christian Theology*, 12–16. Later (99–100) he notes, by way of contrast, that Cyril O'Regan finds Hegel's emphasis on philosophy to diminish his relation to orthodox Christianity. John Burbidge's treatment of this problem takes into

Fall, and genesis, and of resurrection and religious community, become in philosophy: dialectic, otherness, and reciprocity. Shared content trumps different form.

On the other hand, Hegel criticizes picture-thinking. I have decided to retain Miller's outrageous translation of *Vorstellung* as "picture-thinking"[5] to give equal time to Hegel's negative approaches to religion. Stories like the Fall, by including sensible imagery, necessarily contain inconsistencies.[6] Different form implies a different self-consciousness, and will change the content. It is not really possible that the same content has two forms, or that religious thoughts of genesis are mapped directly onto philosophical thoughts of self-development.[7] Different form trumps shared content.

My goal is to explore possible meanings of "same-content different-form." It will become evident that this leads me to lean towards form.

Of course, to say that religion has one attitude and philosophy another, when each has a thousand variations, is shorthand. Both form and content develop in stages, sometimes jointly, sometimes independently.[8] The *Science of Logic* provides the theory. The *matter: wood* can be formed into either a ship or a hat. The *form: hat* is less appropriate for the *matter: wood*, but only for the user; the matter is indifferent. We call formed matters "content," and content is less indifferent to the next level of form. The *formed matter: wooden boat* fits well with oars and less well with heavy artillery. The high-level *content: story about a sea battle* is formed differently into paintings or movies. We might say that content progressively absorbs more forms, by reception or auto-poiesis, as if content drives form. Or instead, we might say that form increasingly absorbs content, that things become more and more formal—not formulaic, which is formally simplified, but more meaningful, as if form drives content.[9] Now, when form forms already formed content,

---

account the changing nature of Christianity itself, and so gives one of the most interesting analyses of the issue, e.g., in "Is Hegel a Christian?"

5. Hegel, *Phenomenology*, 440 (and many other places).

6. Hegel, *Philosophy of Religion*, 215.

7. I.e., as if there were a one-to-one correspondence of contents mapped onto different models. J. N. Findlay almost takes that view when he says that "a religious term like 'God' will, when stripped of pictorial associations, reveal itself as *meaning no more than* the 'I' of self-consciousness." In *Hegel: A Re-examination*, 342; my italics.

8. Might the category prior to both religion and philosophy provide their common content? What precedes religion? Art? In the *Phenomenology*, art is a subheading within religion. In the *Philosophy of Religion*, politics immediately precedes religion. In the *Aesthetics*, art leads to politics more than to religion. Perhaps these are red herrings, and it is simply content specific to religion—genesis, Trinity, Resurrection—that philosophy re-forms.

9. A *Gestalt* is found, but a *Form* is constructed subjectivity (Hegel,

form actually appears. What is at stake in religion is whether the whole truth of this process appears, whether the form of content is revealed as a content in its own right. Hegel's critique of picture-thinking implies that even after form appears as God, it succumbs to still another form, the form of thought.

I propose a formula for philosophy in relation to religion: philosophy is the form of the content of the form of already formed content. There is a phenomenal world: *content*. The world has meaning: *formed content*. Shapes of consciousness organize these forms: *form of formed content*. Through these shapes, the truth of the world appears; religion is the content of this absolute revelation: *content of the form of formed content*. Philosophy thinks the logic whereby truth appears through thought: *form of the content of the form of already formed content*. The simple question of whether shared content trumps different form becomes insanely complicated. But for a dialectician, every sentence has three clauses, and each of the three has three, making nine, 27, 81 . . . I think that 27 is the minimum number of elements qualifying a sentence as worthy of the name Hegelian. My formula is still short by 22.

Religion is in one sense closest to philosophy: the least wrong non-right pathway. Yet since it makes a stronger claim to absolute knowing than preceding categories—perception of a salty cube is nobody's ideal of absolute knowing—if religion is wrong, it is more wrong than perception is. Of course, most imperfect ideas are preserved in absolute knowing, but some come pretty close to vanishing: substrate, for example. So if we want to preserve God in Hegelian dialectic, we need an argument specific to that category. Why does Hegel continue to refer to God even after his chapter on religion is over? Clearly, Hegel's philosophy is in general neither atheism nor a straightforward return to religion. Perhaps Hegel is a deist and his concept of God is not really religious. Indeed, there are endless quasi-religious ways of expressing the idea of God: God is truth, Spirit is humanism, revelation is history, not to mention the neo-Platonic and Spinozistic equations. A systematic philosopher may need to deploy a concept of God, but not decide whether she believes in the existence of God.

The question whether religion is superseded has a parallel in art. If, as Hegel says, art is in the past, is religion also?[10] Neither thesis is strictly chronological. It is said that the Greeks were more art-centered than the moderns, but the issue for Hegel is rather that art cannot explain itself, and is superseded by what can. Analogously, it is not that medieval philosophy

---

Phenomenology, 766).

10. See, e.g., Jaeschke, "Philosophical Theology and Philosophy of Religion," 15. For Jaeschke, philosophy proves religious truths in the form of concepts.

was more religious than modern, but whether religious categories are sublatable in principle. Hegel's metaphor near the end of *Phenomenology* pertains both to the twilight of the Muses and to religion:[11] a girl serving fruit on a platter. From the platter, we can no longer smell the manure or hail the peasants, but we get two things that are better: we get a whole range of fruits, not just the local ones, and we can enjoy the girl's self-conscious smile. The girl is an art gallery in that she separates the art works from their indigenous cultures, but unites them with each other and with herself, i.e., with us. Then the girl is philosophy, in that she divests religions of their cultic chauvinism and serves them up to thinkers. But just *before* she is philosophy, the girl is Christ, fulfilling the prophecies and revealing their kernels while dismissing their parochial laws. Art, religion, and philosophy all historicize natural content and mediate with spiritual form. Still, if religion is already a mediating form, this mediator in turn must be mediated: no exceptions.[12] Philosophy is the form of mediative forming.

Perhaps religion practices form, but as content, whereas philosophy practices form as form. Hegel's dialectic is not Platonism, but it may be a different theory of forms. We need a lot of distinctions. Let us say that a content is factual matter whose shape is a *Gestalt*; an abstraction is not a form but a propositional content; a form (German: *Form*) is a concrete power of the negative that drives a content to develop. Philosophy never posits content, since content is not its content; it formalizes contents, negatively by limiting each, affirmatively by including each, and virtually by rational invention.

In general, content is to form as object is to subject; in religion, as an object of worship is to the mode of worship; in philosophy, as a judgment is to a mode of knowing. From the dozens of passages in *Lectures on the Philosophy of Religion* where Hegel uses content-form vocabulary to distinguish religion and philosophy, we can collect the following variations: content is to form as consciousness is to self-consciousness; as assertion is to explication; as presupposition is to proof; as sensible representation is to thought; as external is to internal; as particular is to universal; as state of affairs is to event; as event is to history; as history is to logic.[13]

Lectures on the Philosophy of Religion begins with philosophy on the defensive. It has the "same object" as religion, and does nothing but

---

11. Hegel, *Phenomenology*, 753–54.

12. Art peaks in finding content adequate to its form, and so becomes discursive; religion peaks with content too great for its form. To avoid peaking and falling, philosophy needs form and content that neither converge nor diverge.

13. A few of Hegel's comparisons do not mention form and content, as when he says "religion and philosophy as a whole turn upon dualism," i.e., upon the creation of otherness (*Philosophy of Religion*, 301), but even these are formal observations.

explicate religion; it "explicates itself in explicating religion."[14] Does philosophy pervert the content of religion by adding form? Religion's form is thin: immediate and personal, whereas philosophy's is thick: mediated and critical. Hegel's answer is that philosophy shows how religion's rightful immediacy must be related to self-consciousness.[15] Bit by bit, philosophy "asserts its rights": it interprets "unsystematic" Scriptures;[16] it "embeds" religion in other phenomena;[17] it makes of religion's division into many faiths a coherent history of divine appearances.[18] The "form of reason" is finally the true *unio mystica*:[19] all God for all people.

However, religion was not always about content. At first it was the raw form of feeling: "The form of feeling is the subjective aspect, the certainty of God. The form of representation [religion's second form] concerns the objective aspect, the content of the certainty . . . 'What is this content?' The content is God."[20] The tricky thing is that there are two kinds of form in religion: the form of feeling and the form of representation. Because both are tied to different sorts of content, they have a common resistance to reason. In fact there is a third form in religion, found in theology: the form of thought,[21] which has the same form as philosophy. But even here, says Hegel, religion thinks in personal experience, while philosophy operates with concepts alone. But this is too simple; philosophy too, like religion, is both experiential content and conceptual form, both phenomenology and logic. Could the move from phenomenology to logic be like the move from religion to philosophy, and vice versa? Or does philosophy contain one subset—a form of pure form—that religion simply does not contain, namely logic?

In *Philosophy of Religion* Hegel often instructs readers to consult his *Science of Logic*. For example, proving the Trinity "is the task of logical exposition."[22] In the transition from the Brahmanic One towards Greek religion, Hegel appeals to definitions of unity and totality, empirical and

---

14. Hegel, *Philosophy of Religion*, 79.
15. Ibid., 88–89.
16. Ibid., 93–94.
17. Ibid., 102.
18. Ibid., 107.
19. Ibid., 105.
20. Ibid., 144.
21. Ibid., 151–52.
22. Ibid., 427–32.

absolute, finite and infinite,[23] concept and objectivity,[24] and insists that these only "get developed in the science of logic";[25] the ontological proof, the only valid one, "belongs to logic."[26] Several times Hegel inserts what he calls "lemmas," "subsidiary propositions" proved separately by logic and then injected into religion.[27] Without logic, religion could not develop, or could not be seen to develop. "As soon as [thoughts go beyond empty words], their content is given a form, more specifically logical form."[28]

This sounds as though philosophy is form without content, and that cannot be quite right for Hegel. But it is not altogether wrong, either.[29] At the beginning of *Philosophy of Religion*, when Hegel is saying that philosophy shares the content that God is One, he says: "[T]hought alone is the soil for this content . . . The form—that within us which apprehends the universal—is for that very reason thought."[30] Hegel often identifies content with the sensible representations in religions, from nature symbols to God's wisdom and wrath to the narratives of Jesus.[31] Even when religion operates with concepts and theories, it is "intertwined with other, impure thoughts . . . developed from other concrete contents."[32] Once Hegel has identified content with representations, he implies that advanced religion, even before philosophy, has to move beyond content—the further the better.[33]

"The religious sphere as such" arises "for the first time" with the death and resurrection of Christ, the renunciation of security and the

---

23. Ibid., 405.
24. Ibid., 420.
25. Ibid., 294.
26. Ibid., 186.
27. Ibid., 114, 294, 331.
28. Ibid., 400.
29. Barth, in *Protestant Theology*, argues that in spite of Hegel's sincere Christian leanings, religion cannot be central for Hegel because in Hegel's philosophy "the only center is the method" (406). Barth thinks Hegel is right to associate truth and history, but wrong to associate truth with knowledge; theological truth should be more "incomprehensible," Barth says (418), and Hegel's emphasis on form "abolishes God's sovereignty" (420).
30. Hegel, *Philosophy of Religion*, 120.
31. Ibid., 145–48.
32. Ibid., 467.
33. It is not that philosophy's form will have a new content; it is as if philosophy permits no content to remain. To be sure, these passages are frequently hard to interpret. Is the anthropomorphic character of the Greek gods due to god-imagery in general, or to the isolation of those gods from each other into ethical traits? It is sometimes difficult to say whether Hegel is closer to maximal pantheism or to subtractive deism.

reconciliation with the other:[34] "This is how the content behaves."[35] That is, it behaves as form. Hegel defines consummate religion as "joining myself as myself in God together with myself."[36] But in the natural religions, where elements in nature are imbued with spiritual meaning, we expect to find a more straightforward theory that contents are representations or picture-thoughts. When we come to particular religions, Hegel's limitations and sometimes prejudices are well known.[37] In any case, what does "representation" mean? I will consider three possibilities.

IS REPRESENTATION A PARTICULAR WITHOUT AN EXPLICATION?

Treating a plant, animal, or food as a divine symbol needs an interpretation, otherwise it is an object without a subject, a content without conceptual form.[38] The commonplace that religion depicts monkey-gods and gardens of innocence would of course relegate religion to a low stage of self-consciousness, and if that is what content is, of course philosophy would want to go beyond it. But if this is content, it makes no sense to say that philosophy and religion share content. And of course, religion never aims at these sensible images for their own sake. If Hegel thought religion was cartoons, his own philosophy of religion would be a cartoon; it isn't.

In discussing Hinduism, Hegel makes the subtler point that the particularities of a religion, its sensible deities and ornate theogonies, are not its content: "The content [of Hinduism] is the one, simple, absolute substance."[39] Not even naturalistic religions that employ nature-images have those images for their real content. Contents are representations, but images are not contents. The nature-images are not the picture-thoughts

---

34. That is, with self-feeling in the Kingdom of God and the beginning of community.

35. Hegel, *Philosophy of Religion*, 463–66.

36. Ibid., 191.

37. The worst are his remarks on African religions in the *Philosophy of History*; see my "Hegel and Ancient Egypt." He does leave himself an out in case he is wrong about particular religions, by noting, consistently with his form-emphasis (particularly in the case of magic religions), that we can grasp the idea behind religions other than our own but cannot feel them subjectively "from within," and so cannot imagine why they do not critique their own religions as we do. "To put oneself in the place of a dog requires the sensibilities of a dog" (*Philosophy of Religion*, 224).

38. See, e.g., *Philosophy of Religion*, 79, 94, 144.

39. Ibid., 274.

of Hinduism; Oneness is its picture-thought (and Threeness is likewise a picture-thought[40]). So representation is not particularity.[41]

IS REPRESENTATION EXTERNALITY?

Hegel identifies five levels of exteriority in religion:[42] the assumed sovereignty of law; verification by miracles; the authority of the text;[43] the contingent history of interpretations;[44] and doctrine in "the form of positivity."[45] But again, religion already insists on overcoming externality. Hegel cites 2 Corinthians 3:6: "The letter kills, but the Spirit gives life." He also takes up the Scripture in which "God himself says 'Behold, Adam has become like one of us'" (Genesis 3:22)—a text that, unlike many readers, he interprets literally because non-literal interpretation is like saying that "God has made a joke."[46] For Hegel, it is actually true that humans become just like God, overcoming externality; Scripture already prophesies the philosophy to come, and the becoming-form of content. When Hegel says that "The content as Idea is the truth,"[47] it sounds as if he has built enough spirit into content for content to be truth. But saying that content *as Idea* is truth suggests that no matter how profound the content, it can never be truth without a formal supplement, a piling on of form *ad infinitum*—not a bad definition of philosophy. So religious content is *not* especially external—and for that matter, even philosophy posits some externality, since the truth of the whole is self-differentiating. Hegel emphasizes God's self-differentiation in revealing himself to his other, but he insists that God's internalized self-differentiation is still only good "content," not "the form of the concept."[48]

---

40. Ibid., 427–31. Assigning a number to God, whether as one, two, three, or five, is "useless" and "superfluous" picture-thinking (*Phenomenology*, 776).

41. Nor can we equate naturalistic images with anthropomorphism. For Hegel, Greek gods in the shape of humans do not philosophize, so "the defect is not that there is too much of the anthropopathic in the Greek gods, but that there is too little" (*Philosophy of Religion*, 348n). Philosophy is more anthropomorphic than religious spirituality, and therefore less a case of picture-thinking.

42. The context of his discussion involves Roman Christianity.

43. This externality will be removed when its "content is given specifically logical form" (*Philosophy of Religion*, 400).

44. "The investigation of these forms of interpretation falls to philosophy alone" (ibid., 401).

45. Ibid., 395–402.
46. Ibid., 444.
47. Ibid., 411.
48. Ibid., 425.

It is true that God the Father-Son is content ready for philosophical form in a way that God the Father is not. But even the former is "understood" as a presupposition instead of reasoned to a conclusion. So a representation need not be external.

IS REPRESENTATION ANY IDEA NOT YET PROVED?

Hegel says that, "to know the rational in God's works . . .—that is philosophy."[49] If the "content" of religion is that "God is everywhere," as Hegel says, "the form of the idea comes to appearance as a result" once we can "prove that 'what is so' is also necessary."[50] This is what makes philosophy of religion "scientific."[51] The most striking formula appears on the penultimate page of *Philosophy of Religion*: the content of religion is revealed *by* consciousness to itself.

> The standpoint of philosophy . . . is free reason, which has being on its own account, that develops the content [of religion] . . . , and justifies the content . . . Therefore, it [I will name this 'it' in a moment] is the justification of religion . . . it knows the *content* [of religion] in accord with its necessity and reason. Likewise it knows the *forms* in the development of this content. The two belong together: form and content.[52]

Justification of the content of religion is not proving the existence of God from assorted premises; it is the deduction of forms of appearance that justifies the content of religion.

The "it" that does the justifying, is, strikingly, the "Enlightenment." We know how the Enlightenment works: the more successfully you prove the Trinity, the more you become Spinozist. In *Phenomenology*, the Enlightenment is as embarrassing to philosophy as superstition is to religion, but in *Lectures on the Philosophy of Religion* it occurs almost as the finale.[53] It

---

49. Ibid., 194.
50. Ibid., 432–33.
51. Ibid., 404.
52. Ibid., 487–88.

53. Charles Taylor is one of the few commentators who notes how close the Enlightenment comes to the end of Hegel's *Philosophy of Religion* (see Taylor, *Hegel*, 509). Taylor in general finds that Hegel's version of religion has little or no room for prayer or God's love, and so is not only a demythologized religion but a "de-theologized" one (ibid., 494–95). But he puts Hegel's terseness on how philosophy can reconcile enlightenment with piety down to his pessimism that it will take hold, rather than to his pessimism about the theory itself.

is not quite the final word, but there are only three paragraphs remaining in the text: a seven-line paragraph in which Hegel says that "piety" is not concerned with justifications;[54] a nine-line paragraph including the statements, "The reconciliation [of Enlightenment and piety] is philosophy. Philosophy is to this extent theology";[55] and an eleven-line paragraph in which Hegel declares that "Enlightenment wants to have nothing further to do with the content," but philosophy does.[56] And without explaining, he signs off till next year's lecture series. Presumably, philosophy will reason out the content of religious forms, avoiding the abstractness of the Enlightenment while retaining its formalism. But then philosophy deduces theology, and the equation of the two will have the distasteful effect for the pious that Hegel predicts it will have, and that it did have in the 1820s when he was accused of atheism and/or panlogism.[57] It is one thing to say that philosophy accepts all the truths of religion and explicates them for conceptual interest, and another to say that philosophy, by demonstrating religion's necessity, is what makes religion true.

Now, whenever Hegel appeals to necessity, freedom cannot be far behind. Deduction is the freedom of self-consciousness to say and be itself. And Hegel is explicit: form is freedom. The issue is not the freedom to choose whichever faith one wishes; that choice is free with respect to the form of faith, but is "indifferent to content."[58] In practice, people often feel that their faith was freely "leapt," but rarely that the content of their faith was entirely up to them. For Hegel, "thought [in philosophy] knows itself to be free not only according to its form but also with respect to its content."[59] If the form of a religion is freedom, the content should be free too.[60] In short, it is not a question of whether religion and philosophy *have* the same form or the same content, but whether they have the same *freedom* of form and content. They may even share the same content (God) *and* the same form (Freedom), but philosophy alone harmonizes the freedom of its form with its content.

54. Hegel, *Philosophy of Religion*, 488–89.

55. Ibid., 489.

56. Ibid.

57. For this history, see Laurence Dickey's very informative "Hegel on Religion and Philosophy."

58. Hegel, *Philosophy of Religion*, 197n.

59. Ibid.

60. At the very least, the content has to exist within the subjectivity of the believer, a situation that Hegel finds in the sublime of Judaism. Judaism expresses "the rationality that subsists as subjectivity—universal subjectivity with respect to its content, and free with respect to its form" (ibid., 357).

But it is not so simple. Harmonizing a content with its most appropriate form is not always the best way to think form and content.[61] Only by separating form and content can diverse religions recognize their common truth-content. Perhaps the *goal* is to make form and content correspond, but that only happens when form is free from content in order to make its own content. (Only a philosopher, and barely even Hegel at that, could envisage the free conceptual development of new religions.) Part of what philosophy adds to religion is the thematization of form and content as distinct forces in their own rights—which is why, for philosophy, their difference of form is so important. The "same-content different-form" thesis depends on their *non*-correspondence.

Now, even if form and content can undergo relatively independent developments for portions of their connected histories, form can never render content entirely superfluous.[62] Content is always present from pre-content feelings to post-content conceptualizations, playing a role in all otherness and synthesis. This is partly why *Phenomenology* is more cautious about whether the Enlightenment can or should rid itself of picture-thinking; Hegel suggests that maybe we "should approve" of the expression of concepts in images.[63] If the topic is creation, for example, thinking pictorially is not a bad model for generating content *ex nihilo*. Nevertheless, in so many passages in *Phenomenology*, Hegel is dismissive of picture-thinking; picture-thinking needs to pin concepts to an actual event, but no actual event can support them. So, for example, it finds the origin of good and evil in Eden, then "pushes it back" to Lucifer, then perhaps back to creation itself, and so on.[64] (Many of Hegel's comments on picture-thinking involve images of good and evil, as if the very topic of good and evil drags philosophy down.)

---

61. Before the union of form and content through subjectivity is accomplished, we remain in Persian religion: "When the content is still not an inwardly developed subjectivity, the personification [of God] is only formal" (ibid., 304–6). In the first clause, it seems that the content of a personified God is opposed to subjectivity; that is, form is subjectivity, and Persian religion does not have it. In the second clause, it seems that without subjectivity, the content is merely formal.

62. We said that content was not a substance parallel to form, but one stage in the history of form. In the chapter on Religion in *Phenomenology*, Hegel calls content "the form of substance" (767).

63. Ibid., 776. Stephen Rocker argues that philosophy, although it is more conceptual, preserves religion so that philosophy's spirit can have an embodied life. See Rocker, "Integral Relation of Religion and Philosophy."

64. Hegel, *Phenomenology*, 775–76.

Where do we stand? Form localizes on content, but each content is outdated by its own justification. Content is the part of form that form shifts back into its past.[65]

Now,[66] there is one case where content contains form instead of form shaping content, namely, when Hegel treats the content of God not as object but as the subject who philosophizes. The so-called predicates of God need to be synthesized in a concept, and "God is the one who resolves the contradictions."[67] Philosophizing *is* God, "what God is for himself."[68] God represents representation, as well as reason, and community; they are the logic of God's own eternal life.[69] The old interpretation of Hegel, according to which Logic is the representations in the mind of God, has fallen out of favor; but maybe it was correct. Of course, it cuts both ways: logic is only what is in God's mind, but what is in God's mind is only logic.

Still, once we get back to topics specific to religion, any preservation of representation is problematic for philosophy. For Hegel, resurrection is the paradigm. That death is overcome in community should be an ontological point about self-consciousness. Indeed, that is what revealed religion wants to say; it knows that actual communities have cultural limitations, and that resurrection trans-forms the content of both death and community. So resurrection *is* already a thought-form: behind picture-thinking's back, picture-thinking's content has become form. Hegel says that at this point in religion, "self-consciousness has ceased to think in pictures."[70] Picture-thinking was responsible for articulating a battle between good and evil, and now picture-thinking itself appears as the evil of idolatry,[71] a holdover from the pagan past. But now, the demonization of picture-thinking uses the same model of good and evil; it is more picture-thinking. Ceasing to think in pictures is not enough to escape pictures. The very fact that content is its past threatens to corrupt form. In different terms, as long as art and

65. Form and content alternate positions, as when a natural impulse (a form) gets pictorialized as a god (a content), and later the form of representation is re-formed by rational theology: a form is transposed onto a content, then the content becomes a form, which another form challenges. There are times when it is difficult to say what is the content and what is the form.

66. When, occasionally, the Greeks shape gods just so they will express ethical form, "the formal element turns over into the content" (Hegel, *Philosophy of Religion*, 331); the content does nothing but embody form.

67. Ibid., 413.

68. Ibid., 414.

69. We might say that God creates form out of content when he bears a Son; see, perhaps, Hegel, *Phenomenology*, 769.

70. Ibid., 780.

71. Ibid., 782.

religion are in the past, philosophy will remain philosophy of aesthetics and theology, and logic will not be free.

Here we need a few words about history. In a sense, the form of content is its history.[72] Revealed religion is the form of redemption of previous prophecies, incorporating both the pre-religious and postmodern. Hegel says that Christianity ascends to God "historically";[73] each religious community has its moment in the "history of the appearances of God."[74] The "history of God . . . is the life that God himself *is*."[75] However, chronological history is not conceptual history. As Hegel says, echoing the Christian new beginning against traditionalism, "any merely historical view comes to an end."[76] Hegel's promise that "finitude and evil are destroyed" echoes 2 Corinthians: "the last enemy will be destroyed." The last enemy is death, or, more generally, time. At a certain point in time, time itself comes to an end in a new, all-at-once, i.e., logical, history. But now, if this second history allows "consummate" religion to place its past into a past that no longer counts as true, religion itself faces the same momentum. In its happy consciousness, faith presupposes that reconciliation is possible, and even that it "has happened."[77] But the promissory future and the assurance of the past are no substitute for the presence of self-conscious demonstration. Chronology comes before or after conceptual history, and in truth, chronology is not history at all. This explains the backhanded role that Hegel assigns to the "teaching church."[78] It is indispensable that children be "born into" the church "while still unconscious," that they be baptized to their "vocation for truth," that they be "cultivated" by "authority."[79] There is a role for habit in Hegel, and yet philosophers are not children;[80] but on the other hand, to say that religion is the childhood of philosophy cannot be right either, for that mimics once again the model of the chronological past.

In fact, the critique of the chronological past is the first success that Hegel attributes to the critique of picture-thinking, which is not to condemn religion but to save it from history. Hegel says it is dangerous to attribute

---

72. Hegel, *Philosophy of Religion*, 391–92.
73. Ibid., 468.
74. Ibid., 469.
75. Ibid., 470.
76. Ibid., 467n.
77. Ibid., 471. Even those who do not practice "speculative thinking" can receive this certainty.
78. Ibid., 476.
79. Ibid., 477.
80. Ibid., 476.

resurrection only to the historical Jesus, and not to the "self of everyone."[81] If resurrection is not an equally distributed universal, it is "not yet the form of the concept."[82] The revealed content must die, i.e., must become past, if it is to become form and spirit, but it is a mistake to think that becoming-past happens in the past. A resurrection-event "remote in time and space"[83] permits the false view that religion is a thing of the past. It is picture-thinking to assume that religion is an event of the past, and the critique of picture-thinking is what saves religion.

But how does religion get out of pictures of the past, free from content, free from self-images? How does philosophy do so? If philosophy is the form of things that cannot get out of picture-thinking, how does it get out of that of which it is the form? After each step to escape picture-thinking, the escape has still not been effected.[84] The model of the past is picture-thinking, and every time philosophy rejects the image of the past, it puts religion and its picture-thinking into the past, thereby conceding the model of the past and reviving picture-thinking, which contradicts the form of resurrection. Revealed religion is "the true absolute content";[85] this is not disputed. But just because it is in movement, picture-thinking still always "attaches" to it and "burdens" it.[86] Content is a stain that cannot be washed off.

To go beyond picture-thinking supposes that there is a beyond, and so does not go beyond it. To go beyond the beyond, to go meta-beyond, to affirm a meta-resurrection, invokes a different sort of form-beyond-content than mere superiority. For philosophy to be higher than religion is not to put religion into its past, but to recapitulate the moments of religion in an entirely formal schematic. As for the image, perhaps the best that can be done is to treat it *as* image, to keep an intellectual "distance" from it.[87] It's my picture, but it's only a picture. My Mother is human, but my Father is divine. The content treats the image as if it is real, but the form treats it as

81. Hegel, Phenomenology, 762.

82. Ibid., 762–63. See also 784: even the idea that God is self-consciousness is too particular!

83. Ibid., 764.

84. Somewhat paradoxically, near the end of the Religion chapter of *Phenomenology*, having argued that he who is resurrected, the mediator and source of the beyond, must in turn be mediated and "got beyond," Hegel reverses his statement five paragraphs earlier (780) that "self-consciousness has ceased to think in pictures," and now says that resurrection too remains an "imaginative idea" (784) which is "no longer beyond picture-thinking" (785). Having ceased, it is no longer not.

85. Ibid., 776.

86. Ibid., 787.

87. Ibid. The key is to treat the image as "a distant past" or a "distant future," which amount to the same thing.

a contingent, though self-conscious, "seeing-as": as-if content vs. seeing-as form. If the movement *through* content is self-knowing Spirit, it can hardly pause to commit itself to any of the contents as such, nor cause them to be succeeded by some new content. Of course, this is true of anything; philosophers do not make sugar cubes or live Roman lives, we think about thinking about them. The trick is that religion already articulates thought, representation, and synthesis. Its only flaw is that it lives thought in specific ways, limiting itself to the appearances of forms and not the forms themselves.

To sum up, I think the same-content different-form thesis intensifies the formal side of philosophy. However, it is not clear how the formal side of philosophy preserves the content of religion. The text shows us how philosophy *thinks about* religion, but not how it uses religious content for its own work—assuming there is such a thing as its own work, which may not be obvious. Perhaps philosophy deduces from pure being not just the forms but also all the contents of all the religions; but not likely. Or perhaps philosophy designs its concepts to include parallels to every passage of Scripture: equally unlikely, because too submissive. Perhaps philosophy just looks in religious images for clues that might be useful for logic? No; too minimal. Perhaps philosophy is an operation and not a subject-matter, and merely uncovers the form of pre-existing contents, of which religion is the best. No, that is too formalist even for me. Perhaps philosophy is a mode of embodied, historical, and social life—yes, but not necessarily religious. Perhaps philosophy takes something on faith? No. Perhaps philosophy needs its prior standpoints like religion to be autonomous so that it can surpass them[88]—yes, of course, but that's the problem.

Or perhaps when philosophy takes up religion in the concrete, it really is informed only by the forms of oneness, resurrection, and the like, and not by the contents after all. Perhaps philosophy simply takes every thing in the world as a form: Isis, Job, and Jesus; tonkas and the Eucharist; Gothic cathedrals and Hegel conferences. These are all concrete forms: forms of genesis and structure, forms of logical thought, forms of life.

It is as if philosophy surpasses religion just by judging that religion is the truest *content* there can be. Hegel does not challenge the correctness of any religious propositional content, not even symbolic propositions about animal gods. Yet conceding truth, causal power, or even absolute reality to a sphere of reality is hardly praise in Hegel's system. Nature too, after all, exists unconditionally, yet knowing nature correctly is not an absolute standpoint. Religious doctrines may be entirely accurate, prayer might be efficacious,

---

88. James Doull has a good approach along these lines, in his "Comment on Quentin Lauer."

and theology the best way to theorize about absolute being, about the givenness of the given, or about loving recognition; but the instant we ask, "What is the form of that proposition?" or "What is that the content of?" we are in another form, the science of logic. And it is not as though Hegel introduces criteria of form and content only to achieve a partisan result; they are logically indispensable in order for consciousness to change, and be changed by, the world of objects.

As Hegel is aware, religion may wonder, "If the truth is before us, subjectively, objectively, and absolutely, why does it matter what form it takes?" The question whether religion and philosophy share content but not form is of concern only to form; it is a question that philosophy asks, not religion. Even where Hegel acknowledges that religion and philosophy are the same, he is clearly *doing* philosophy, as I am today, and not doing religion. Comparing religion and philosophy for their form and content is comparing apples and oranges. But the point of the fruit-girl is that apples and oranges roll around on the same plate.

BIBLIOGRAPHY

Barth, Karl. *Protestant Theology in the Nineteenth Century*. Translated by Brian Cozens. London: SCM, 2001.

Burbidge, John. "Is Hegel a Christian?" In *New Perspectives on Hegel's Philosophy of Religion*, edited by David Kolb, 93–107. Albany: State University of New York Press, 1992.

Dickey, Laurence. "Hegel on Religion and Philosophy." In *The Cambridge Companion to Hegel*, edited by Frederick C. Beiser, 301–47. Cambridge: Cambridge University Press, 1993.

Doull, James. "Comment on Quentin Lauer's 'Hegel on the Identity of Content in Religion and Philosophy.'" In *Hegel and the Philosophy of Religion*, edited by D. E. Christensen, 279–83. The Hague: Nijhoff, 1970.

Findlay, J. N. *Hegel: A Re-examination*. London: George Allen & Unwin, 1958.

Hegel, Georg Wilhelm Friedrich. *Lectures on the Philosophy of Religion: One-volume Edition—The Lectures of 1827*. Edited by Peter C. Hodgson. Translated by R. F. Brown, P. C. Hodgson, et al. Berkeley: University of California Press, 1988.

———. *Phenomenology of Spirit*. Translated by A. V. Miller. Oxford: Oxford University Press, 1977.

———. *The Philosophy of History*. Translated by J. Sibree. 1956. Reprint. Matrix: Dover Philosophical Classics. Mineola, NY: Dover, 2004.

———. *The Science of Logic*. Translated by George Di Giovanni. Cambridge: Cambridge University Press, 2010.

Hodgson, Peter C. *Hegel and Christian Theology: A Reading of the Lectures on the Philosophy of Religion*. Oxford: Oxford University Press, 2008.

Jaeschke, Walter. "Philosophical Theology and Philosophy of Religion." In *New Perspectives on Hegel's Philosophy of Religion*, edited by David Kolb, 1–18. Albany: State University of New York Press, 1992.

Kline, George L. "Hegel and the Marxist-Leninist Critique of Religion." In *Hegel and the Philosophy of Religion: The Wofford Symposium*, edited by D. E. Christensen, 187–202. The Hague: Nijhoff, 1970.

Lampert, Jay. "Hegel and Ancient Egypt: History and Becoming." *International Philosophical Quarterly* 35 (1995) 43–58.

Lauer, Quentin. *A Reading of Hegel's Phenomenology of Spirit*. New York: Fordham University Press, 1976.

Rocker, Stephen. "The Integral Relation of Religion and Philosophy in Hegel's Philosophy." In *New Perspectives on Hegel's Philosophy of Religion*, edited by David Kolb, 27–37. Albany: State University of New York Press, 1992.

Taylor, Charles. *Hegel*. Cambridge: Cambridge University Press, 1975.

9

"Truth Is Subjectivity"
The Religious and the Secular within the Bounds of Kierkegaard and Kant[1]

BRAYTON POLKA

"Truth is subjectivity." Such is the dramatic avowal made by Kierkegaard in *Concluding Unscientific Postscript* (published in 1846).[2] Yet, by the end of this huge and sprawling work he has bound both truth and subjectivity to Christian faith, to Christianity. Still, in sharply distinguishing Christianity from Christendom, with Christendom understood to be the reduction of Christian faith to the idolatry of objective certainty, Kierkegaard rigorously

1. See my related studies on Kant, Kierkegaard, and modern philosophy: "*Works of Love*"; "Who Is the Single Individual?"; "Metaphysics of Thinking Necessary Existence"; "Hermeneutics of the Single Individual in Kierkegaard"; and "Modern Philosophy, The Subject, and the God of the Bible." This present study is a revised version of the paper that I gave at the 11th Biennial Conference of the International Society for the Study of European Ideas, held at the University of Helsinki from July 28 to August 2, 2008.

2. While it is important to take into account the pseudonymous authors in whose name Kierkegaard presents many of his works, it is far more important to account, as many scholars fail to do, for the common framework of ideas that shapes the totality of his work both pseudonymous and authored. The hermeneutical challenge posed by Kierkegaard's texts is no different in principle from the hermeneutical challenge posed by all texts (whether by, say, Spinoza or Shakespeare). For purposes of economy I therefore refer in this study to Kierkegaard as the author of both his pseudonymous and his authored works.

identifies Christianity with what he calls the single individual, inwardness, indirect communication, the invisibility of infinite spirit as metaphor, the art of existing, dialectic, paradox, and the historical, the last of which he associates in *Philosophical Fragments* with coming into existence. In *Works of Love* the truth of subjectivity, the truth of the subject, is linked not only with God but also with the neighbor, with conscience, with action—with what Kierkegaard calls the upbuilding practice of loving the neighbor as yourself, the metaphorical "like for like" of spirit. "God is actually himself this pure like for like, the pure rendition of how you yourself are," he writes there.[3] One of the most engaging "Christian deliberations" in *Works of Love* is entitled "Love Believes All Things—and Yet Is Never Deceived." Love believes all things subjectively true and truthfully subjective. Love, in believing that the subject is all things truthful and that truth is all things subjective, is never deceived by claims that identify either subjectivity with the certainty of objects or truth with objective certainty. Love, like subjectivity, like truth itself, is neither certain nor uncertain. Love is the "like for like" of subjects, of human beings, all of whom are without exception commanded to love the neighbor as themselves, as the likeness in whose truthful image they are created.

Kierkegaard's avowal that truth is subjectivity—that the subject, whether human or divine, constitutes the truth of existence—underlies and in that fundamental sense altogether structures the critical philosophy of Kant. This relationship has been little understood. Let me indicate it by calling upon two of the principal formulations in which Kant articulates his critique of pure reason. In the first, he writes that "it is indeed very illuminating that I cannot know as an object itself that which I must presuppose in order to know an object at all. . .."[4] In other words, that by which (or through which) I know something I do not and cannot know in the same way in which I know that something; I can only think, will, and practice it as a subject, as a human being. Kant systematically demonstrates this in both the *Critique of Pure Reason* and the *Critique of Practical Reason*. While I can, indeed, know myself as an object or thing (what Kant calls an object of "possible," that is, empirical or sensible, experience), the "I" or subject by (and through) which I know myself as an object or thing I cannot know as

---

3. Kierkegaard, *Works of Love*, 384. In the "Conclusion" of the same work Kierkegaard writes: "Just one more thing, remember *the Christian like for like, eternity's like for like*. This Christian like for like is such an important and decisive Christian specification that I could wish to end, if not every book in which I develop the essentially Christian, then at least one book, with this thought" (376).

4. Kant, *Critique of Pure Reason*, 442. Guyer and Wood translate *erkennen* ("to know") as "to cognize." See their Glossary.

an object or thing. He artfully calls upon the old-fashioned term "thing in itself" as a means of distinguishing between the thinking subject and the knowable object. We can know the thing in itself only as it appears to us as an object of possible (empirical) experience. We cannot know, and shall never know, *what* the thing is in itself. For what the thing in itself is we must think, will, practice as a subject. What the thing in itself is *is* the subject, the human being whose subjectivity constitutes the critique of pure reason.

Thus we arrive at the second principal formulation of Kant. In the Preface to the second edition of the *Critique of Pure Reason* he points out that, while mathematics and the natural sciences have, in modernity, effected the revolution that has allowed them to secure a critical path of knowledge, metaphysics has failed to secure for itself a revolutionary path of critique and has remained, instead, premodern and uncritical. Kant puts it this way:

> Up to now it has been assumed that all our knowledge must conform to the objects; but all attempts to find out something about them *a priori* through concepts that would extend our knowledge have, on this presupposition, come to nothing. Hence let us once try whether we do not get farther with the problems of metaphysics by assuming that the objects must conform to our knowledge . . .[5]

Let me summarize, in elementary terms, the revolution that Kant demonstrates in the *Critique of Pure Reason* to be the critical path of metaphysical thinking. It is a case of either/or. *Either* the mind conforms to objects, with the result that human beings remain powerlessly ignorant not only of things, the objects of nature, but also of themselves as subjects, as persons; *or* objects conform to the mind, with the result that human beings can justify the sciences of nature—for knowledge is empowerment—and human subjects are liberated from conformity to objects with the result that they can make justice for all the standard of human relations. As Rousseau puts it, we judge fact by right, not right by fact. We judge the fact of human degradation by right, not right by the fact that human degradation exists, concluding that it is and so must be right. We argue from "ought" (the duty to love our neighbor) to "is" (the lack of neighborliness in the world), not from "is" to "ought." That by (or through) which I know—myself as a human subject, a thinking, willing human being—I cannot know as an objective fact or thing according to the methodology of the natural sciences. Indeed, Kant later observes in the *Critique of Pure Reason* that, given his critical distinction between the thinking subject and the knowable object, it is not

---

5. Ibid., 110. Guyer and Wood translate *Erkenntnis* ("knowledge") as "cognition." See n4.

to be feared that, if the matter of nature were removed, "then all thinking and even the existence of thinking beings would be abolished . . ." On the contrary, he remarks, "If I were to take away the thinking subject, the whole corporeal world would have to disappear, as this is nothing but the appearance in the sensibility of our subject and one mode of its representations."[6]

I bring Kant and Kierkegaard together in my paper to argue for the abiding significance of both metaphysics and religion in sustaining a critical conception of human being, of the truth of human subjectivity, in modernity and in its latest avatar, postmodernity. In order to develop this argument I shall pursue two lines of thought, each of which readers may find paradoxical and which, when taken together, may strike them as representing what Kierkegaard calls the absolute paradox. The first line of thought involves Kant's metaphysics. I shall argue that the revolutionary insight allowing Kant to put metaphysics on a critical path—whereby objects conform to the mind of the subject and not the mind of the subject to objects—is radically biblical. What we shall see, then, is that modern philosophy will be faithful to the truth of human subjectivity, to what Kant calls the dignity and worth of all human beings, only insofar as it systematically appropriates biblical theology, which is also biblical anthropology: the relationship of God and human beings in the covenant of existence.

The second line of thought involves Kierkegaard's religion. I shall argue that Kierkegaard's radical claim that truth is subjectivity, that every human being is the neighbor whom we are commanded to love as constituting the truth of our own subjecthood, is no less secular than religious; indeed, that it is religious only insofar as it is secular. It will be seen, then, that my two lines of thought converge. Kant's argument that it is the subject—human, yes, but also divine—who constitutes or creates the world of our subjective relationships is as religious as it is philosophical; and Kierkegaard's argument that truth is subjectivity, that truth belongs equally to the divine subject and to the human subject, is as secular as it is religious.

My overall purpose, then, in showing that Kant and Kierkegaard share a common framework that is at once historical and ontological, is to argue for the importance of seeing that (a) the philosophical, when identified with the secular, is truly religious; and (b) that the religious, if it is opposed to the secular, collapses into what Kierkegaard calls Christendom, the subjection of human beings to the idolatry of objectification or reification. I argue, then, that philosophy and religion together constitute the secular realm of subjective human values, or what Kant calls the kingdom of ends. It is not, in other words, the objective sciences of nature that constitute the secular realm of

6. Ibid., 433.

human values. For what empowers the certain (scientific) knowledge of objects for us human subjects is our commitment to the truth of subjectivity. If knowledge is power, then it is thinking that empowers human subjects. It thus turns out, weirdly, and consistently with what Nietzsche calls "the revaluation of all [modern] values," that what we normally associate with objectivity (with, say, fairness or fair-mindedness) is in its truth subjectivity, and that what we normally associate with subjectivity (with, say, subjectivism or uncritical opinion or bias) is in its untruth objectivity.

When, to take up my first line of thought, Kant argues that metaphysics can enter securely upon the revolutionary path of modernity only when objects are understood to conform to the critical reason of subjects, and not subjects to objects as things unknowable in themselves, it is important to see that the modern path of metaphysical revolution on which he sets rational critique is what the biblical prophets call the way of the Lord.[7] The God of the Bible is not an object that is knowable solely in itself and consequently unknowable relative to us, to recall Aristotle's formulation of the contradictory opposition between divine and human knowledge. Indeed, god for Aristotle is the unmoved mover, that which—thought thinking itself—moves all beings as their unknown and unknowable end but is unmoved by them in their ignorance of their end. The God of the Bible is not the first or the final cause of Greek ontology. The biblical God, rather, is the way of the covenant, the way of love, the way in which human beings as subjects are to relate to their fellow human beings as their neighbor. "God is love," John tells us, "and he who abides in love abides in God, and God abides in him" (1 John 4:16). "Love," Paul writes in his epistle to the Romans, "is the fulfilling of the law," the law of walking in the critical way of the Lord (Romans 13:10). And James urges his readers to "be doers of the word, and not hearers only, deceiving yourselves" (James 1:22).

So we shall now see that the question containing what Kant calls "the real problem of pure reason" articulates biblical ontology: "How are synthetic judgments *a priori* possible?"[8] Kant's use of formidable, even rebarbative, philosophical terms doubtless reflects the enormous effort he had to expend to overcome the oppositional or dualistic logic of Greek ontology so deeply entrenched in Western metaphysics: the opposition between appearance and reality, between the many and the one, between body and soul, between what is knowable relative to us and what is knowable in itself, between inductive logic (which, as synthetic or experiential, is powerless to

---

7. The prophecy of Hosea ends with the lines that "the ways of the Lord are right, and the upright walk in them, but transgressors stumble in them" (Hosea 14:9).

8. Kant, *Critique of Pure Reason*, 146.

establish priorities among appearances) and deductive logic (whose analytical priorities, in remaining hypothetical, are powerless to command action: love God above all others and your neighbor as yourself). Kant shows that pure reason, in being constituted by synthetic *a priori* judgments—that is, in being constituted by the relationship of subjects whose actual existence is established as the priority of all human beings—is practice first and last, the practice of categorically willing the good (the love of God and neighbor) as true for all. The paradoxical relationship of analytic or deductive logic (which is powerless in the world) and synthetic or inductive logic (which is no less powerless in the world) Kant calls transcendental logic: the logic or *logos* whose content constitutes and is constituted by pure reason as the practice of bringing the kingdom of human ends into existence.

As noted above, Kant asks, How are synthetic judgments *a priori* possible? When he makes this the fundamental question of metaphysics, it is important to see that he does not ask *whether* they are possible. For, as he explains, the primal question of metaphysics is always: given that something exists, how is it possible? How do we interrogate (in other words: what does it mean to interrogate) the possibilities of what actually exists? We do not ask if something exists or why something exists. For our very question—the action of thinking, of willing, of existing—presupposes existence. It is existence itself—and so, consequently, human willing, human thinking, human loving: in short, human practice—that comes into existence with our critical interrogation of its possibilities. Existence or, in other words, all concepts of human (and divine) existence are synthetic *a priori* judgments, for they can be thought (willed, loved . . .) solely as the priorities of our existence, with the first priority commanded above all others as the love of neighbor and God. This is the way of critical reason as practice. Human practice constitutes the transcendental logic of synthetic *a priori* judgments. In being neither merely analytic *a priori* (i.e., deductive, without relationship to existence) nor merely synthetic *a posteriori* (i.e., inductive, without relationship to priority), human practice unites both kinds of logic in that transcendentally unique yet also universally binding relationship of human love and justice. The *logos* of the biblical Word—love your neighbor as yourself—replaces Greek logic as the critical way of demonstrating that pure reason is first and last the practice of human subjects.

I suspect that by now readers will have recalled that Kant is famous for having demolished what he was the first to name the ontological argument for the existence of God. He definitively shows that any demonstration purporting to prove that God, or any being, necessarily exists as an object that is knowable either in itself (i.e., prior to human thought and practice) or relative to human beings (i.e., posterior to human thought and practice) is illusory. The necessity of existence, whether divine or human, cannot be established on the basis of either deductive (*a priori*) logic or inductive (*a posteriori*) logic. What is necessary analytically has no existence, and what exists synthetically is not necessary. As Hume points out, there is no being in existence whose non-existence is contradictory. That is, it is not necessary.

However, Kant conclusively refutes Hume when he reconstitutes metaphysics, which Hume had consigned to the flames, by means of what he calls the fiery ordeal of critique, whose very basis is the synthetic *a priori* judgment. Another name for the synthetic *a priori* judgment is existence constituted as necessary, that is, necessary existence. Necessity constitutes the priority of existence; existence constitutes the priority of necessity. Necessity of existence describes neither logical necessity (A is A) nor the causal necessity of hypothetical inference (if P, then Q). Rather, necessary existence describes the categorical necessity of agency, of will, of practice, of self-determination—in other words, of freedom. There is one being that cannot be thought (or willed or loved) by human beings without existing necessarily, or freely, and that being is God—and equally the neighbor. In other words, Kant silently embraces the ontological argument, as formulated earlier by St. Anselm, Descartes, and Spinoza (and later also by Hegel), in linking existence and necessity as the very basis of his metaphysics of transcendental thought and practice. God and neighbor do not exist either *a priori* in themselves or *a posteriori* relative to others. They exist, rather, in and through the necessary existence of the relationship that the Bible knows as the covenant.

So, then, when I take up my second line of thought, Kierkegaard's religion (or Christianity), we find that the critical path, which is the way of prophetic revelation, has already been cleared for us by Kant. We have learned from Kant that metaphysics, as centered on the synthetic *a priori* judgment, articulates the ontological argument proving the necessary existence no less of the neighbor than of God. We shall now learn from Kierkegaard that it is the neighbor who, together with God, is the truth of subjectivity, the "like for like" structuring the covenantal relationships of human beings. The proposition that truth is subjectivity indicates that truth is not a contradictory object which, in being sought by you in your ignorance, can be known solely in itself as your self-contradiction. Rather, the notion that truth is subjectivity, in embodying the categorical imperative of ethics that you are to love your neighbor as the truth of your very own subjectivity, shows us, consistent with Kant, that truth involves and expresses the paradoxical relationship of subjects.

The simple point I am making here is this: while Kant's metaphysics, in embodying reason as truthful practice, articulates the values of biblical rather than Greek ontology, so Kierkegaard's Christian metaphysics is to be understood as both secular and religious. The distinction between Christianity and Christendom central to Kierkegaard's demonstration that truth is subjectivity is *not* the distinction between the religious and the secular. Rather, it is the distinction between, on the one hand, (a) the truth embodied by human subjects in their relations with each other in believing all things while never being deceived (never deceived, that is, by the illusory claims of objective knowledge to describe the human or divine subject); and, on the other hand, (b) the false and deceptive claim that truth is objective, that truth describes objects as knowable either in themselves or in their empirical connections with us (i.e., relative to our use of them). Indeed, when Kant demonstrates that the critical path of pure reason involves making objects conform to subjects, it follows that what he calls the assumed conformity of subjects to objects (of which we human beings are ignorant or have knowledge that is merely relative to us) is equivalent to what Kierkegaard calls Christendom.

We have seen Kant demonstrate that within the natural sciences we can have certain and reliable knowledge of objects solely insofar as it is clearly grasped that objective knowledge presupposes the subjectivity of truth. Truth, then, is understood to inhere in the relationships that human beings establish with each other as willing, thinking, loving agents. We shall now see that Kierkegaard, in elaborating what he calls the three stages of human existence, shows us that the truth of subjectivity is a concept no less secular than religious. Indeed, the point for which I am arguing here is that what he terms the religious stage of human existence (or, in *Fear and Trembling*, "the absolute relation to the absolute") can be religious only insofar as it is understood to be secular—that is, only insofar as secular values are not reduced to the scientific knowledge of objects or (to the say the same thing in different words) reified within Christendom as the conformity of subjects to objects. There is an enormous amount of confusion on the part of scholars regarding what Kierkegaard understands by the three stages of existence—the aesthetic, ethical, and religious, as formulated in *Fear and Trembling*—primarily because they fail to see that the "first" two stages are not stepping stones to but idolatrous departures from the "third" stage as their necessary priority.[9] In elementary terms, the aesthetic stage

9. Kierkegaard also obscures (indeed, he frequently mystifies) his presentation of the three stages of existence in two ways. (1) While he shows in *Fear and Trembling* that the aesthetic and the ethical stages of existence are fundamentally opposed to the religious stage of existence, he also points out in that work that there is a completely different concept of ethics, "for example, that love to God may [sic!] bring the knight of faith to give his love to the neighbor . . ." (70) But this concept of ethics, in being identified

of existence represents self-centered egoism: the subordination of the other (the universal) to the single individual's temporal, sensate self. The ethical stage of existence (also called the "universal" in *Fear and Trembling*) represents the subordination of the single individual to the universal (to the other as psychically eternal).[10] The religious stage of existence represents the single individual in absolute relationship to God. However, what Kierkegaard does not tell us is that the absolute relationship of the single individual with God is not found outside the individual's relationship with every human being whom, as the neighbor, he is absolutely commanded to love as himself. The so-called "third" or religious stage of existence is really the first or, in other words, the only *true* stage of existence. The religious stage of existence is the necessary priority of all human beings "on Life's Way," to recall the title of another of Kierkegaard's works. It is necessarily prior to the aesthetic and ethical stages of existence in that these two stages are deviations characterizing the idolatrous transgressors who stumble on the "critical path" of the Lord, to recall the prophet Hosea.[11]

---

with love of neighbor, is not only opposed to the "ethical" stage of existence, in which love of neighbor is absent, but also altogether indistinguishable from the religious, although Kierkegaard does not acknowledge this. Further, the content that Kierkegaard associates with the "ethical" (which he makes central to *Either/Or*, Part II, and which he elaborates in the *Postscript*, especially in the earlier sections of that work) is, in being indistinguishable from the content of what he calls the "religious" in *Fear and Trembling*, clearly to be distinguished from the "ethical" stage of existence in that work. But, again, he does not acknowledge this. (In the *Postscript* Kierkegaard refers to "the absolute ethical distinction between good and evil" and states that "the ethical is absolutely and for all eternity the highest . . ." 134, 149). (2) In the *Postscript* Kierkegaard reiterates his commitment to the tripartite division of the stages of existence—aesthetic, ethical, and religious—yet obfuscates it by imposing on it further distinctions like the ethical-religious (also found in *Either/Or*, Part II), the dialectical, and the difference between Religiousness A (the immanence of paganism) and Religiousness B (Christianity), etc. The pseudonymous author of the *Postscript* also criticizes his pseudonymous predecessors, the authors of, for example, *Fear and Trembling* and *Either/Or*, Part II, for not having a true grasp of the religious as Christianity. But a clear indication that all this is simply a smoke screen on the part of Kierkegaard is the fact that, in the *Postscript* (as in *Fear and Trembling*), he does not make love of neighbor central to the religious, while in *Works of Love* (as in *Either/Or*, Part II) he makes love of neighbor the very center of the ethics of Christianity. Indeed, he writes in *Works of Love* that "Christianity is the true morality . . ." (51). It is also noteworthy that the three stages of existence are absent from *Works of Love* (as also from *Either/Or*, Part II), indicating further that love of neighbor is the only stage of existence that counts as the necessary priority of all human beings.

10. In *Fear and Trembling*, *Works of Love*, etc., Kierkegaard distinguishes systematically between the sensate-psychical and the spiritual—in other words, between body-soul and spirit. Spirit, whether divine or human, religious or secular, is what he calls in *Works of Love* the "third" (or middle) term that constitutes the truthful relationship of subjects, the truth of subjects in loving their neighbor as themselves.

11. The relationship between the religious stage of existence and the two "prior"

The religious stage of human existence represents, then, the overcoming of the opposition between the aesthetic and the ethical stages together with the opposition between the individual and the universal. It signifies, in other words, the appropriation of aesthetic individuality and ethical universality in and through loving the neighbor as the single individual who is the universal truth for all human beings.[12] The religious stage of existence, in overcoming the opposition between the individual as temporal and the universal as eternal, thus no less appropriates the temporal as eternal and the eternal as temporal. In *Philosophical Fragments* Kierkegaard describes the dialectic of the temporal and the eternal as coming historically into existence; in the *Postscript* he points out that the dialectic of historical existence embodies the paradox that, as soon as it is temporal, it must necessarily have been (always already) eternal.[13] We see, then, that the religious stage of existence, in appropriating the singular (and temporal) as universal and the universal (and eternal) as singular, makes subjectivity, the relationship of subjects, the necessary truth of historically existing human beings. The religious stage, in representing the necessary existence of human beings, not only embodies the dialectic that underlies the transcendental logic of Kant's synthetic *a priori* judgment[14] but also articulates the ontological argument

aesthetic and ethical stages corresponds to the distinction that Spinoza and Rousseau make between the social pact (the civil state of human relations) and the "prior" state of nature (the natural or uncivil state of human relations in which individual and universal are opposed to each other). The civil state of the social pact presupposes the state of nature yet, as its priority, is not derived from or based on it. The state of nature (which is what Kierkegaard calls Christendom) characterizes the deviance (sin) on the part of those who transgress the social pact or covenant (which is what Kierkegaard calls the religious stage of existence).

12. Just as Kierkegaard presents opposed concepts of ethics in his works (see n7), so he also presents opposed concepts of the "universal" in them. The "universal" (or ethical) stage of existence in *Fear and Trembling* (and also in the *Postscript*) represents the subordination of the single individual to the other as the eternal *telos* that is external to him. However, in *Either/Or*, Part II, *Works of Love*, and *Purity of Heart Is To Will One Thing*, etc., Kierkegaard explicitly identifies the single individual with the universally human, that is, with the neighbor whom it is one's absolute duty to love (consistent with the Kantian concept of universal duty as the ethical responsibility of every individual to treat all human beings as ends in themselves).

13. Kierkegaard, *Postscript*, 573. In the language of Hegel: actual historical existence is—must become—rational necessity; rational necessity is—must become—actual historical existence.

14. Kierkegaard's religious (i.e., secular) stage of existence, in overcoming and thus in appropriating the opposition between the aesthetic (i.e., the sensately individual) and the ethical (i.e., the psychically universal), bears the same dialectical spirit as Kant's synthetic *a priori* judgment, which overcomes and thus appropriates the opposition between the universality of analytic priority and the singularity of synthetic (experiential) posteriority.

demonstrating that there is one being that cannot be thought (or willed or loved) by human beings without necessarily existing, and that is the neighbor (and God).

I shall conclude my paper with the observation that I have brought Kant and Kierkegaard together for two closely related reasons. First, in his distinctive fashion each shows that it is only as we see objects as conforming to subjects, and not subjects to objects—that is, as we see the neighbor as the subject whom we must love as ourselves—that we come to understand that love believes all things and yet is never deceived. Love, the love of subjects in relationship, is never deceived by the claim of the natural sciences, masquerading behind the idols of secular certainty, that conformity to objects constitutes the standard of truth for subjects. Second, to consider Kant and Kierkegaard together helps us to make clear the way of the prophets. Only on their critical path do we come to see, on the one hand, that philosophy must be understood to embrace biblical values if it is not to lose the truth of subjectivity, and, on the other hand, that religion—specifically Christianity, in the case of Kierkegaard—must be understood to embrace secular values as truly biblical if it is not to lose the distinction between "Christianity" and "Christendom." Either both the religious and the secular together constitute "Christianity" as love of neighbor, or both are lost to the idolatry of Christendom in which subjects, human or divine, conform to objects. Only in acknowledging that philosophy articulates both theological and anthropological values central to the Bible, and that biblical religion is faithful to the subject only insofar as it is truly secular, do we avoid sacrificing the subjectivity of truth, the truth of subjects, to the idolatry of having subjects conform to objects. We see that the subject is the secular and religious truth by which we determine the certain place, in our lives, of objects as studied by the natural sciences.

BIBLIOGRAPHY

Kant, Immanuel. *Critique of Pure Reason*. Translated by Paul Guyer and Allen W. Wood. Cambridge: Cambridge University Press, 1998.

Kierkegaard, Søren. *Concluding Unscientific Postscript*. Vol. 1. Translated by Howard V. Hong and Edna H. Hong. Kierkegaard's Writings 12. Princeton: Princeton University Press, 1992.

———. *Fear and Trembling*. Translated by Howard V. Hong and Edna H. Hong. Kierkegaard's Writings 6. Princeton: Princeton University Press, 1983.

———. *Philosophical Fragments*. Translated by Howard V. and Edna H. Hong. Princeton: Princeton University Press, 1985.

———. *Works of Love*. Translated by Howard V. Hong and Edna H. Hong. Kierkegaard's Writings 16. Princeton: Princeton University Press, 1995.

Polka, Brayton. "The Hermeneutics of the Single Individual in Kierkegaard: Religious or Secular?" *The European Legacy* 19 (2014) 442–55.

———. "The Metaphysics of Thinking Necessary Existence: Kant and the Ontological Argument." *The European Legacy* 17 (2012) 583–91.

———. "Modern Philosophy, the Subject, and the God of the Bible." In *Biblical Philosophy? Exploratory Essays*, edited by Mark Cauchi and Avron Kulak. Continuum, forthcoming.

———. "Who Is the Single Individual? On the Religious and the Secular in Kierkegaard." *Philosophy and Theology* 17 (2005) 157–75.

———. "*Works of Love* and the Structure of Interpretation: The Like-for-Like of Neighbour and Metaphor." *Toronto Journal of Theology* 9 (1993) 79–94.

10

We Have Never Been Secular
The Politics of Reading Scripture and Practicing Theology

Mark Alan Bowald

I am a native Michigander, which means I grew up in Michigan in the U.S. Thirteen years ago my wife and I moved to Canada to study and then teach. In that time I have learned the nuances of the differences between the two cultures. One subtle but substantial contrast is the character and perception of secularism in each. Canadians take great pride in the belief that they have a secular state and society with less of the poisoning impact of religion on their political life than the United States. The average resident of Toronto or Vancouver is troubled by any hint of prayer or biblical references in political contexts, election speeches, and such in the U.S. The pride that Canadians take in their version of secularism is on display every election season. On May 2, 2011, just ten months ago, Canada held a general federal election. All of you hearing this paper knew that, right? How many of you followed the election? Or know the results, which were utterly unprecedented and have significant implications for the future of Canada? Are the British as oblivious to Canadian affairs as Americans are? We can talk about that later.

As the elections approached there were, as usual, news shows with round-table discussions. On one such show in April, 2011,[1] the panelists were debating whether public funding should be appropriated for religious private education. Also on the table was the related controversy over Muslim and Christian political candidates who had publicly appealed to their having been shaped by their religious heritage as relevant to their political platforms. The panelists were generally agreed that in both cases, the tread was too heavy on the sacred secular doctrine of the absolute separation of politics and religion. One panelist, a member of the faculty of the University of Toronto, concluded with a short speech praising the record of Canadian secularism. He then paused, and proclaimed matter-of-factly, even smugly: "Everyone knows that religion has nothing to do with politics."

I was stunned. I, like many of you, found this shockingly reductionist and antiquated, almost quaint. I looked around my living room, seeking to confirm what I had heard, to share this surreal moment with someone. I managed to make eye contact only with our cat, who was indifferent as only cats can be. This evidence is not anecdotal; as I read Canadian newspapers[2] and make my way through the streets, restaurants, and shopping malls of southern Ontario, I regularly encounter (as you may also) rigid declarations about the "place" of religion as sequestered in the home.

It is remarkable that this claim can be made today with no hint of qualification or irony. Even a cursory and honest and look at world history confirms the ingredient relationship and struggle between religion and politics even in the most intentionally secular of states. The remarkable events under the umbrella of the Arab Spring and the deep struggles in the UK and Europe to deal with growing Muslim minority communities are just two recent examples that press the recognition of the intimate historical waltz of faith and politics.

Bruno Latour, in his popular and now classic work from 1993 titled *We Have Never Been Modern*, spoke directly to the dualisms of modernity, including that of religion and politics. He argues that each is, in fact, a chimera; that despite popular contemporary perceptions, reason and faith, science and humanities, subject and object, have always possessed deep, intimate, and organic relationships to one another, and always will. The interrogation of the dualisms and other boundaries of modernity has been

---

1. The show aired on TVOntario. I have not been able to identify the exact date or participants' names.

2. As I was writing this paper a particularly narrow and egregious example was published in *The Globe and Mail*. See column by Doug Saunders at: http://www.theglobeandmail.com/news/world/doug-saunders/the-problem-in-public-life-isnt-islam-but-religion-itself/article2342413/

vigorously pursued by thoughtful people in the various fields that fly under the "post-" banner: postmodern, post-liberal, post-critical, post-structural, post-colonial, etc. In academia the boundary testing between religion and politics has come to reside under the broad canopy of "post-secularism."[3]

There is a simple way to organize the animating dynamics of these various "post-" movements; namely, as the tension between the internal and external. This spatial metaphor is utilized by thinkers in all these "post-" fields, and with similar rhetorical effect. Jacques Derrida's now-famous aphorism, "There is nothing outside the text," is one. A person could quite effectively teach a course on post-structuralism and postmodernism beginning with this quote. By it Derrida wished to signal something about location, something profoundly political: that the space "outside" the text is in one important sense a myth; that language itself, and the holders of hermeneutical or political power, do not stand outside or above and beyond texts and political structures, but within them. Thomas Nagel famously castigates this myth as the "view from nowhere"[4]—again, drawing on the spatial metaphor.

Charles Taylor's recent interrogation of secularism in *A Secular Age* also draws on this model; he employs the simple but effective comparison between the "buffered self" of the modern secular and the "porous self" of the pre-modern and post-secular.[5] The difference between the buffered and porous self is their fundamental orientation; the modern secular person sees herself as constituted by a pure and self-sustaining spring within, having a relationship with the world that is purely voluntary and ad hoc; the pre- and post-secular persons see their constitution as originally and perennially porous, given to them from "outside" themselves, and regard any sense of singular independent integrity as deeply qualified and highly unstable.

The employment of the internal-external spatial metaphor is common and prevalent among the "post-" movements—and now that I've pointed it out, I've probably ruined you for reading them. You will notice this metaphor everywhere; if you think of it, email me when this happens. We could talk about how much work the metaphor does in the phenomenological

---

3. One of the chief catalysts for this was the seminal book *A Secular Age*, written, ironically, by Canadian philosopher Charles Taylor. A primary meeting place for discussions related to debates surrounding post-secularism can be found at the blog sponsored and hosted by the Social Science Research Center: *The Immanent Frame*.

4. Nagel, *The View from Nowhere*.

5. Taylor, *A Secular Age*, 27. For one adept reading of the implications of Taylor for Christian theology see Long, "How to Read Charles Taylor." On Taylor's significance for the social sciences, described with a theological sensitivity and a response from Taylor, see Lyon, "Being Post-secular in the Social Sciences."

tradition, in people like Jean-Luc Marion and his notion of the "saturated phenomena." We could also look at the post-liberal theological movement that originated at Yale University in the last half of the last century with Hans Frei and George Lindbeck, whose work was animated by a concern for the emergence of meaning from within Scripture and the emergence of truth from within the practices of the Christian community. And finally we could note how the work of Pierre Bourdieu, defined succinctly in his book *The Logic of Practice*, employs the internal-external metaphor to uncover the methodological colonialism that has operated quietly beneath the surface of much of the work done in modern anthropology and social science.

The net result of the employment of the internal-external metaphor in all these movements is an interrogation of the hubris and hegemony that can so easily characterize the varieties of methodological externalism. This is accompanied by an equally insistent call to listen and to observe with more intent and patience to the internal voices and practices of religions and texts and cultures.

Today we will see how this cue from Taylor and Bourdieu has come to sharpen one aspect of the post-secular critique: the political administration of policies regarding religious practices and tolerance.[6] We will start with a sample from one of its rising stars: Saba Mahmood, whose notoriety begins with her accomplished first book, *The Politics of Piety*. Mahmood is an Arab woman, is not a practicing member of any religious tradition, and teaches in the anthropology department at the University of California, Berkeley. She employs an "inside/outside" metaphor when interrogating the relationship of the practitioners of particular religions and the social and political entities that seek to influence or administer those religions. With regard to a common liberal secularist argument that all religions be allowed equal space and voice in the public domain, she notes that it often produces a kind of flattening of religious faiths, that typically secularism "remains blind to its own normative framing of what constitutes 'inclusion' by ignoring the fact that a particular religious group's demand for inclusion or recognition itself requires that such a group is able to recognize itself, and articulate this self-recognition, within the terms of liberal national discourse. Religious sensibilities that do not yield to such protocols of legibility cannot be heard in the public domain."[7]

In the same article Mahmood examines a similar mode of secularism that underwrites U.S. foreign policy regarding Muslim communities in

---

6. The best entry point to engage the literature on postsecularism is the blog sponsored by the Social Science Research Center, *The Immanent Frame*, at http://blogs.ssrc.org/tif/.

7. Mahmood, "Secularism, Hermeneutics, and Empire," 328.

the wake of 9/11. She focuses specifically on how the U.S. has developed policies in consultation with key documents obtained and funded by the Rand Corporation, which resulted in the report *Civil Democratic Islam: Partners, Resources, and Strategies*.[8] The focus of these documents is an evaluation and critique of how Muslims read Scripture: the Rand report identifies certain ways of reading the Qur'an that are purportedly conducive to extremism, and other ways of reading it that are not. The U.S. government has received the recommendations of the Rand report and applied them in its foreign policy and funding decisions; the concrete steps taken in this process are detailed by Mahmood,[9] and I will not trace them here. She holds this up as an example of how political institutions that presume to operate in religiously neutral, secular spheres annot help but employ religious reflection and judgments in the course of administering religious practices.[10] She employs the internal-external critique here, as well as in her earlier work, to uncover the religious ideological contours of the supposed secular and neutral external judgments of the Rand Corporation report and subsequent U.S. foreign policy. Citing the example of the Rand report, she asserts the following:

> [S]ecularism [seeks] not so much to banish religion from the public domain but to reshape the form it takes, the subjectivities it endorses, and the epistemological claims it can make. The effectiveness of such a totalizing project necessarily depends upon transforming the religious domain through a variety of reforms and state injunctions. This has meant that nation-states have had to act as *de facto theologians*, rendering certain practices and beliefs indifferent to religious doctrine precisely so that these practices can be brought under the domain of civil law.[11]

---

8. Benard, *Civil Democratic Islam: Partners, Resources, and Strategies*. This report is easily obtainable on the Internet.

9. Mahmood, *Politics of Piety*, 330ff.

10. Mahmood traces one significant example of this in the administration of funding in the Muslim World Outreach program, an arm of the White House National Security Council. See Mahmood, "Secularism, Hermeneutics and Empire," 330–32.

11. Ibid., 326; emphasis mine. See also Mahmood's gesture in this direction, p. 328: "The political solution offered by the doctrine of secularism resides not so much in the separation of state and religion or in the granting of religious freedoms, but in the kind of subjectivity that a secular culture authorizes, the practices it redeems as truly (versus superficially) spiritual, and the particular relationship to history that it prescribes." See also, p. 329: "In addition to its military 'war against terror,' the United States has embarked upon an ambitious theological campaign aimed at shaping the sensibilities of ordinary Muslims . . ." and a description of the U.S.'s "theological prescriptions" on p. 330.

Nation-states acting as theologians? What are we to make of this? First off, we need to note that her point is not meant as a criticism *per se:* She is not criticizing the fact that theology informs these policies, but the self-perception of secularism that the practice of regulating religious practices could somehow *not* be theological.[12] This is so insofar as such practice has to assume boundaries and definitions for the religious subject. In other words, it must assume that there are certain ways of being religious that are correct, tolerable, or true, and others that are not. Let's dig deeper here to see the point.

First of all, we need to acknowledge that the term "theology" as it is used here is not tied to either intention or consciousness. Indeed, the sharpness of the point is felt when we consider that the Rand report has a "theological" character despite the self-perception and intention of both its composers and the U.S. government that sponsored it. These activities have been undertaken in a secular realm that perceives itself to be neutral to religion; their intention is to *not* be "confessional" or "theological." In other words, the "theological" character of these reflections and assertions is not tied to a narrow understanding of theology as a vocation or profession, but resides in the simple fact that there are lines drawn here that demarcate and define the religious dimensions of human subjectivity. Discerning and describing those dimensions *is* the vocation of theology.

Underlying the Rand report and the policies on which it is built are strong assumptions about the character of Muslim Scripture and the hermeneutic according to which it *should* and *should not* be read. The Rand report recommends that modernist historical-critical methods used by some Christians for reading the Old Testament be promoted as a hermeneutic for Muslims to use in reading the Qur'an. Here is a quote from the report describing what it sees as the optimal modernist hermeneutic to be applied to sacred texts so as to promote the ideal form of liberal democracy:

> Modernism, not traditionalism, is what worked for the West. This included the necessity to depart from, modify, and selectively ignore elements of the original religious doctrine. The Old Testament is not different from the Quran in endorsing conduct and containing a number of rules that are literally [sic] unthinkable, not to mention illegal, in today's society. This does not pose a problem because few people would today insist that we should all be living in the exact literal manner of the Biblical patriarchs. Instead, we allow our vision of Judaism's and Christianity's true

---

12. For an interesting account of how this basic insight of postsecularism translates into the field of international relations see Thomas, "Living Critically."

message to dominate over the literal text, which we regard as history and legend.[13]

The ideal hermeneutic described here rests upon very strong assertions about the nature of the sacred texts, both Judeo-Christian and Muslim, their origin, the kind of truth claims they can and cannot make, and so forth. With very broad, wooden, and reductionist strokes the report defines a "literal" way of thinking, a "literal" way of living, and a "literal" way of reading, and neatly dismisses all three. All of these assertions and definitions are highly contested and debated in theological circles in both Christianity and Islam.

Based on these assertions the report goes on to recommend promotion of a very specific hermeneutic. The government is advised to find ways to discourage conservative and moderate literal and historicist readings of Muslim Scripture and encourage more "enlightened" metaphorical and progressive readings. The report also identifies specific progressive and reformist Muslim scholars who may be seen as potential partners in this work. Tellingly, one of the reformist Muslim scholars that Mahmood names among those that have received sympathetic attention from the U.S. government, Abdul Karim Soroush, is "often hailed as the Martin Luther of Islam."[14]

The Rand report is theological in that it must assume a set of judgments related to several key elements of religious practice. It assumes something concrete about the nature of Scripture (both the Christian Bible and the Qur'an); it also assumes the character of the ideal reader of Scripture, a very particular religious hermeneutic and anthropology. This reader will believe certain things about Scripture and not other things. He or she will have a specific understanding of the relationship of God to history and to Scripture: how and why and when God does and does not "speak" and so forth. The ideal religious subject will also observe a specific set of religious and ethical practices. All of these elements—the character of God, of history and text, of the reader and reading community—will, ideally, resonate harmoniously with each other.

Now, a footnote is in order here. In this discussion we are not evaluating the correctness or usefulness of the Rand report, nor the justice or appropriateness of the policies embraced and undertaken by the U.S. Those are important questions, but our interest, which parallels Mahmood's, is simply to examine an instance of the administration of religious practices in order to highlight a fiction of secularism—namely, that it manages to

---

13. Benard, *Civil Democratic Islam*, 37.
14. Mahmood, *Politics of Piety*, 338.

sequester religion from the political administration of public life. So: we see here how the conclusions that the Rand report draws, the recommendations it makes, and the policies that result rest upon theological judgments about Scripture and its interpretation, about the character of the ideal reader of Scripture, and about particular religious practices as observed by individuals and faith communities. These are the very clay with which theologians wrestle and get dirty.

Taking this observation one step further presents us with the kernel of the post-secular critique: If government policies regarding religious practice necessarily employ theological frames of thought, this illustrates how the relationship between political and religious spheres is not stable, fixed, or buffered. Rather, it is porous, shifting, and fluid.[15] The point bears emphasizing, as the full import of our argument turns on it. The question is whether the political machinations of nation-states necessarily employ theological judgments in the development and administration of policies and laws regarding religious practice. If these are judgments regarding the idealized shape of religious subjectivities, then the answer must be "yes."[16] What follows below will be a consideration of the implications of this fact.

First, insofar as this is true, secular liberal democratic governments occupy an awkward and ironic stance: *Administering religious tolerance is inherently a religiously and theologically invested and interested activity.* The natural response we will have to this, the quintessential human response, is to try and resolve this irony. But what are our options? One is to reconsider the possibility and legitimacy of theocracy. Regardless of the theoretical prospects of such, practically speaking this is simply not an alternative, and is contestable on grounds other than utility; it is doubtful any of us here would see this as a live opportunity. Another would be the reassertion of a purer form of secularism. There are some who call for this, but their influence seems to be waning under the post-secular critique in inverse proportion to the shrillness of their protests.[17] The upshot of post-secularism is that any simple resolution of the ingredient relationship and tension between the political and theological realms is impossible. It is a

---

15. Both Saba Mahmood and Charles Taylor employ such terms when talking about this relationship.

16. I am tempted to note here how one of the theological traditions that has been deeply formative for me has been making this same point for over a century: the Dutch Reformed tradition, with its notion of worldview and the work of Abraham Kuyper and Herman Bavinck, of Reformed philosophers such as Nicholas Wolterstorff and Alvin Plantinga, and others. I will resist the temptation to gloat.

17. See the back-and-forth between Stathis Gourgouris and Saba Mahmood in their respective articles in *Public Culture* 20 (2008) for an example.

tension that requires us to be respectful of its complexity and irresolvability. Insofar as it is true we can only accept it, and work with it as best we can given the political options we have presently.

The line we have taken today, then, should not be interpreted as a denunciation of liberal democracy, nor as an argument for anarchy or theocracy; some form of democratic rule remains the best option for the possibility of religious freedom and human justice. Nor are we advocating abandonment of the administrative role of the political realm in promoting tolerance. Mahmood, Charles Taylor, Talal Asad, and most others associated with post-secularism share a commitment to that role even as they seek to redefine the secular.[18] The future of post-secular political practice is the acceptance of the mutuality of religion and politics and the commitment to a chastened and deeply qualified small-*s* secular space in which people of different faiths and philosophies meet to discuss and decide on the common good.

Second, this irresolvable tension, which reveals the awkward instabilities at the intersection of the political and religious spheres in this space, points to a fundamental limit on the side of government. It points to a clear and deep qualification of the capacity of liberal democratic governments to undertake, comprehensively and intentionally, all of the reflective activities required to ensure religious tolerance and justice. A democratic government simply cannot engage in theological reflection and articulation in the manner and depth that is required to guarantee these. Those who are interested should read the Rand report as an example; it is supposed to represent the highest level of political reflection, yet its theological form is embarrassingly awkward, distorted, and shallow.

Under this deep qualification and limit, liberal democracies must recognize that they are dependent upon the religious traditions active in their jurisdictions to recommend, articulate, and promote the necessary theology of the common good. It is only from the deep well of confessional voices that the full rationale for what constitutes human rights and justice can be articulated with any real substance.[19]

Now let's be clear. At this point we may feel that we are taking a risk, making a substantial wager on the probability that the religious traditions informing government policy and practice will be able to articulate theologies of tolerance that are truly just. The prospect should arouse considerable

18. See Charles Taylor's, *A Secular Age*; Talal Asad's, *Genealogies of Religion*; Saba Mahmood's "Can Secularism be Other-wise?" and the various conversation lines developed at the blog *The Immanent Frame* for the key contributions to the redefinition of the secular.

19. Wolterstorff makes this point in "Between the Pincers."

nervousness, as human history witnesses clearly to the comical and tragic failures of religion here. The way we *feel* about the historical record is however, certainly distorted;[20] historians are fickle reporters, and everyone knows that drama, tragedy, and horror are what gather crowds, sell books, and raise ratings.

But regardless of how we feel about this prospect, the implication of post-secularism compels much more than just a wager on the possibility of confessional theologies of justice. If post-secularism is correct and the administration of religious practices is in fact an inherently theological affair, then there is no gamble, since there is no other option: nation-states must honor their role as the preserver of the public good, and to do so requires certain self-limiting practices, including the division and balance of political powers, with full awareness of their accountability to the theological traditions comprised by their constituency.

Third: If the administration of religious practices is inherently theological, and if nation-states cannot, by virtue of their administrative function, undertake thick theological reflection, then the responsibility for articulating and promoting religious tolerance and human justice shifts necessarily to religious and theological traditions themselves. This renders older, rigid forms of secularism untenable: they are revealed as not simply an innocuous myth of religious and theological neutrality, but more graphically as a temptation to default on our basic responsibilities as human beings—namely, care for the other. Let's unpack this just a bit more.

If the proper administration of religious practices and tolerance requires the kind of deep theological reflection properly undertaken only from within religious traditions, then insofar as the doctrine of secularism creates tensions and walls between religious and political spheres, it subtly introduces temptations on both sides. On the political side, in countries that have been ruled by some form of secular government, there is a temptation to a false sense of self-sufficiency: insofar as the government perceives itself as purely secular, it will communicate in more and less obvious ways that the advice and contributions of Christians or Muslims or other communities of faith are not welcome or even appropriate to its deliberations on domestic and foreign policy. The temptation is to assume that the government is fully capable of undertaking the promotion of the common good apart from the deep articulations of theology. On the religious side, the temptation is, ironically, to make the same assumption: to lay the responsibility for religious tolerance and justice solely at the door of the political realm. In the interest of full disclosure, it is not only secularism that gives rise to

---

20. See Griffith, *The Myth of Religious Violence*.

this temptation; religious traditions struggle perennially with the instinct to spend all their efforts on self-protection and self-promotion. According to Scripture this is a basic human temptation as old as the creation narratives: "I am not my brother's keeper." I can tell, as many others can, stories about inhuman acts of emotional violence committed within and between church denominations, intramural battles waged over theological minutiae in the interest of maintaining community purity and control.

Thus the sinful penchant for control on the one hand, and on the other a secular narrative that discourages theological reflection on the public good, combine to produce both a false and arrogant self-sufficiency on the part of government and a passive indifference to the rights of other faiths among the confessionally and traditionally minded.

Concrete outcomes are suggested by the line of argument we have taken above. To close this paper I will highlight specific points of action to be undertaken in response to the temptations of secularism in light of the post-secular critique. Of the many we could discuss, I will mention just three.

1. THE NEED FOR READING PRACTICES AND DEEP THEOLOGIES OF JUSTICE AND TOLERANCE

One of the subtle but significant implications of post-secularism is the increasing political gravity recognized in the practices of reading Scripture and doing theology. The argument we have followed above insists that political administration is religiously and theologically informed. From the other side the gravity is more immediate and compelling: reading Scripture and doing theology are politically charged practices. This, in turn, should compel those who are deeply committed to their religious and theological traditions, who also believe in the importance of tolerance, to be more proactive and assertive in practicing reading and theology to this end—specifically, and with passionate intention, in speaking out of the deep wells of their religious traditions to promote tolerance and justice.

There are a variety of reasons why theologians who understand their work as emerging from the clear voices of tradition have not been drawn to work on theologies of religious tolerance. We alluded to some above. Another that bears mention is pluralism. We need to be clear here, as there are presently two very disparate and ultimately incompatible definitions of pluralism operating in academic and religious circles. These produce great confusion.

One form of pluralism employs the form of methodological externalism we mentioned at the outset: it stands and observes the goings-on in all the various religious traditions of the world and claims to have a unique insight into what is really going on behind and beneath them. It then proceeds to sort out which bits of these religions are dispensable and which are to be preserved and, after discarding the unnecessary bits, produces a grand identity of all religions unified in either a universal historical process or an ontology of universal religious subjectivity.[21] In so doing its nominal pluralism devolves into something like a religious monism.

This form of modern religious pluralism, which mirrors modern secularism in interesting ways, has created the false impression that developing theological arguments for religious tolerance and justice somehow equals the embrace and approval of the practices and beliefs of other religions. This is not the case. On the contrary, tolerance implies disapproval of at least some elements of another's practices: I do not agree with this or that in your practice, but I tolerate it on the basis of some mediating principle. Indeed, as Nicholas Wolterstorff has argued, the embrace and approval of all religions under a large P modern pluralism is more accurately indifferent to its perceived unifying elements of religions, and intolerant of those religious beliefs and practices it has judged dispensable in the process.[22] The thinness of theological arguments for justice and tolerance within the social and cultural *ethoi* of nation-states is only redressed and remedied by learning to speak out of the fullness of traditional voices and resources, including the honest acknowledgment of the sometimes painful and deep irreconcilable differences between religions.

The other definition of pluralism arises from the low-flying observation that one lives in a culture and in a world in which there is diversity. This version of pluralism seeks not to explain, rationalize, or dissolve diversity but to work out ways of co-existence and mutual respect. It readily accepts that there will be irresolvable dimensions to that diversity. This second chastened and *ad hoc* form of pluralism underwrites the post-secular conversation, and from it there are signs of progress. A vibrant and evolving field of political theology is emerging.[23] There are also collaborative inter- and intra-faith efforts under way that work intentionally toward religious toler-

---

21. Representatives of this version of modern pluralism are common and have been effectively critiqued by such as Gavin D'Costa, Joseph Dinoia, Paul Griffiths, and others.

22. See Wolterstorff, "Religious Intolerance."

23. Examples include Stanley Hauerwas, Paul Griffiths, Alasdair Macintyre, Jeffrey Stout, Radical Orthodoxy Graham Ward, John Milbank, the renewed interest in Augustine political theology, etc.

ance and justice out of the fullness of their traditions and differences. These do not operate under the guise of older forms of pluralism, which seek to boil and strain the rich gumbo of religions down to some common essential broth; rather, they invite practicing confessional members of different religions to speak out of the distinctiveness of their traditions to identify points of common interest for the pursuit of justice and public good. The Cambridge Inter-faith Programme, named a flagship project by Cambridge on the occasion of the university's eight-hundredth anniversary, is an example. Another is the recent inter-faith conference on religious tolerance at the Berkeley Center at Georgetown.[24]

On this first point, one last comment is in order. In any nation-state that has liberal democracy, the majority religious group bears unique responsibility for working toward justice for religious minorities. This is a simple byproduct of the way democracies function: majority voices obtain a greater hearing and possess greater influence. Here in the West, this means that Christians bear the greater responsibility for articulating and promoting theologies of tolerance. The future of tolerance in the West depends on promoting tolerance for all religious minorities, from Jewish business owners to Muslim factory workers, and, yes, even for Mormon presidential candidates.

2. THE NEED TO RECOVER THE PUBLIC CHARACTER OF THEOLOGICAL REFLECTION

On February 2, 2012, Barack Obama delivered a speech[25] at the National Prayer Breakfast in Washington D.C., making significant reference to biblical passages and themes. He referred to two biblical themes that were formative for him in his commitment to legislative changes ensuring that wealthy Americans pay proportionately more tax: "Thou shalt love thy neighbor as thyself" (for which no chapter-and-verse reference was indicated) and Luke 12:48, "To whom much has been given, of him much will be required." The responses to Obama's speech were widely varied, but can be sorted to some effect.[26] Here we will focus on the negative responses, which raised two discrete dimensions of the speech for criticism while often conflating the two.

---

24. Papers from this conference were published by Yale University Press in 2012 under the title *Abraham's Children: Liberty and Tolerance in an Age of Religious Conflict*, edited by Kelly James Clark.

25. http://www.washingtonpost.com/politics/national-prayer-breakfast-president-obamas-speech-transcript/2012/02/02/gIQAx7jWkQ_story.html

26. Since this paper was drafted, the leading Republican candidate in the 2012

First, there were those who focused on Obama's line of theological argument and simply disagreed with it. This was less common, and often accompanied by a criticism of the second variety, which characterized the vast majority of negative responses. In this second category, regardless of whether they agreed with Obama's political views or not, were those commentators who felt that it was inappropriate for Obama to appeal to Scripture or to his theological beliefs in order to explain or support his taxation policy. This opinion was often expressed quite strongly and was supported by several different lines of reasoning. Some insinuated that Obama was being disingenuous in his appeal to Scripture, that he was feigning a Christian rationale as a political ploy to attract the sympathy of fiscally liberal-minded Christians. We can set this argument aside, as the accusation of lying is a political non-starter and does not address either the question of whether Scripture indeed supports the idea of higher taxation for those with greater wealth, or whether we should talk about that connection in public debates.

Others were critical of Obama's appeal to Scripture on no other basis than an alleged violation of the terms of secularism, that theology had no place in discussions of domestic financial policy. Let's interrogate this. First we can ask whether Obama's understanding of these Bible passages could, in fact, be a rationale for his political views. Obviously, the answer is Yes. Many presidents and politicians are and have been shaped deeply by their religious beliefs about humanity and society. And if this is so, then the biggest elephant in the secular room is why we cannot or should not talk about these connections, why we should not work toward greater transparency for the sake of more substantive political dialogue.

But more to the post-secular point: not only *might* Obama's theological views be informing his political platforms, these views *must* be operating in the conscious and unconscious horizons of his reflections and practices; it cannot be otherwise. And if so, then we must regain the comfort to talk about them publicly in a way that is honest, critical, respectful, and gracious. To do otherwise is to leave those deeply formative religious dimensions of the political sphere dangerously unexamined: hidden, unarticulated, unacknowledged, and therefore not amenable to reform or improvement. Poor theology is worked out quietly in bad political practices. Open and free discussion and debate, the greatest strength of liberal democracy, is foreclosed and compromised by misguided secularist policing of religious speech.

---

election, Rick Santorum, has responded specifically to the theology of Obama's administration. He has done so assuming, in agreement with Obama, that these connections are fair game for public debate.

3. THE NEED FOR A REINVIGORATED COMMITMENT TO LIBERAL ARTS EDUCATION

We have engaged in an abstraction in this talk by referring to governments and religions as if they were personal agents. The truth is that they are made up of many persons, all having their own characters, traditions, and histories. The U.S. government is not an entity that can consciously and intentionally adopt a religious mode of reflection pursuing the connections between theology and policy. However, individual politicians and lawmakers can make those connections in their own thinking and discourse. Indeed, if Saba Mahmood and Charles Taylor, Talal Asad and Nick Wolterstorff, and others associated with post-secularism are correct, then (as established in point 2 above) individuals *necessarily* engage political practices with theological and religious frameworks and vice versa.

This means it is paramount for those who enter political vocations to be educated with the ability to reflect on the interdisciplinary connections between theology, philosophy, and governance and law. And this, in turn, means that it is of the utmost gravity and importance to foster education in the liberal arts. There are significant pressures on liberal arts education in the West: the attractiveness of professionalized studies is well-known, and professionalized higher education is unquestionably efficient in terms of supplying market demand. But efficiency without direction is blunt and blind. Nuclear weapons, abortion, genetic modification, unfettered capitalism, totalitarianism: all of these are, in their own way, highly efficient.

The decline of the liberal arts results in a dearth of holistically formed students and citizens and drains the social well of substantive reflection and character. The decline of the liberal arts is inversely proportionate to the rise of an efficient and shallow polis. The pools of broad and deep political reflection have slowly been drained. Political leaders capable of profound reflection and possessing substantive character have become a rare and endangered species, as have members of the public who can understand with depth and clarity the nature of political questions. It is no wonder that we are pessimistic about the political process and the quality of the candidates in every election.

Modern secular doctrine, which wishes to employ and enforce strict— and artificial—separation between politics and religion, is blind to its own hegemony in silencing much-needed theological and religious voices. In so doing, it fosters the mechanism of blind efficiency in all spheres and denies itself the unique ability of theological self-critique to expose violence and articulate policies that promote tolerance and justice. The future of such policies in liberal democratic societies depends on politicians who, on the contrary, understand how their faith can be engaged to foster the common good. Only the liberal arts can properly train young men and women to reason and speak out of the fullness of their religious and theological traditions, so that they can see the forms of justice and common good that flow out of these traditions to inform public practice—political, financial, legal, and other.

CONCLUSION

Admittedly the picture we have painted here remains unfinished: there are many more questions to pursue, other avenues to explore. And there are tensions that we will have to live with as we go. Christians, and especially those of my own Reformed tradition, expect some messiness in the working-out of our faith; we believe that Scripture speaks to this moral and philosophical ambiguity, that this life will always be lived in the tension between the ideal and the real, the transcendent and the mundane, the light and the darkness, the religious and the secular: in short, between sin and redemption. This is not something to lament, however; rather, it is an opportunity to express the vocation of our humanity, to tend the Garden, to pull weeds and plant trees, to prune and to harvest the cultural and political vineyards.

The Reformed theological tradition also possesses resources from which to build a substantive theology of tolerance. A Reformed anthropology is built upon the idea of humankind created in the image of God, and in that image is conferred an uncompromised status ingredient within human nature. Creation and humanity were created very good, and this goodness is inherent to each of us human beings in our porous relationship to God and to the world despite the distorting and violent effects of sin.

A Reformed doctrine of humanity affirms the basic value of human life while simultaneously recognizing the human tendency to distort and destroy its inherent goodness, even to the point of pursuing practices of death and incurring judgment. God, however, is patient and tolerant, desiring that all who are called might respond by turning away from the practices of violence and redeem their humanity in practicing justice.

This divine tolerance should be mirrored in our tolerance of each other. John Calvin, in his *Commentary on Genesis*, comments on the passage in Genesis 9 where God sends Noah and his sons out to pursue once again the creation mandate to multiply and fill the earth. God warns them that they are accountable for each other, and accountable to God if they injure or commit violence on one another. Calvin comments on this passage as follows:

Men are indeed unworthy of God's care, if respect be only had to themselves; but since they bear the image of God engraven on them, he deems himself violated in their person. Thus, although they have nothing of their own by which they obtain the favor of God, he looks upon his own gifts in them, and is thereby excited to love and to care for them. This doctrine, however, is to be carefully observed, that no one can be injurious to his brother without wounding God himself. Were this doctrine deeply fixed in our minds, we should be much more reluctant than we are to inflict injuries.[27]

God himself is injured when we injure each other. This is the foundation for a Reformed theology of tolerance. The Reformed vision of the intrinsic value of human life in all its spheres, the ambivalence of the present age, and the patient tolerance of God, forms a gift of political pragmatism characterized by a high standard of justice and respect for life. It is a timely gift we can offer to public discourse about the common good—because, as everyone knows, religion has *everything* to do with politics.

BIBLIOGRAPHY

Asad, Talal. *Genealogies of Religion*. Baltimore: Johns Hopkins University Press, 1993.
Benard, Cheryl. *Civil Democratic Islam: Partners, Resources, and Strategies*. Arlington, VA: Rand Corporation, 2003.
Bourdieu, Pierre. *The Logic of Practice*. Translated by Richard Nice. Stanford: Stanford University Press, 1990.
Clark, Kelly James. *Abraham's Children: Liberty and Tolerance in an Age of Religious Conflict*. New Haven: Yale University Press, 2012.
Gourgouris, Stathis. "Antisecularist Failures: A Counterresponse to Saba Mahmood." *Public Culture* 20 (2008) 453–59.
Latour, Bruno. *We Have Never Been Modern*. Translated by Catherine Porter. Cambridge: Harvard University Press, 1993.
Long, Stephen D. "How to Read Charles Taylor: The Theological Significance of *A Secular Age*." *Pro Ecclesia* 18/1 (2009) 93–107.
Lyon, David. "Being Post-secular in the Social Sciences: Taylor's Social Imaginaries." *New Blackfriars* 91 (2010) 648–64.
Mahmood, Saba. "Can Secularism Be Other-wise?" In *Varieties of Secularism in a Secular Age*, edited by Michael Warner et al., 282–99. Cambridge: Harvard University Press, 2010.
———. "Is Critique Secular? A Symposium at UC Berkeley." *Public Culture* 20 (2008) 447–52.
———. *The Politics of Piety: The Islamic Revival and the Feminine Subject*. Princeton: Princeton University Press, 2005.

---

27. Calvin, *Commentary on Genesis*. Thanks to Nick Wolterstorff for alerting me to this passage.

———. "Secular Imperatives." *Public Culture* 20 (2008) 461–65.

———. "Secularism, Hermeneutics, and Empire: The Politics of Islamic Reformation." *Public Culture* 18 (2006) 323–47.

Nagel, Thomas. *The View from Nowhere*. New York: Oxford University Press, 1989.

Taylor, Charles. *A Secular Age*. Cambridge: Harvard University Press, 2007.

Thomas, Scott M. "Living Critically and 'Living Faithfully' in a Global Age: Justice, Emancipation, and the Political Theology of International Relations." *Millennium: Journal of International Studies* 39 (2010) 505–24.

Wolterstorff, Nicholas. "Between the Pincers of an Increased Diversity and Supposed Irrationality." In *God, Philosophy and Academic Culture: A Discussion between Scholars in the AAR and the APA*, edited by William J. Wainwright, 13–20. New York: Oxford University Press, 1996.

———. "Religious Intolerance and the Wounds of God." In *Abraham's Children: Liberty and Tolerance in an Age of Religious Conflict*, edited by Kelly James Clark, 141–59. New Haven: Yale University Press, 2012.

11

Why Spinozists and Kierkegaardians Should Love Each Other

Michael Strawser

"One man may do the very opposite of what another does; but if each one does the opposite out of love, the opposites build up."

—Søren Kierkegaard[1]

INTRODUCTION

As consistently presented by "professors" of philosophy, there appear to be numerous reasons for Kierkegaardians and Spinozists to be at odds. Given that "from the mere fact that we imagine a thing to have something similar to an object that is wont to affect the mind with pleasure or pain, we shall love it or hate it" (according to proposition 16 of Part 3 of Spinoza's *Ethics*), it follows as a corollary that imagining significant differ-

---

1. Kierkegaard, *Works of Love* (1962), 202. Note that Howard V. Hong and Edna H. Hong have provided two different translations of this text issued by two different publishers, the first in 1962 and the other in 1995. As I refer to both in this paper, I have included the date of the respective translation in each citation.

ences between one thing and another that is wont to affect the mind with pleasure will lead us to hatred of the different object. In other words, if we love Kierkegaard's philosophy—which we all surely must, otherwise there would be no reason for the present celebration[2]—and imagine another philosophy, such as Spinoza's, to be significantly different from it, then we will be led to hate the other philosophy and to endeavor that it should be hated by everyone.[3]

Consider, then, their differences. Kierkegaard, born a Danish Christian, is, as those "professors" teach us, a great "existentialist" thinker—one who advocates an unsystematic leap into irrationalism through faith in an absurd transcendent God. Whereas we are taught that Spinoza, born a Dutch Jew, is a rationalist par excellence—one who is focused on the pursuit of systematic objective knowledge of an immanent God. Could the difference be any greater?

Although briefly expressed, these differences would seem to preclude any serious scholarship connecting the two thinkers; hence the secondary literature on the relationship between Spinoza and Kierkegaard is scant. Clare Carlisle's 2009 article on Spinoza, which offers the best and only overview of this relationship, concludes with a list of "Secondary Literature on Kierkegaard's relation to Spinoza"[4] consisting of only eight sources: three in French, two in German, one in Spanish, and two in English, both of which are PhD dissertations from the early 1960s. Although Carlisle's list may not be exhaustive—after all, my 2007 article "The Ethics of Love in Kierkegaard and Spinoza" published in *Philosophy Today*[5] is not included—it does express a serious lack of interest and a perceived lack of connection between these two thinkers. I contend that, at the very least, this double lack deserves critical attention.

After all, although the references to Spinoza in Kierkegaard's writings are "relatively few and far between,"[6] he did read "the philosopher of Amsterdam" and engaged with his ideas. *The Auction Catalogue* of Kierkegaard's Library includes the 1830 Latin edition of Spinoza's complete works as well as 51 works that discuss Spinoza. Carlisle shows that "Kierkegaard read Spinoza's obscurer works in addition to the well-known *Ethics* and *Tractatus Theologico-Politicus*, and most of his own pseudonymous texts contain some

2. This paper was first presented at the Kierkegaard Circle Conference: Celebrating SK at 200, Trinity College, University of Toronto, Canada, April 6, 2013.

3. Spinoza, *Ethics*, 3:31c.

4. Carlisle, "Spinoza," 194.

5. Parts of this paper are based on my earlier article. See Strawser, "Ethics of Love," 438–46.

6. Carlisle, "Spinoza," 184.

mention of Spinoza."⁷ Carlisle examines these passages in Kierkegaard to show what he thought of Spinoza's philosophy; however, as this work has already been well done, and since my main focus is not on the historical question, I wish to pursue a different path. A path of love.

Perhaps another reason for the esteemed professors' silence on the question of the Spinoza-Kierkegaard relationship is their even more regretful silence on love. If we begin our approach to the Spinoza-Kierkegaard question from an inquiry on love—an attempt to overturn the history of philosophy (which, having divorced itself from its origin, has been a disaster as far as love is concerned, and has even, as Jean-Luc Marion persuades us in *The Erotic Phenomenon*, hated love⁸)—we shall find that we are able to offer a new interpretation. This interpretation will show that Kierkegaard and Spinoza should be understood first and foremost as philosophers of love, who in their own ways endeavor to raise their readers' awareness of what is required in pursuing the path of eternal love. This path is expressed most clearly in Kierkegaard's *Works of Love* and Spinoza's *Ethics*.⁹ If my interpretation is successful, then Spinozists and Kierkegaardians will not only have a reason to love each other through a perceived similarity, but even more importantly through an adequate understanding of the eternal love that lies at the heart of the vision held in common by Spinoza and Kierkegaard. Let us start with Spinoza.

SPINOZA'S STAGES ON LOVE'S WAY

The fact that Spinoza entitled his *magnum opus* "Ethics" is significant, for it highlights what is most central in Spinoza's vision: not metaphysics or epistemology as commonly interpreted, but rather a practical ethics of life. Had Spinoza wished to highlight something else, he could have entitled his greatest work "Truth," "True Knowledge," or "The Way of Reason," but he did not. Nor did he call it "God" or "Nature," neither of which would have been unreasonable. Instead, his work is simply entitled *Ethics*. This signifies that the heart of Spinoza's philosophy and the key value of this work lie in communicating the proper way of living or acting in the world. Not surprisingly, then, an understanding of "love" can be found in the heart of this work.

7. Ibid., 167.
8. Marion, *Erotic Phenomenon*, 3.
9. Most quotations from Spinoza's *Ethics* are from G. H. R. Parkinson's translation (2000), and are cited according to the common practice indicating Part, proposition, and scholium respectively.

We all know that coming to terms with love is difficult. To complicate matters, there is some ambiguity in Spinoza's presentation of love in his *Ethics*. Careful readers will find that there are three seemingly distinct conceptions of love at work within his text, which can appropriately be understood in Kierkegaardian terms as aesthetic, ethical, and religious. In his *Ethics* Spinoza writes of love in the following ways: (1) love as a passion defined as "pleasure accompanied by the idea of an external cause";[10] (2) love as an action, equated with "nobility" (*generositas*), which conquers hatred[11] and is defined as "the desire by which each person, in accordance with the dictate of reason alone, endeavors to help other men and join them to him in friendship";[12] and (3) love as an action based on understanding God—the intellectual love of God (*amor dei intellectualis*)—understood as "pleasure, accompanied by the idea of God as its cause."[13] Let us consider some of the details.

Although the term "love" is not geometrically defined and discussed until Part Three of *Ethics*, the ambiguity appears earlier in the text. The first use of "love" occurs parenthetically in proposition 31 of Part One, where it is claimed to be "related to passive and not to active Nature." "Love" does not appear again until it is found in the lengthy and significant scholium that closes Part Two. This scholium is significant because in it Spinoza, responding to criticisms of determinism and explaining the practical benefits of that doctrine, projects themes that are central in the last part of his work. The mention of "love" is in the following sentence: "This doctrine, therefore, besides the fact that it makes the mind entirely calm, has the further benefit that it teaches us in what our supreme happiness, or, our blessedness, consists: namely, solely in the knowledge of God, from which we are led to do only those things which love and piety advise."[14] So love advises. Love advises us to do only those things that will lead to our blessedness. Consequently, this is clearly not the kind of love that belongs to our passive nature, as initially mentioned in Part One and further explained in Part Three. It is rather the kind of love that acts rather than reacts, that prevents or weakens the passive emotions of hate, anger, and envy. This love advises us to help our neighbors "not from effeminate pity, bias, or superstition, but solely

---

10. Spinoza, *Ethics*, 3:13.
11. Ibid., 3:43:s.
12. Ibid., 3:59:s.
13. Ibid., 5:32:c.
14. Ibid., 2:49:s.

from the guidance of reason."[15] Clearly, love of this kind is not without rationality, and the lover will continually strive to make such love intuitive.

What is primary in Spinoza's philosophy of love is not the conception of love initially defined by him as "pleasure with the accompaniment of the idea of an external cause."[16] It is therefore not necessary for us to distinguish the different manifestations of this kind of love as determined by its various objects (e.g., the love of sports, food, etc.). Such love is egoistic, and Spinoza clearly moves beyond this conception when, in the course of explaining the supposedly passive dynamics of love and hate, he writes: "Hatred is increased by reciprocal hatred, and conversely can be destroyed by love."[17] This proposition should give readers pause for at least two reasons: first, because of the powerful idea expressed—there is a way to remove hatred—and second, because of the ambiguous use of "love." It seems obvious that we are now dealing with a different kind of love; one cannot substitute Spinoza's "essential" definition into this proposition and have it fully make sense. The love that is now being referred to is active rather than passive.

There is another term Spinoza uses to refer to what we may understand as active, ethical love, and that is "nobility." This term is repeatedly equated with love. After 57 propositions in Part Three that explain "the origin and nature of the emotions" and categorize 46 passive emotions, Spinoza writes only two propositions explaining active emotions rather than passions. Proposition 58 reads: "Besides the pleasure and the desire which are passions there exist other emotions of pleasure and desire which are related to us in so far as we act." Then in the scholium to the following proposition Spinoza writes that all the active emotions are related to fortitude, which covers two categories of emotions: courage and nobility.

> For by "courage" I understand "the desire by which each person endeavours to preserve his being in accordance with the dictate of reason alone", and by "nobility" I understand "the desire by which each person, in accordance with the dictate of reason alone, endeavors to help other men and join them to him in friendship".[18]

Thus for Spinoza it is essential for an active person to try to help others, and it should be pointed out that the notion of "friendship" is not that which we normally consider to be based on personal preferences. It cannot be, since it is commanded by reason alone. A "friend" in Spinoza's sense is what

15. Ibid., 4:37:s1.
16. Ibid., 3:13:s.
17. Ibid., 3:43.
18. Ibid., 3:59:s.

Kierkegaard calls "the neighbor," and what philosophers today generally designate as "the other."

Nobility has now been defined, but what's love got to do with it? Is it possible to ground our interpretation of nobility as love in the text itself? In a significant proposition in Part Four Spinoza writes: "Someone who lives in accordance with the guidance of reason endeavors, as far as he can, to repay the hatred, anger, contempt, etc. that another has for him with love, [that is] with nobility."[19] So, now, it is clear that by "love" Spinoza means nobility, *amor sive generositas*. (Moreover, in the demonstration of this proposition Spinoza directs readers to the initial reference to nobility as well as to the proposition, quoted above, that hatred can be extinguished by love.) Love is now a purely internal movement of the self, although intended to have external effects; namely, the decrease of hatred, anger, contempt, etc. Here we have works of love leading to fruits of love, if you will. Following the command of reason, it is clear that one shall love, and it is through acts of love that one strengthens and preserves one's own being. Without love one lives miserably.[20]

In the final scholium in Part Four Spinoza writes:

> These and similar things that I have demonstrated about the true freedom of man are related to fortitude, that is, to courage and nobility. I do not think it worthwhile to demonstrate here, one by one, that a free man hates no one, is angry with no one, envies no one, is indignant with no one, despises no one, and is far from being proud. For these, and all the things that relate to true life and religion, are easily demonstrated from Props. 37 and 46 of this Part: namely, that hatred is to be conquered by love, and that each person who is led by reason desires that the good that he seeks for himself should also exist for others.[21]

There are other passages in the *Ethics* where Spinoza indicates the equivalence of love and nobility, but we do not need to continue our exposition of this point. We are now justified in reading Spinoza's *Ethics* as a philosophy of love.

---

19. Ibid., 4:46.
20. Ibid., 4:46:s.
21. Ibid., 4:73:s.

KIERKEGAARD'S LOVER SUB SPECIE AETERNITATIS

Kierkegaard, as we all know and as Irving Singer has written, "writes book after book about love."[22] In other words, like Spinoza, Kierkegaard is most edifyingly read as a philosopher of love rather than an irrational existentialist, Christian moralist, etc. And like Spinoza, Kierkegaard also understands the stages on love's way. In *Either/Or* we find both an illustration and a description of erotic love that is fleeting and dependent on an external object; there also, in volume II,[23] we read about marital love, conceived as an ethical love and marked by its eternal validity. But it is clearly *Works of Love* that most directly expresses Kierkegaard's philosophy of love. In *Works of Love* the religious conception of the love of God is surely all-important, but it is not the central focus of the text. For example, Kierkegaard writes that "fundamentally love to God is decisive; from this arises love to one's neighbor."[24] Spinoza makes a similar point in *Ethics* when he writes: "From this we clearly understand in what our salvation or blessedness or freedom consists, namely in the constant and eternal love towards God, that is, in God's love towards men."[25] The central focus of Kierkegaard's text is, of course, neighborly love, the highest ethical conception of love, and if we keep our focus on this practical conception rather than on abstract theological reflections, the common watermark of love found in both Spinoza and Kierkegaard becomes evident. Let us now consider Kierkegaard's conception in more detail.

In the ecstatic lecture in *Either/Or* A writes "I, as Spinoza says, view everything *aeterno modo*."[26] I wish to suggest that this expression can even more appropriately be applied to the author of *Works of Love*. Undoubtedly, we have transformed our understanding of these words, but it is easily demonstrated that for Kierkegaard the true lover "is continually *aeterno modo*." What exactly does this mean?

First, it means that in our conception of "you *shall* love" the "shall" signifies duty or obligation. Where this duty comes from, where its foundation lies, is a mystery. Whether we consider it a divine command or a law of reason, we come no closer to unveiling its origin; in either case we are dealing with an *a priori* source grasped intuitively. Such is the nature of both Kierkegaard's and Spinoza's visions. Kierkegaard explains: "this

---

22. Singer, *Nature of Love*, 38.
23. See "The Esthetic Validity of Marriage," in *Either/Or*, 3–154.
24. Kierkegaard, *Works of Love* (1962), 70.
25. Spinoza, *Ethics*, 5:36:s.
26. Kierkegaard, *Either/Or*.

obligation to love is an alteration of the eternal," and through this "all things are made new."[27] "Spontaneous love [i.e., the aesthetic conception of love, i.e., pleasure accompanied by an external cause] has, according to the beautiful understanding of the imagination [i.e., Spinoza's first and lowest kind of knowledge based on inadequate ideas] the eternal in itself, but it is not *consciously* grounded upon the eternal and consequently can be changed."[28] "*Only when it is a duty to love*," Kierkegaard writes, "*only then is love eternally secure*."[29] Thus for Kierkegaard the duty to love is understood as "a change of eternity" and the goal of the lover is to love *sub specie aeternitatis*, which secures her against every change and against despair, freeing her in blessed independence. Let us consider an example.

If I love my beloved with only preferential love and not eternal love, then I can indeed love my beloved passionately, and I may even claim that I love her more than I love myself. But if my beloved changes and says she no longer loves me and wants to separate, what happens to my preferential love? It may easily change and become hate—in fact, for Spinoza, insofar as I am passive it would necessarily change into hate—in which case I could hardly be conceived as independent of my beloved, but highly dependent indeed. Or, it could happen that I am cast into despair, which for Kierkegaard is a "misrelation in a person's innermost being."[30] The only way to avoid or prevent such despair is through "eternity's shall," which is to say, by transforming preferential love into eternal love. When my beloved says she hates me and I recognize that it is my duty to love nonetheless—that nothing changes or revokes this duty—then, and only then, can I freely respond with love. Whether we speak of an eternal duty or a dictate of reason matters little in practice. Kierkegaard recognizes that preferential love involves a misrelation, and so too does Spinoza, who writes: "Then it is to be noted that the sicknesses and misfortunes of the mind derive their origin chiefly from an excessive love for a thing that is subject to many changes, and which we can never possess."[31] The corrective to the faulty, excessive, passive love is eternal love, i.e., *Kjerlighed*. As is well known, Kierkegaard distinguishes *Kjerlighed* from *Elskov*, which refers to "self-love," "spontaneous love," "preferential love," "erotic or romantic love," and "friendship." *Elskov*, like Spinoza's aesthetic *amor* as initially conceived, is passive and defined by external objects (e.g., an attractively curved physique, or my spouse, my sibling, my

27. Kierkegaard, *Works of Love* (1962), 41.
28. Ibid., 46; my italics.
29. Ibid., 47.
30. Kierkegaard, *Works of Love* (1995), 40.
31. Spinoza, *Ethics*, 5:20:s.

child, etc.). *Kjerlighed*, however, which like Spinoza's nobility is the kind of love that essentially defines the ethics of love, is referred to by Kierkegaard as "self-denial's love," "eternal love," "the spirit's love," or "true love." This love is not defined by external objects, but rather the innermost center of a person (what we commonly refer to metaphorically as the heart). *Kjerlighed* is active rather than passive, and inclusive rather than exclusive. This love is not an unfree reaction caused by external forces; it is a free action produced from within the inner self (the true self)—an action that we may consider to be "as difficult as it is rare"[32] or "more difficult . . . than to capture a city."[33]

If we now consider what is signified by "the neighbor," we rightly understand it to mean the "nearest," not in the sense of "preferential love," but in the sense of essential love. In that case I understand myself not as he, a man, teacher, husband, father, or coach, but rather as "one who is equal" or similar to all others. Conceptually, Kierkegaard tells us, the neighbor is "a redoubling of your own self," but this is difficult to clarify because of the ambiguous term "self." Kierkegaard writes that "self-love cannot endure 'redoubling,'"[34] suggesting two different notions of the self. The point is that the "true self" found in redoubling is the eternal self common to us all. Kierkegaard illustrates this nicely in the following passage:

> Every human being is the neighbor. In being king, beggar, rich man, poor man, male, female, etc., we are not like each other—therein we are indeed different. But in being the neighbor we are all unconditionally like each other. Dissimilarity is temporality's method of confusing that marks every human being differently, but the neighbor is eternity's mark—on every human being. Take many sheets of paper, write something different on each one; then no one will be like another. But then again take each single sheet; do not let yourself be confused by the diverse inscriptions, hold it up to the light, and you will see a common watermark on all of them. In the same way the neighbor is the common watermark, but you see it only by means of eternity's light when it shines through the dissimilarity.[35]

This notion of the (true) self in Kierkegaard, which is equal and similar in us all, can be seen as equivalent to Spinoza's understanding of the (true) self, for after all, in Spinoza's thought we are all essentially one, united in our *conatus*, our desire to persevere. Clare Carlisle also recognizes an affinity here:

32. Ibid., 5:42:s.
33. Kierkegaard, *Works of Love* (1995), 218.
34. Ibid., 21.
35. Ibid., 89.

> [T]he ontological interpretation that has eventually emerged from our focus on the theme of movement, and which captures the essence of Kierkegaard's thought—the self as a center of power, and God as the source of all power—is integral to Spinoza's Ethics too.[36]

Carlisle goes on to explain that for Kierkegaard, "'the essentially human is passion,' and . . . passion is a movement of intensification that can be equated with inwardness itself." She continues by suggesting that this view of Kierkegaard shares an ontological similarity to Spinoza's conatus. Carlisle then writes that "to become religious is to understand that this power which spontaneously pours forth is a loving power."

These are important points by Carlisle that complement my reading of Spinoza and Kierkegaard. When readers miss the unity of Spinoza's and Kierkegaard's philosophy of love—and many fine ones have—it may be because they accentuate the differences and consequently obstruct or marginalize the sameness. In Merold Westphal's thought-provoking book entitled *Transcendence and Self-Transcendence: On God and the Soul*, he adopts this more common position, arguing that Spinoza's "alternative ethics" differs "dramatically from that of theism."[37] While there may be theological differences regarding the status of ethical claims (such as whether they are divine commands or not), the emphasis on the philosophy of love is of a practical, not theoretical, nature. This emphasis is clearly found in Kierkegaard, who focuses on the practical works of love and does not wish to speak of love itself, since it is essentially indescribable and unspeakable. There can be for Kierkegaard no theory of love, for, as noted, its origins are essentially mysterious. Similarly, as suggested above, the title of Spinoza's greatest and most important work clearly indicates the primacy of human relations and a concern for others in his thinking. Consider the following proposition (referred to but not cited above), which is a crucial point in Spinoza's philosophy of love: "The good which each person who follows virtue seeks for himself he also desires for all other men, and the more so, the more he has a greater knowledge of God."[38]

While I can conceive of reasons why some commentators might not focus on Spinoza's philosophy of love, one can hardly maintain, as Westphal does, that "nothing in Spinoza's therapeutic ethics requires that I concern myself with the happiness of others, forbids me to be indifferent to the

---

36. Carlisle, *Kierkegaard's Philosophy of Becoming*, 134.
37. Westphal, *Transcendence and Self-Transcendence*, 61.
38. Spinoza, *Ethics*, 4:37.

widow, the orphan, and the stranger."³⁹ Such a claim fails to acknowledge the active emotions of fortitude and nobility, i.e., love, that figure so prominently in Spinoza's ethical vision. To imagine Spinoza's moral exemplar of human nature as lacking the desire to help others is to form an inadequate idea in Spinoza's terms. Only when I endeavor to help others to become stronger, and join them in friendship—or better, "neighborship"—by wanting the same good for them that I desire for myself, do I approach what Spinoza understands as an exemplar of human nature. Although a metaphysical foundation for Spinoza's ethics is given in his unfolding of a particular conception of God (and one could also argue that Kierkegaard's view presupposes a certain metaphysics), the practical love ethic in Spinoza's work centers on the ideal of a moral exemplar and the active emotion he calls "fortitude."

Let us return to this emotion once more. Fortitude, as we have seen, has a twofold essence. First, it is a way of being for oneself or "a desire by which each person endeavors to preserve his own being by the dictate of reason alone," which Spinoza calls "courage." Second, it is a way of being for others, or "a desire by which each person endeavors to help others and join them to him in friendship," which is called "nobility."⁴⁰ It is important to understand the unity of these two sub-concepts of fortitude.⁴¹ In desiring to preserve one's own being one endeavors to help others, and by helping others one preserves one's own being. This is similar to the Christian command as explained by Kierkegaard: "to love your neighbor as yourself" means "that you shall love yourself in the same way that you love your neighbor when you love him as yourself."⁴² In other words, the love of neighbor teaches us to love ourselves in the right way—in a way that causes ourselves to flourish and increase in loving power. Further, consider this passage from *Works of Love* that clearly resonates with Spinoza's view: "You ought to preserve the love and you ought to preserve yourself and in and by preserving yourself to preserve the love."⁴³ Readers who see Spinoza's ethics as essentially egoistic miss this point—namely, that for Spinoza being for oneself is essentially being for others. Further supporting this view is the fact that, for Spinoza, one is less free alone than with others in a community.⁴⁴

---

39. Westphal, *Transcendence and Self-Transcendence*, 65, my italics.

40. Spinoza, *Ethics*, 3:59:s.

41. A parallel position is found in Spinoza in his understanding that the sub-concepts of thought and extension are united in the concept of substance.

42. Kierkegaard, *Works of Love* (1995), 23.

43. Kierkegaard, *Works of Love* (1962), 57.

44. Cf. Spinoza, *Ethics*, 4:73.

CONCLUSION

It is unfortunate that Kierkegaard, like most of his contemporaries and many philosophers still today, interprets Spinoza primarily as a metaphysician. Even so, he clearly appreciated the profundity of Spinoza's ideas, although he failed to focus on the ethical import of Spinoza's philosophy of love: while there are numerous references to Spinoza in other works by Kierkegaard, there is no reference to the "philosopher from Amsterdam" in *Works of Love*. As I have suggested above, any reading of Spinoza that misses his philosophy of love is a grave distortion. Certainly Spinoza was keenly interested in metaphysical and epistemological questions, and certainly he attempted to present his philosophy in as systematic manner as possible; but his conatus—his spirit, his "passion" in the Kierkegaardian sense—would not let him rest there. It led him to affirm a practical philosophy of life and love in a way that no other modern philosopher did.

So, we must now conclude that both of our philosophers endeavor to conceive a philosophy of love under the aspect of eternity. When we imagine this similarity—and it is hard to conceive a more meaningful one—between Spinoza and our beloved Kierkegaard, then (as explained in the proposition cited at the beginning of this paper) we shall be moved to love. More deeply, however, when we adequately understand this common watermark with eternity's light, we shall feel pleasure accompanied by love as its cause.

BIBLIOGRAPHY

Carlisle, Clare. "Baruch de Spinoza: Questioning Transcendence, Teleology and Truth." In *Kierkegaard and the Renaissance and Modern Traditions, Tome 1: Philosophy*, vol. 5 of *Kierkegaard Research: Sources, Reception and Resources*, edited by Jon Stewart, 167–94. Aldershot, UK: Ashgate, 2009.

———. *Kierkegaard's Philosophy of Becoming: Movements and Positions*. New York: State University of New York Press, 2005.

Kierkegaard, Søren. *Either/Or*, Parts I and II. Translated by Howard V. Hong and Edna H. Hong. Kierkegaard's Writings 3 and 4. Princeton: Princeton University Press, 1987.

———. *Works of Love*. Translated by Howard V. Hong and Edna H. Hong. New York: Harper & Row, 1962.

———. *Works of Love*. Translated by Howard V. Hong and Edna H. Hong. Matrix: Kierkegaard's Writings 16. Princeton: Princeton University Press, 1995.

Marion, Jean-Luc. *The Erotic Phenomenon*. Translated by Stephen E. Lewis. Chicago: University of Chicago Press, 2006.

Nun, Katalin, Gerhard Schreiber, and Jon Stewart, eds. *The Auction Catalogue of Kierkegaard's Library*. Matrix: Kierkegaard Research: Sources, Reception and Resources 20. Aldershot, UK: Ashgate, 2009.

Singer, Irving. *The Nature of Love*, vol. 3: *The Modern World*. Cambridge, MA: MIT Press, 2009.

Spinoza, Baruch. *Ethics*. Edited and translated by G. H. R. Parkinson. Matrix: Oxford Philosophical Texts. Oxford: Oxford University Press, 2000.

Strawser, Michael. "The Ethics of Love in Spinoza and Kierkegaard and the Teleological Suspension of the Theological." *Philosophy Today* 51 (2007) 438–46.

Westphal, Merold. *Transcendence and Self-Transcendence: On God and the Soul*. Bloomington: Indiana University Press, 2004.

PART 2
Science and Theology

12

Thinking of Everything
Scientific and Theological Challenges of the Multiverse

Robert B. Mann

The growing level of interest amongst cosmologists and theoretical physicists in the multiverse[1]—the idea that our observable universe is a small part of a much, much larger structure—is ample reason for those interested in the relationship between science and theology to take notice. It raises new challenges for theological thinking that may indeed lead to differences with science that are not reconcilable. However, the multiverse also raises new challenges for scientific thinking, challenges that have led a number of prominent scientists to suggest that perhaps we need to modify the foundations of science itself.[2]

The origin of the theological challenges can be understood by considering omnipotence, one of the central attributes of God.[3] Simply put, omnipotence asserts that God is capable of doing anything, where "anything" is taken to mean "anything that is logically self-consistent," thereby putting aside such trivial conundrums as whether or not God could make a stone too heavy for him/her/it to lift. From a theological perspective, the observable universe is regarded as owing its origin to this God, not existing in

---

1. A recent overview of this subject is given in Carr, *Universe or Multiverse?*
2. See for example the article by Weinberg in ibid., 29.
3. Aquinas, *Summa Theologica*, Article 3; see also Luke 1:37.

and of itself, but rather as a deliberate manifestation of the limitless power that flows from the Almighty. It is also regarded as a specific manifestation of God's omnipotence—whence (as we shall see) emerges the theological challenge.

The scientific challenge is rooted in unification, a key motivator of all scientific thought. The idea here is that apparently disparate phenomena can be understood as different aspects of the same phenomenon at some deeper level. While there is no proof of this, historically this path has been enormously fruitful in science, particularly in physics. Newton posited a single law of gravity that governed both the motion of stars in the heavens and of apples falling to earth, thereby uniting celestial phenomena with terrestrial phenomena. Maxwell produced a theory that described electricity and magnetism as manifestations of a single force now known as electromagnetism. A little more than forty years ago the weak interactions governing radioactivity were united with electromagnetism in a single theory—electroweak theory—that made a number of new predictions subsequently confirmed by experiment. By the end of the 1970s a Standard Model of particle physics[4] had emerged that described all known subatomic particles (quarks and leptons) and their interactions due to the electroweak and strong nuclear forces.[5] While comprehensive in its descriptive scope, it depends on 27 distinct parameters (12 of which are the different masses of the 12 elementary subatomic particles, for example), suggesting to many that a deeper level of unification is required. These and many other examples have motivated physicists to search for a "Theory of Everything," a single theory that would describe all known (and yet to be discovered) particles and forces in a coherent, unified whole. Many regard superstring theory as holding the most promise for a concrete realization of this ideal.[6]

The multiverse is sometimes understood as a "theory of everything," but the meaning and context of the phrase so used are quite different from those of the Theory of Everything described above. The multiverse is better understood as a "theory of anything,"[7] since at its core it posits the physical existence of all possible configurations of our observable universe permitted by the laws of physics. In other words, anything that can happen does happen. Furthermore, it posits the possibility of new laws of physics, leading to physical systems and configurations that could not exist in our universe

---

4. For a non-technical introduction see Lederman and Teresi, *The God Particle*.

5. For an introduction at an undergraduate level, see Mann, *Introduction to Particle Physics*.

6. Ellis, "Superstring."

7. Albrecht, *Theory of Everything vs Theory of Anything*. Lect. Notes Phys. 455:323–332 (1995).

given its physical laws. In other words, anything that might happen will happen. This radically different ontological stance presents dual challenges to science and theology as they are traditionally understood.

But wherein lie these challenges? Couldn't an omnipotent God create all possible laws of physics, and enough matter and energy to realize all possible configurations that these laws permit? And shouldn't science be as comprehensive as possible, subsuming all of reality—even that which lies outside observation—into a coherent, descriptive whole? Shouldn't the multiverse be regarded as the culmination of the grand ideas of theology and science?

Tempting though it may be to answer this question in the affirmative, intellectual honesty compels us to recognize two key issues before doing so. (1) Scientifically, a theory of everything is not the same as a theory of anything.[8] (2) Theologically, a God who can do anything is not the same as a God that does everything.[9] It is the distinction between anything and everything in both science and theology that gives rise to the challenges presented by the multiverse. The purpose of this paper is to clarify and expand on these distinctions so that the nature of the challenges presented by the multiverse are better understood.

PERPLEXED BY PARTICULARITY

Both science and theology are engaged, each from their own perspective, with particularity. Why do some things exist and not others? Why do some events take place and not others? It is a two-sided problem. First, why is there something instead of nothing? Why does the universe bother to exist at all? Second, why don't all things exist? Why don't all events take place? The empirical foundations of both questions appear superficially to be on equal footing, but this is not quite the case. The first question is motivated by straightforward observation: clearly particular things and events exist. The second question, however, presumes particularity—that there are some things and events that logically could exist but don't. The multiverse paradigm challenges this latter assumption, asserting that the logically permissible is also the physically actualized. In so doing it suggests the second question is ill-posed. It is here that its challenges for science and theology emerge.

---

8. John Polkinghorne, as quoted in Folger, "Science's Alternative to an Intelligent Creator."

9. Mann, "Puzzle of Existence."

The question of existence is theology's oldest question;[10] it has been discussed and debated in various forms for centuries. The emergent response is the doctrine of *creatio ex nihilo* (creation out of nothing): the notion that all that exists originates due to a Creator who is its first and ultimate cause.[11] The question of specificity, on the other hand, is typically never asked nor addressed in theological terms, though it could have been asked centuries ago since it is the converse of the previous *creatio ex nihilo* question. I contend this is theology's newest question:[12] why are there some things instead of everything? The multiverse paradigm, in rejecting the premise of the question by asserting that the possible is the actual, suggests here that something along the lines of *creatio ex omnia* (creation out of everything) is theologically required.

Modern cosmology puts these issues into sharper focus. I use the expression "cosmic theology" to refer to theological reflection on, and interpretation of, the science of cosmology. Cosmic theology deals with three main issues emerging from our current understanding of the cosmos: injection, direction, and selection. Injection has to do with the origin of the cosmos: how and why did it all get started? Direction refers to the developmental history of the cosmos: how and why did we develop from our primordial state to our present state? And selection refers to the configuration of the cosmos. What specific features does our present state of existence have, and are these of any significance?

One of the meta-findings of science in the latter half of the twentieth century has been the particularity of our cosmos.[13] Its origin evidently depends upon special initial conditions and physical properties, its subsequent development is contingent upon special features of the laws of physics, and its present state contains special structures and configurations. In other words, our universe is not a typical specimen out of the vast range of universes that the laws of physics permit. Moreover, this atypicality is connected with the existence of life, or at least of life as we know it[14].

How? Clearly we can live only in a universe whose initial conditions—for example, its initial rate of expansion and its thermodynamic entropy—allow life to exist. Similarly, the laws of physics and their associated constants of nature (such as the speed of light, mass of the electron,

10. For a discussion in the context of modern cosmology see Craig, "Philosophical and Scientific Pointers to Creation ex Nihilo," 191.

11. For an introduction see May, *Creatio ex nihilo*.

12. Mann, "Inconstant Multiverse."

13. For the first comprehensive discussion of this see Barrow and Tipler, *Anthropic Cosmological Principle*.

14. For a philosophical analysis of these issues see Leslie, *Universes*.

strength of the nuclear force, and many others) must be such as to permit life to develop. And the configurations of matter and energy allowed by these laws—planets with water in the liquid state, for example—must actually come into existence so that life can survive. This much is fairly obvious and essentially tautological—analogous, if scientists were fish, to their finding that the universe contained large quantities of water surrounding them: if this were not so, there would be no fish to discover it! What is neither obvious nor tautological is that the conditions permitting life are not typical. The life-permitting (or biophilic) initial conditions, physical laws, and particular configurations of our cosmos are all rather special, a very tiny subset of the vast range of possibilities we might scientifically contemplate.

It is natural to ask if there is any theological significance associated with this situation. To address this question it will be helpful to consider the scientific concept of potentiality.

POTENTIALITY

The approach of science has been to understand particular situations or configurations in the context of generality. The paradigm for doing so relies on the concept of potentiality, the idea that many alternatives are available for the development and configuration of a given system. Within this paradigm the job of science is first to describe the potential: all the configurations and developments that are possible under a given system.

Note that this does not mean all of these possibilities must be actualized. Actualization depends on two things: the underlying laws of physics, dependent on the symmetries and dynamics associated with the system under consideration; and the boundary conditions—the particular configuration a system has at a given time and place. Boundary conditions are set by an agent and/or by the environment, though even in the latter case a scientific understanding of the system is possible only when an agent (often called an observer in the scientific literature) has sufficient knowledge of the boundary conditions set by the environment. To the extent that this knowledge is limited, the scientific description is impoverished.

Two examples should suffice to illustrate this concept. Consider the motion of a tennis ball in a game of tennis. The laws of gravity near the earth force the ball to follow a parabolic trajectory. (Air resistance modifies this to a small extent, and can be neglected for the present discussion.) This parabola might be high and narrow, or low and long, or any of a number of infinite possibilities. Which of these possibilities is realized depends on the initial position and velocity of the ball at the instant it leaves the racket, conditions set by the tennis player in hitting the ball. A good tennis player is able to adjust these conditions to a rather precise level to achieve a desired trajectory out of this infinite range of possibilities.

Conversely, consider the motion of an air molecule, say oxygen, in the vicinity of the tennis game. To the best of our knowledge only the laws of gravity and electromagnetism, the latter being more important as the molecule collides with others in its neighborhood, govern the motion of the molecule. Even though these laws are very well understood, predicting the motion of a given oxygen molecule is effectively impossible since it would require, at any given time, knowledge not only of that molecule's position and velocity but also those of all the other air molecules in the atmosphere. The boundary conditions here are set by the environment (and, to a tiny extent, by the tennis players and the ball as they move around). Obtaining, storing, and processing this information about these boundary conditions is not feasible. However, it is possible to obtain knowledge of these boundary conditions for *large groups* of such molecules by averaging (or coarse-graining as it is sometimes called) the configurations and interactions of the individual molecules, affording a scientific description of the gas as a whole. In this manner the sub-discipline of statistical mechanics can turn limited knowledge of initial conditions into a scientific advantage, provided one is willing to settle for answers to a different (and less precise) set of questions.

How do potential situations become actualized? While the answer is not fully understood in all circumstances, some general scientific principles have emerged. Systems generally seek out configurations of lowest energy, largest entropy (or disorder), and maximal stability. In physics these situations are commonly illustrated by means of a graph in which the potential energy of a system (its stored energy that can be used to effect change) is drawn as a function of some other parameter (call it X) such as the position of a body in the system or the strength of an electric field. The potential will typically have peaks and valleys (maxima and minima) that depend on the values of X. Values of X where the potential is minimized correspond to stable, static configurations of low energy; values of X for which the potential is maximized correspond to static but unstable configurations of high energy. All other parameter values correspond to situations that are not static, in which the system is changing from one configuration to another. During such changes heat is typically dissipated to the environment, maximizing the entropy of the system plus environment as a whole. More generally a potential depends on many parameters of a system (such as the positions and charges of its constituents) whose actual configurations are attained for a choice of parameters that optimizes the requirements of stability, minimal energy, and maximal entropy.

The role of agency is tacitly ignored throughout, used implicitly as needed depending on the situation. The most common implicit use of agents is as observers who interpret the results of experiments. However, the contrivances involved in setting up an experiment also require agents, who select the appropriate boundary conditions to ferret out the behavior of a given system as predicted by a given class of theories. Agents also make the distinction between what constitutes the system and what constitutes the environment, a distinction without which there is no context for either observation or interpretation.[15]

Now, what of cosmological actuality? In this case the system under consideration is taken to be the entire (observable) universe. There are many possible configurations of our universe. Is there any significance to the particular configuration we observe it to have in fact?

One item of significance associated with our cosmos is life. By the 1970s it was known that the present state of our universe, with its particular biophilic properties, is highly sensitive both to the conditions obtaining at its origin and to the laws of physics (including many of the 27 parameters of the Standard Model) that govern its 13.7 billion year development. Very small changes in any of these conditions, laws, and parameters yield universes that look very different from our own, prohibiting the conditions for life as we know it. Evidently the particular configuration of our universe is significant insofar as it is "fine-tuned" so that life can exist.

Note that this situation is not logically necessary. It might very well have been the case that the biophilic properties of our universe were rather *in*sensitive to small changes in its laws and initial conditions. If this were the case, then the particular state of our universe would be a generic one out of all the possibilities. But this is not the case—the actual situation is as if our universe were perched at the top of a very steep, sharp peak of some potential curve.

There are several responses one might make on becoming aware of this situation.[16] One might say that the parameters of our universe, with its particular constants of nature, laws of physics, and initial conditions, simply exist arbitrarily and without reason. Another is to say that there is some

---

15. For a short discussion of some of these issues in a theological context, see Polkinghorne, *Is Science Enough?*

16. For a pro-and-con analysis of these responses, see Manson, *God and Design*.

"meta-law" of nature that governs both the boundary conditions of our universe and its laws of physics, so that rather than the boundary conditions being "added" to the laws of physics (as in the case of the tennis ball), they are instead part of the laws of physics, determined by a deeper meta-principle. This is the view advocated by practitioners of quantum cosmology in the context of a Theory of Everything. It is driven by a perspective of necessity, an assumption that the observed properties and evolution of our universe follow deterministically from some underlying basic principle. From this perspective the universe stably sits at the bottommost part of some potential curve, its biophilic parameters attaining their observed values as a result of this meta-principle of which we are so far ignorant; at present our ignorance of this principle leads to the mistaken impression that our universe is unstably situated at the top of a sharp potential peak. The challenge faced by advocates of this viewpoint is to find this meta-principle.

Yet another response is to regard the atypicality of the biophilic properties of our universe as the result of an Agent (whom we might call "God") that selected them for some reason.[17] Apart from being in accord with monotheistic faith traditions—especially the Judeo-Christian tradition, which regards the existence of life as resulting from the intentions of a Creator—this view is not without scientific precedent. As noted above, agents implicitly play roles in both establishing experiments and in interpreting their results, entailing special contrivances of matter and energy to achieve the desired goal. Perhaps the atypical biophilic features of our cosmos indicate something similar. Why not regard the cosmos itself as being established by an Agent? From this viewpoint our universe has indeed a special configuration akin to being at the top of a potential, but it is due to the intentions of an Agent who both selected and sustains the conditions that make this possible. Advocates of this Agency viewpoint face a challenge akin to that faced by neuroscientists studying the mind-brain relationship: what is the causal link between the intentions of the Agent and the action that originated the cosmos?

A fourth response is to regard the particular features of our universe as analogous to those of the oxygen molecule in the example above. The atmosphere has very large numbers of oxygen molecules, each with its own properties that differ slightly from every other molecule's. Perhaps our universe, with its special biophilic properties, is one out of many universes, each of which has its own particular properties (most of which will be biophobic, or life-prohibiting). The entire collection of universes is referred to as the multiverse, which plays the role of the atmosphere in this metaphor. From

---

17. For further discussion see Collins, "God, Design and Fine-Tuning."

this standpoint, our universe is indeed at a "special place in the potential," in this case because all other places in the potential are occupied by other universes. This explanation relies upon randomness (or chance, as I shall call it) insofar as it asserts a statistical ensemble of universes, all of which exist. In other words, all potential states of the cosmos, typical and atypical, biophobic and biophilic, are physically realized, hence even our atypical universe must exist. The remarkable biophilic features of our universe are inevitably realized, much as a person repeatedly playing poker for a long enough time would eventually be dealt a royal flush. Multiverse proponents face their own set of challenges, one of which is to provide any evidence in support of this viewpoint given that, by definition, our universe is the only observable member of the collection of universes.

In summary, the philosophical premises underlying each of these perspectives can be succinctly stated as follows.

1. *Necessity*: There is a single universe, whose special properties and features are the result of some underlying physical principle. No other universes can exist.

2. *Agency*: There is a single universe, whose special properties and features are the result of selection and actualization by an Agent (God). Other universes that could have existed do not, because of the Agent's intent.

3. *Chance*: There is a vast statistical ensemble of universes known as the multiverse. All possible universes permitted within the bounds of the ensemble exist, and so our universe with its special properties and features must also exist.

The first of these perspectives has generally been regarded as the goal of scientific inquiry, whereas the second has been regarded as the root principle of theological reflection. The third perspective introduces new elements for consideration in both disciplines, and will be explored in the remainder of this essay. Of course they are not mutually exclusive: one can consider variants of these perspectives, mixing and matching them, and I shall briefly consider that option in the concluding section of this paper.

MULTIVERSE MOTIVATIONS AND MULTIPLICITY

The multiverse paradigm regards our universe as a small part of a much larger whole, its atypicality being an unavoidable consequence of the statistical features of this ensemble, much in the way that our atmosphere will have a few oxygen molecules with unusual properties (e.g., high speed or slow rotation). This idea has become increasingly popular among cosmologists and theoretical physicists in recent years. Why?

There are several reasons. One is a frustration with standard approaches to unification. The simplest model of grand unification—a model that united electromagnetism, the weak nuclear force (governing radioactivity), and the strong nuclear force (binding quarks into neutrons and protons, and those into nuclei)—predicted that the proton would decay over a very long but feasibly observable lifetime.[18] Subsequent searches for proton decay in the 1980s found no evidence for this decay process and instead set lower bounds on proton lifetime.[19] As these experiments were being carried out, many more Grand Unified Theories (GUTs) were constructed, each making their own predictions for proton decay and low-energy particle physics. Many more experiments were carried out, confirming with increasing precision our theories of the strong, weak, and electromagnetic forces but finding no evidence whatsoever for their unification. All that has been done so far is to set empirical limits and bounds on GUTs. Explaining the origin of the 27 parameters of the Standard Model and the biophilic character of the cosmos through a clever deployment of natural law, symmetry, and dynamics has not been successful after more than three decades of hard effort by large numbers of theorists.

Agency remains a viable explanation for both the existence of the universe and its finely-tuned biophilic complexion, yet it sits rather uncomfortably with the current scientific mindset, which generally regards the assumption of Agency as an unproductive scientific strategy.[20] The contention that there are no firm criteria for making use of this notion (with its accompanying concepts of purpose and meaning) leads to the assertion that explanations of observable phenomena are productive only when they hypothesize specific natural causes rather than agent-driven action (including indeterminate miracles).

Proceeding by elimination, the multiverse paradigm would seem to be the default explanation. While this is certainly part of the reason for the growing interest in the multiverse, there are four avenues of scientific inquiry that its proponents contend provide positive reasons for considering it seriously. Two of these emerge from a "bottom-up" approach: inductive inference based on observations that the existence both of life as we know it and of the cosmos as a whole are "finely tuned." In other words, a significant number of physical parameters of the universe—such as the mass of the

---

18. Georgi and Glashow, "Unity of All Elementary-Particle Forces."
19. Amsler et al., "Review of Particle Physics."
20. See, for example, Wilczek, "Model of Anthropic Reasoning," 151.

electron and the rate of expansion of the universe[21]—are in a state of very delicate balance; a small change in any one of them yields a universe that is inhospitable to life[22] and looks nothing like the one we see.[23] The other two emerge from a "top-down" perspective: deductive reasoning based on axioms. Here the case in point is cosmic inflation[24] and string theory,[25] two theoretical paradigms favored by many physicists as the best descriptions, respectively, of our cosmos and of the union of gravity with quantum theory. Inflation is regarded by many as most naturally described in a multiverse context, whereas recent calculations in string theory suggest the emergence of an enormous number—or landscape—of low-energy kinds of universes (at least 10^{500} kinds), each with its own particular properties.

There are also several kinds of multiverse paradigms, corresponding to increasing levels of "size" or generality.[26] The simplest (or "smallest") of these is the Initial Condition Multiverse (ICM). An ICM can be generated by cosmic inflation: an exponentially expanding false vacuum spontaneously yields bubbles of true vacuum, each of which has an initial configuration that subsequently evolves into a universe.[27] As more bubbles of true vacuum are generated, more initial configurations are realized and thus more universes evolve. Each evolves according to the same laws of physics that govern our universe; only the initial conditions change from bubble to bubble. Since there is no limit either to the duration of this process or to the amount of energy involved, all possible initial conditions are eventually realized. This leads to an infinite ensemble of universes, each member of which could have been our universe but for its initial conditions. Each member is also replicated an arbitrary number of times, since initial configurations can be repeated from bubble to bubble. Although cosmic inflation is the generating mechanism for this ensemble, it is not required; a space of infinite extent with an arbitrarily large amount of randomly distributed matter and energy will also yield an ICM, sometimes called a Level 1 multiverse.

---

21. See Kaufman, *Universe*; also Weinberg, "Cosmological Constant Problems."

22. Carter, "Large Number Coincidences."

23. Carr and Rees, "Anthropic Cosmological Principle"; see also Collins, "Fine-Tuning Design Argument."

24. Guth, "Inflationary Universe"; Linde, "New inflationary universe scenario"; see also Guth, *Inflationary Universe*.

25. Green and Schwarz, "Anomaly cancellations"; for some readable introductions to string theory, pro and con, see respectively Greene, *Fabric of the Cosmos* and Smolin, *Trouble with Physics*.

26. Tegmark, "Multiverse Hierarchy."

27. For a non-technical description see Vilenkin, *Many Worlds in One*.

Beyond this there are four other levels of multiverse. Level 2 has distinct regions of space and time that are governed by different laws of physics. Level 3 is the Many Worlds Multiverse, in which all distinct quantum possibilities for a given set of conditions yield distinct universes (as opposed to a single universe that might be obtained upon measurement). Level 4 contains every mathematically conceivable universe possible, the only constraint being internal self-consistency. Level 5 is a computer-simulated multiverse (CSM), in which our universe is a small part of a much larger computer simulation, controlled by some agency external to our universe. Unlike Level 4, the CSM may or may not have any meaningful scientific or mathematical constraints. It is well known how to simulate magic, monsters, time travel, and other phenomena, all by means of computer graphics (this is after all how the movie industry makes its money); what then prevents similar manifestations in our own universe, if it is part of a computer simulation?

These different levels illustrate that the multiverse paradigm comprises a variety of multiverse theories. A given multiverse theory may posit limits to what is physically possible, as is the case with other scientific theories. Such theories in this sense are not "theories of anything," since they posit that certain things do not exist. Levels 1 to 3 share this feature, whereas Levels 4 and 5 do not. However, all multiverse theories rely on a certain degree of unbounded potentiality, coupled with the assertion that there is no distinction between the potential and the actual. Consequently all multiverse theories rely on "unbounded actuality" to achieve their goals. In this sense they are indeed "theories of anything" and have important implications for both science and theology.

SCIENTIFIC IMPLICATIONS OF THE MULTIVERSE

Elegance

Since a multiverse theory is not a singleverse (single-universe) theory, one must give up the hope that a unique and elegant "Theory of Everything" exists that will unite all observable forces and particles into a coherent, unified whole. Rather, as a "Theory of Anything," the multiverse paradigm subsumes all observable *and unobservable* forces and particles together, rendering the basic laws of physics neither unique nor elegant.[28] It has an arbitrarily large number of free parameters associated with the different kinds of universes, and so the specific character and features of our universe have no deeper explanation than the weather conditions on a certain day in a particular neighborhood on earth.

Cosmology thus becomes an environmental science. This is not a contradiction, and would also not be the first time that basic scientific expectations had to be revised (classical determinism yielded to quantum probability, for example). However, it does run contrary to the historical meta-lesson of science, which points to disparate phenomena being united by a more coherent understanding. If empirical particularity does not follow from mathematical uniqueness, is the epistemic price demanded by the multiverse paradigm worth the payoff?

Duplication

A strange implication of the multiverse paradigm is the phenomenon of rampant duplication.[29] Consider an ICM. Since DNA has a finite number of configurations, there will be an exact copy of yourself a finite distance away, provided there is sufficient matter or energy and an actualization of all possible initial conditions. Crude estimates of this distance can be carried out. For example the closest copy of any given human is about $10^{10^{29}}$ meters away from here, far larger than the size of our observable universe (or Hubble volume), which is 1026 meters in radius. Of course, all other material structures can be replicated as well: for example, the closest copy of our cosmos within 100 light years of earth is $10^{10^{91}}$ meters away, and the nearest copy of our observable universe is $10^{10^{118}}$ meters away.

While such numbers are ridiculously large, they are nevertheless finite. If the universe is unbounded in size and matter or energy, duplicates will appear not just once or twice, but arbitrarily often. Furthermore, all possible variants of duplicates will appear in the ICM (and all other levels of multiverse for that matter) arbitrarily often. In this sense the multiverse undermines one of its original motivations: in attempting to explain the special biophilic features of our cosmos by considering it to be a small part of a large ensemble, one is led to the strange conclusion that the ensemble contains all possible biophilic environments arbitrarily often. In particular, there are infinitely many earths, with all possible variations emerging from

---

28. Susskind, *Cosmic Landscape*.

29. See Ellis and Brundrit, "Life in the Infinite Universe"; also Tegmark, "Parallel Universes."

any given set of observed conditions. Hence all possible social, psychological, and experimental outcomes occur somewhere in the multiverse. The principle of induction is undermined: one cannot reliably infer a general law based on particular outcomes, or rule out unlikely possibilities on the basis of chance.[30] Quantum-mechanical probabilities are no longer given by the absolute squares of quantum amplitudes (i.e., the Born rule becomes non-operative), and the replacement prescription for making predictions is uncertain.[31]

Creationism and Boltzmann Brains

Another strange multiverse feature is the propensity for complex structures to emerge by chance, due either to thermal fluctuations or to quantum fluctuations. Since entropy increases with time, an infinite universe in thermal equilibrium would consist of disordered particles in a state of maximal entropy. No complex structures (such as intelligent life) could exist. However over a long enough period of time (or large enough distance in an ICM), random fluctuations occasionally form regions of lower entropy. If the fluctuation is large enough, a human brain can temporarily form, complete with a set of memories and perceptions. Such a Boltzmann brain[32] (named after Ludwig Boltzmann, who pointed out this kind of phenomenon)[33] can presumably be regarded as an "observer" just as much as any other human (or bio-brain) could be.

If we take current geological and biological knowledge seriously, bio-brains have a long developmental history that is ultimately embedded in our big-bang cosmos. In a multiverse, however, our cosmos, with its much higher mass-energy complexity, is much less likely than a Boltzmann brain to emerge from a fluctuation (either per unit time or per unit volume). Hence bio-brains are much less typical than Boltzmann brains in a multiverse scenario, contrary to the original intent of the paradigm. This is an unsolved problem for multiverse practitioners.

It gets worse. Given the multiverse scenario, one can ask how seriously one should take current geological and biological knowledge. For example,

---

30. For a discussion of the principle of induction in the context of the multiverse, see Leslie, *Infinite Minds*.

31. Page, "Born's Rule."

32. Rees, *Before the Beginning*, 221; see also Albrecht and Sorbo, "Can the Universe Afford Inflation?"; and Page, "Is Our Universe Likely to Decay within 20 Billion Years?" For a recent non-specialist discussion see Overbye, "Big Brain Theory," 306.

33. Boltzmann, "Theory of Gases."

there is some probability that an earth 6,000 years old, complete with a fossil record, fluctuated out of equilibrium. In this sense a creationist scenario finds a home in the multiverse; it can't be ruled out, given the premises of the paradigm. Furthermore, it is presumably a more likely fluctuation than a cosmos 13.7 billion years old, since it has much less developmental history. Can this scenario be ruled out on non-sociological grounds?

Testability

Since the special features of our universe are "explained" in the multiverse paradigm by positing it to be one of a very large ensemble of companions, multiverse practitioners contend that there is a weak test of the idea insofar as we can perhaps determine whether these features are typical among the possibilities statistically spread across the ensemble.[34] The Copernican principle is thereby extended to the "Principle of Mediocrity," which states that most of the foundational constants of nature should attain typical values within some normal distribution.

The idea is as follows. Select an observer at random from the multiverse. If this observer is in a typical region of the multiverse, then the physical constants in the region measured by the observer can be predicted from a statistical distribution. We can thereby test our own "typicality" by observing constants of nature that are apparently bio-irrelevant: things like neutrino masses or the couplings of unstable quarks to one another. In much the same way that we would expect the first adult human male we see on leaving a building to be somewhere between 5'10" and 6'2" tall (one standard deviation about the average height), we expect the values of these constants to be about one standard deviation away from their average values.

However, this approach begs the question of typicality. By what criteria are such normal distributions constructed? If a test fails, does that mean the multiverse paradigm is wrong, or does it mean the normal distribution should be adjusted to ensure typicality? More generally, should the rules of science be weakened to admit such a radical change in what we accept as a legitimate foundation for a physical theory?

---

34. Vilenkin, "Anthropic Predictions," 163.

Unboundedness

I have noted above that the multiverse paradigm opens up a Pandora's box insofar as it relies on arbitrarily large amounts of physical resource (space, matter, energy, time) to do its job. This is quite unlike any other scientific theory, and therefore merits a certain degree of philosophical scrutiny. Consider Occam's Razor, which states that the simplest explanation of a given phenomenon is the most likely. In modern scientific parlance this translates into assumptive parsimony: the best theories are those with the fewest assumptions. Does the multiverse paradigm, with its purported reliance on only a false vacuum and basic quantum physics, respect this principle? Or does the unbounded nature of the false vacuum yield an implicit reliance on an arbitrary number of outcomes that can emerge from this unboundedness? Does this render the paradigm effectively solipsistic? More generally, what are the foundations of the paradigm? Does one allow time travel? Alternate quantum physics? Magic? The rules of the game here are less than clearly defined,[35] particularly in a CSM.

THEOLOGICAL IMPLICATIONS OF THE MULTIVERSE

Justice and Morality

Do some universes have different principles of justice? Are the apparently deep moral principles of the universe[36] merely local by-laws? While it can be argued that encounters between different cultural groups and civilizations raised questions of moral relativism in the past (and will in the future should we encounter alien civilizations), the multiverse raises the theological stakes of the discussion. Can there be a theological foundation for morality in a multiverse? If so, on what is such a foundation based, given that rampant duplication ensures that all possible outcomes of a given social phenomenon will occur? The multiverse would appear to be a game of moral Plinko, in which all moral alternatives are statistically realized.

Does an embodied moral agent mean anything in a multiverse? Given the rampant duplication phenomenon, all decisions that any given human can make at any particular time have each been acted upon. Hence all

---

35. See the article by Ellis, "Issues in the Philosophy of Cosmology."
36. Murphey and Ellis, *Moral Nature of the Universe*.

possible moral consequences of all actions are realized somewhere, sometime. Do morality and justice mean anything in this context?

Free Will

Since every potentiality is an actuality in the multiverse, every choice that any sentient being can make is also realized. If we accept this scenario, on what basis should we make decisions? What role ought reason, experience, and emotion play in the making of any given decision in a context where the decider accepts that all choices will be made? With no genuine selection amongst alternatives, is free will[37] a meaningful concept?

Many other theological problems emerge from similar considerations. Concepts such as love, creativity, salvation, and sacrifice all depend on making selections amongst a range of alternatives. Consider creativity. Normally one thinks of an artist as making a sequence of choices with brush and paint so as to actualize on canvas the creative idea she has; da Vinci's "Last Supper," for example. Now suppose that elsewhere in the multiverse (or here; we don't know for sure) many copies of da Vinci randomly splatter paint on canvas. Most of these will be a mess, but there is a very tiny nonzero chance that one such splattering produces the "Last Supper." Can one genuinely ascribe creativity to this da Vinci?

Christology provides another example of a multiverse theological conundrum. Since there are many copies of our earth, with all possible variants, there presumably will be some earths in which Christ dies on the cross and others in which Christ rejects the cross. The latter would seem intolerable to Christian theology. Does one then impose theological constraints on a multiverse, requiring that all duplicate Christs go the way of the cross (thereby eliminating any free choice Christ had in the matter)? Whichever way one answers this question leads to a very difficult set of problems concerning the relationship between science and theology.

Theodicy

One of the features of actualizing all potentialities is that that there are many more evil potentialities than good ones. The theodicy problem[38]—why a good God allows evil—is amplified to an arbitrarily large extreme. Since history indicates that it is considerably more likely that humans follow

---

37. For a discussion of free will in a Christian context see Boyd, *Is God to Blame?*
38. Leibniz, *Theodicy*.

paths of violence, oppression, and injustice, most of the earths populating the multiverse contain more evil than good. Torture, slavery, the holocaust, and other horrors will be replicated arbitrarily often, and with all possible variants.

Can such limitless evil be theologically tolerated? It is difficult enough to accept the goodness of God in the face of evil in a single universe. The multiverse would appear to make this situation infinitely more difficult. Perhaps one should instead argue that evil and good are irrelevant concepts in a multiverse. If so, what then do we make of moral choices? How can one reasonably act on a belief in moral irrelevancy?

Purpose

Why do we live in a cosmos of change? The Judeo-Christian theological response to this question has generally been grounded in the Creator's purpose. For example, one reads in Isaiah 46:9–10: "I am God, and there is none like me. I make known the end from the beginning, from ancient times, what is still to come. I say: My purpose will stand." The assertion is that the cosmos will fulfill the purpose its Creator envisioned for it, so that its developmental history (and those of its inhabitants) is endowed with meaning. Christian theology asserts there will be a new heaven and a new earth, since the present cosmos itself is in need of redemption. The theological challenge here is that of reworking these concepts in a multiverse context. Does each universe within the multiverse have its own purpose to fulfil, with one new heaven for each? Will two different universes fulfill the same purpose? Do some universes have a purpose, others none? Does the multiverse as a whole have a purpose?

What of individual purpose? Humans are creatures of purpose, and those open to a theological understanding of reality generally wish to understand what God's purpose is for their lives. In Christianity this notion is best expressed in the concept of the *imago Dei*, that we are made in the image of God.[39] This entails an awareness of being that part of the creation through whom God's plans and purposes can best be made known and actualized. Striving to bring about the *imago Dei* in one's life can be seen as the quest for wholeness of purpose, or one's "essential" self, as pointed to in Christ's life and teachings. Yet can this concept retain any meaning in a multiverse of rampant duplication and extreme theodicy? Does God have a distinct purpose for each duplicate? Or are all duplicates and near-variants

---

39. Erickson, *Christian Theology*.

moving toward the same purpose? More bluntly, how does one avoid a nihilistic pointlessness in a scenario where all possibilities are actualized?

Divinity

In a CSM, fake universes—those that are simulations—substantially outnumber real ones. Such universes presumably have fake gods, and these are more probable than real gods. All possible scenarios can be realized,[40] with some universes having gods, others not, gods creating gods, etc. The picture that emerges after sufficient extrapolation is one of theological chaos. Can this picture be avoided? Or can one somehow make sense of a transcendent God amidst such chaos?

SUMMARY

Is the multiverse a satisfactory answer to the "something instead of everything" question? The preceding (and non-exhaustive) sketch of its scientific and theological implications illustrates that the multiverse paradigm is a conceptual Pandora's box: once one begins to implement the idea it is not clear how or where to stop. The Level 5 CSM nicely illustrates this problem: one loses track of the rules of science in this case.

How do we determine what is and is not possible in a multiverse paradigm? Since we are still discovering new phenomena, it is clear that what exists is a larger set than what is observed.

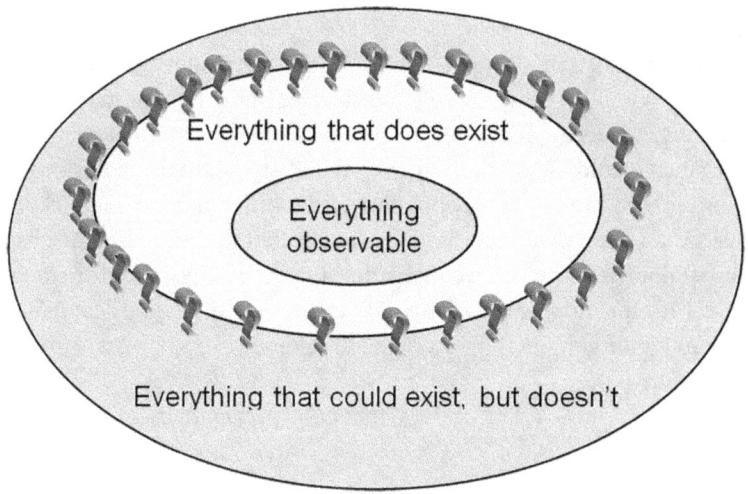

40. Davies, "Universes Galore," 487.

The diagram above illustrates the situation. The smallest circle represents our observable universe: the collection of everything known to exist, at least by humans up to now. (One can make more refined distinctions by restricting/extending the set of observers.) Since the amount of matter and energy in our observable universe is finite, this collection will have a finite amount of energy and information. Of course what exists is larger than what we can detect; indeed there is good reason to believe that our universe extends well beyond what can be observed via astronomy.

What about the boundary between the possible and the existent? Since the multiverse paradigm (in any of its five manifestations) posits that the universe-generating mechanism *will* generate whatever it *can* generate, the dashed line in the above diagram is eliminated: whatever can exist, does exist. But as we have seen above, there is more than one multiverse theory, and therefore competing claims as to what is possible. Consider a few examples. Should possibility be maximized (as in the CSM) or minimized (as in the ISM)? How are we to choose between contradictory multiverse scenarios based on mutually exclusive premises? Furthermore, if we accept the multiverse paradigm, by what criterion do we proclaim something to be impossible within our own observable universe?

These questions cannot be decided by experiment and observation. Notwithstanding the Principle of Mediocrity, by definition the multiverse asserts that all that exists extends well beyond the capacity of observation, and so there is no adjudication between them using normative scientific observational and experimental methods. Mathematical self-consistency arguments are being deployed to see if there is some means of selecting amongst multiverses, though the prospect of this program's success is far from clear.

Finally, must one choose between the paradigms of Agency and multiverse? Couldn't God create a multiverse? Some have argued just that, contending, for example, that God in his desire for maximal mathematical elegance would create the multiverse that string theory describes.[41] Of course this scenario is logically possible, and merits a more complete critical analysis than I can give here. Suffice it to say that the preceding discussion indicates that this kind of reconciliation between science and theology is fraught with formidable difficulties. Whether such difficulties can be overcome or signify genuinely irreconcilable differences remains a subject for further study.

Robert Mann is grateful to Don Page for valuable comments and discussion.

---

41. For example see Page, "Does God So Love the Multiverse?"

BIBLIOGRAPHY

Albrecht, Andreas. "The Theory of Everything vs the Theory of Anything." *Lecture Notes in Physics* 455 (1995) 323–32.

Albrecht, Andreas, and Lorenzo Sorbo. "Can the Universe Afford Inflation?" *Physics Review* D 70 (2004) 063528.

Amsler, Claude, et al. (Particle Data Group). "Review of Particle Physics." *Physics Letters* B 667 (2008) 1–6.

Aquinas, Thomas. *Summa Theologica*. New York: Benziger, 1947.

Barrow, John D. and Frank J. Tipler. *The Anthropic Cosmological Principle*. New York: Oxford University Press, 1988.

Boltzmann, Ludwig. "On Certain Questions of the Theory of Gases." *Nature* 51 (1895) 413–15.

Boyd, Gregory A. *Is God to Blame?: Moving beyond Paat Answers to the Problem of Evil*. Downers Grove, IL: InterVarsity, 2003.

Carr, B. J. and M. J. Rees, "The Anthropic Cosmological Principle and the Structure of the Physical World." *Nature* 278 (1979) 605–12.

Carr, Bernard, ed. *Universe or Multiverse?* Cambridge: Cambridge University Press, 2007.

Carter, Brandon. "Large Number Coincidences and the Anthropic Principle in Cosmology." In *IAU Symposium 63: Confrontation of Cosmological Theories with Observational Data*, edited by M. S. Longair, 291–98. Dordrecht: Reidel, 1974.

Collins, Robin. "God, Design and Fine-Tuning." In *God Matters: Readings in the Philosophy of Religion*, edited by Raymond Martin and Christopher Bernard, 54–65. New York: Longman, 2002.

———. "A Scientific Argument for the Existence of God: The Fine-Tuning Design Argument." In *Reason for the Hope Within*, edited by Michael Murray, 47–75. Grand Rapids: Eerdmans, 1999.

Craig, William Lane. "Philosophical and Scientific Pointers to *Creation ex Nihilo*." In *Contemporary Perspectives on Religious Epistemology*, edited by R. Douglas Geivett and Brendan Sweetman, 185–200. New York: Oxford University Press, 1992.

Davies, P. C. W. "Universes Galore." In *Universe or Multiverse?*, edited by Bernard Carr, 487–505. Cambridge: Cambridge University Press, 2007.

Ellis, George F. R. "Issues in the Philosophy of Cosmology." In *Philosophy of Physics*, edited by Jeremy Butterfield and John Earman, et al., 1183–286. 2 vols. Amsterdam: North Holland, 2006.

Ellis, George F. R. and G. B. Brundrit. "Life in the Infinite Universe." *Quarterly Journal of the Royal Astronomical Society* 20 (1979) 37–41.

Ellis, John. "The Superstring: Theory of Everything, or of Nothing?" *Nature* 323 (1986) 595–98.

Erickson, Millard J. *Christian Theology*. 2nd ed. Grand Rapids: Baker, 1998.

Folger, Tim. "Science's Alternative to an Intelligent Creator: the Multiverse Theory." *Discover Magazine* (December 2008). Online: discovermagazine.com/2008/dec/10-sciences-alternative-to-an-intelligent-creator/article_view?b_start :int=2.

Georgi, Howard, and S. Glashow. "Unity of All Elementary-Particle Forces." *Physical Review Letters* 32 (1974).

Green, Michael B., and John H. Schwarz. "Anomaly Cancellations in Supersymmetric D = 10 Gauge Theory and Superstring Theory." *Physics Letters* B 149 (1984) 117.

Greene, Brian. *The Fabric of the Cosmos: Space, Time, and the Texture of Reality*. New York: Vintage, 2005.
Guth, Alan H. *The Inflationary Universe*. Reading, MA: Addison-Wesley, 1997.
———. "Inflationary Universe: A Possible Solution to the Horizon and Flatness Problems." *Physical Review* D 23 (1981) 347–56.
Kaufman, William J., III. *Universe*. 4th ed. New York: Freeman, 1993.
Lederman, Leon M., with Dick Teresi. *The God Particle: If the Universe Is the Answer, What Is the Question?* New York: Houghton Mifflin Harcourt, 2006.
Leibniz, G. W. *Theodicy: Essays on the Goodness of God, the Freedom of Man, and the Origin of Evil*. Edited by Austin Farrer. Translated by E. M. Huggard. Open Court Classics. Chicago: Open Court, 1985.
Leslie, John. *Infinite Minds: A Philosophical Cosmology*. Oxford: Clarendon, 2009.
———. *Universes*. New York: Routledge, 1996.
Linde, Andrei D. "A New Inflationary Universe Scenario: A Possible Solution of the Horizon, Flatness, Homogeneity, Isotropy and Primordial Monopole Problems." *Physics Letters* B 108 (1982) 389–93.
Mann, Robert B. "Inconstant Multiverse." *Perspectives on Science & Christian Faith* 57 (2005) 302.
———. *Introduction to Particle Physics & the Standard Model*. Boca Raton, FL: CRC, 2009.
———. "The Puzzle of Existence." *Perspectives on Science & Christian Faith* 61 (2009) 139–50.
Manson, Neil. *God and Design: The Teleological Argument and Modern Science*. London: Routledge, 2003.
May, Gerhard. *Creatio ex Nihilo: The Doctrine of 'Creation out of Nothing' in Early Christian Doctrine*. Translated by A. S. Worrall. London: T. & T. Clark, 2004.
Murphy, Nancey, and George F. R. Ellis. *On the Moral Nature of the Universe: Theology, Cosmology and Ethics*. Theology and the Sciences. Minneapolis: Fortress, 1996.
Overbye, Dennis. "Big Brain Theory: Have Cosmologists Lost Theirs?" *New York Times*, January 15, 2008; reprinted in *The Best American Science Writing 2009*, edited by Natalie Angier and Jesse Cohen, 306–13. New York: HarperCollins, 2009.
Page, Don N. "Born's Rule is Insufficient in a Large Universe." *arXiv* 1003.2419 (2010).
———. "Does God So Love the Multiverse?" *Science and Religion in Dialogue*, edited by M. Y. Stewart. Oxford: Blackwell, 2010.
———. "Is Our Universe Likely to Decay within 20 Billion Years?" *Physics Review* D 78 (2008) 063535.
Polkinghorne, John. "Is Science Enough?" *Sewanee Theological Review* 39 (1995) 11–26.
Rees, Martin. *Before the Beginning: Our Universe and Others*. New York: Simon & Schuster, 1997.
Smolin, Lee. *The Trouble with Physics: The Rise of String Theory, the Fall of a Science, and What Comes Next*. New York: Houghton Mifflin, 2006.
Susskind, Leonard. *The Cosmic Landscape: String Theory and the Illusion of Intelligent Design*. New York: Little, Brown, 2005.
Tegmark, Max. "Multiverse Hierarchy." In *Universe or Multiverse*, edited by Bernard Carr, 99–126. Cambridge: Cambridge University Press, 2007.
———. "Parallel Universes." *Scientific American* 288 (2003) 40–51.

Vilenkin, Alexander. "Anthropic Predictions: The Case of the Cosmological Constant." In *Universe or Multiverse?* edited by Bernard Carr, 163–180. Cambridge: Cambridge University Press, 2007.

———. *Many Worlds in One: The Search for Other Universes*. New York: Hill & Wang, 2006.

Weinberg, Steven. "The Cosmological Constant Problems." In *Sources and Detection of Dark Matter and Dark Energy in the Universe: Fourth International Symposium Held at Marina del Rey 2000,* edited by David B. Cline, 18–26. Berlin: Springer, 2001.

Wilczek, Frank. "A Model of Anthropic Reasoning: the Dark to Ordinary Matter Ratio." In *Universe or Multiverse?*, edited by Bernard Carr. Cambridge: Cambridge University Press, 2007.

13

Galileo's Hermeneutical Model
The Reconciliation of Scripture and Science

Jennifer Hart Weed

The case of Galileo Galilei (1564–1642) is perhaps one of the most colorful and well-known cases of conflict between theology and science. The way in which Galileo navigated this conflict and his attempt to reconcile theology and science is lesser known. Surprisingly, Galileo engages both theologians and scientists in a philosophical discussion of interpretation, using several principles articulated by St. Augustine. In this paper, I will focus my attention on the method that Galileo uses in order to determine whether or not this approach holds any promise for current debates between theology and science.

WHY HERMENEUTICS?

Galileo adopted heliocentrism prior to its condemnation by the Church in 1616.[1] Once his view became public, a group of philosophers and astronomers began to circulate scathing articles about Galileo's research.[2] Eventually, those academics were joined by theologians who objected to

---

1. Blackwell, *Galileo, Bellarmine, and the Bible*, 5.
2. Drake, *Discoveries and Opinions of Galileo*, 148, 150.

heliocentrism on scriptural grounds;[3] thus Galileo's belief in heliocentrism faced challenges from both natural science and theology. Not wishing to concede either objection despite the fact that he was not a specialist in theology, Galileo defended heliocentrism using scientific and theological arguments. In 1615, he presented some of his arguments in a letter to the Grand Duchess of Tuscany, who was the mother of his patron, Cosimo II de Medici.

In his letter Galileo boldly puts forth a view of how theological claims based on Scripture are rightly related to scientific claims. More specifically, he offers a model in which theology and science are assumed to be compatible, provided each is understood properly. Although he recognizes the uniqueness of both disciplines, he doesn't assume that theology and science are incommensurate; he takes Scripture and church tradition seriously on the one hand, while recognizing on the other that scientific demonstrations are valid.[4]

On the relation between science, nature, and Scripture, Galileo writes the following:

> In discussions of physical problems we ought to begin not from the authority of scriptural passages, but from sense-experiences and necessary demonstrations; for the holy Bible and the phenomena of nature proceed alike from the divine Word, the former as the dictate of the Holy Ghost and the latter as the observant executrix of God's commands. It is necessary for the Bible, in order to be accommodated to the understanding of every man, to speak many things which appear to differ from the absolute truth so far as the bare meaning of the words is concerned. But Nature, on the other hand, is inexorable and immutable; she never transgresses the laws imposed upon her, or cares a whit whether her abstruse reasons and methods of operation are understandable to men. For that reason it appears that nothing physical which sense-experience sets before our eyes, or which necessary demonstrations prove to us, ought to be called into question (much less condemned) upon the testimony of biblical passages which may have some different meaning beneath their words.[5]

---

3. Ibid., 150.

4. Galileo is influenced by St. Augustine and by Johannes Kepler's *Astronomia Nova*. The connection between Galileo and Kepler was suggested to me by Owen Gingerich.

5. Galileo, "Letter to the Grand Duchess Christina," 182–83.

There are a lot of philosophical assumptions in this text that deserve our attention. I will only highlight a few of them. Notice first of all Galileo's view that nature proceeds from God and executes God's commands; in this respect Galileo views nature in general and laws of nature specifically as part of God's revelation. Also, Galileo believes that nature is intelligible, predictable, and immutable. Although nature does not readily give up her secrets, sense experience of nature can give rise to demonstrations whose conclusions are certain and necessary.[6]

In contrast to science is Scripture. In the conflict with Galileo, Scripture was the primary weapon in the theologians' arsenal; church authority and tradition were less used. Galileo agreed with the theologians that Scripture was part of God's revelation; however, he points out that Scripture accommodates itself to human understanding and hence contains different levels of meaning. Scripture is more obscure than nature. Consequently, the conclusions of science should not be subordinated to a particular reading of Scripture when it is possible that such a reading might not be correct. Given this view of matters, Galileo turns his attention to hermeneutics:

> The interpretation of the Bible is a serious business, and normally the proper meaning of its statements about natural phenomena can be determined only after we know what is true in nature; thus, the business of biblical interpretation is dependent on physical investigation, and to base a controversial physical conclusion on the Bible is to put the cart before the horse.[7]

As I have described Galileo's views thus far, one might conclude that Galileo is in favor of subordinating theology to science. But that conclusion would be premature. In his letter to the Grand Duchess, Galileo identifies several hermeneutical principles that he argues should resolve the conflict between theology and science. Taken together, the principles address some cases in which theology is subordinated to science and some cases in which science is subordinated to theology. But each of these cases presupposes Galileo's acceptance of the logical principle of the unity of truth, such that truth never contradicts itself; truth only contradicts falsehoods.[8] Of course, Galileo believes that truth can be found through theology and through science. For my purposes in this discussion, I will focus on four of Galileo's principles:

1. Restraint or caution

---

6. I would like to thank Richard Blackwell for drawing this point to my attention.
7. See Finocchiaro, *Galileo on the World Systems*, 38–39.
8. Galileo, "Letter to the Grand Duchess Christina," 186.

2. Harmonization of scriptural interpretation with demonstration
3. Harmonization of scientific theories with Scripture
4. The church as the interpretive authority in matters of faith and in practical matters[9]

RESTRAINT

Galileo charges his opponents with quoting Scripture for their own purposes. In so doing, they used passages that they failed "to understand properly, and which were ill suited to their purposes."[10] As a rejoinder, Galileo quotes St. Augustine, who urges restraint with respect to the interpretation of Scripture:

> We should always observe that restraint that is proper to a devout and serious person and on an obscure question entertain no rash belief. Otherwise, if the evidence later reveals the explanation, we are likely to despise it because of our attachment to error, even though his explanation may not be in any way opposed to the sacred writings of the Old or New Testament.[11]

St. Augustine is concerned with the conjunction of Christian doctrine and scientific theory. The interpretation of Scripture occasionally has scientific implications, which might then be assumed to be entailed by Christianity; however, if such a scientific view were to be falsified, it would prove embarrassing to Christianity. St. Augustine therefore advocates restraint. When interpreting Scripture on obscure questions, one should hold one's interpretation cautiously until "evidence reveals the explanation."

Galileo was optimistic that scientific theories could be demonstrated conclusively to be true or false. Because of this, he was confident that if one followed St. Augustine's advice and interpreted Scripture provisionally with respect to scientific matters, recognizing that the interpretation could turn out to be mistaken, eventually conclusive evidence would decide the matter. Because Galileo accepts that truth is unified, there is no possibility that a truth of Scripture and a truth of science would contradict one another.

---

9. For a more extensive discussion, see my "*De Genesi ad litteram.*" See also Ernan McMullen, "Galileo on Science and Scripture."

10. Galileo, "Letter to the Grand Duchess Christina," 175.

11. St. Augustine, *De Genesi ad litteram*, II.18.38. Galileo's quotations of St. Augustine are imprecise and unreferenced in the original. For this reason I am citing this text of St. Augustine directly. See Galileo, "Letter to the Grand Duchess Christina," 176.

With respect to the conflict over the status of geocentrism, Galileo would argue that, until conclusive scientific evidence is produced, theologians should exercise caution in interpreting passages of Scripture that appear to support geocentrism.[12] Of course, it is not clear what would count as "conclusive evidence," which brings us to Galileo's next hermeneutical principle.

HARMONIZATION OF SCRIPTURAL INTERPRETATION WITH DEMONSTRATION

Galileo argues that scriptural interpretation should be subordinated to and harmonized with scientific demonstration. Sometimes scientific demonstrations are geometrical; sometimes they are arguments from effect to cause. According to Galileo, scientific demonstration amounts to a proof.[13] His concept of proof would either be a diagram, in the case of geometry, or something like the following syllogism, in the case of a causal argument:

All A are B.

All B are C.

Therefore, All A are C.

In syllogistic reasoning, if the premises are true and the form of the syllogism is valid, then the conclusion must be true; the conclusion cannot be false. The possibility of certitude in scientific demonstration is the reason Galileo places so much confidence in science. If science uses demonstrative reasoning and meets all of its conditions, then scientific conclusions are indisputable. Returning to the principle of restraint as articulated by St. Augustine, scientific demonstration would provide conclusive evidence on a particular matter that could then be compared with a given scriptural interpretation. If there was a conflict between an interpretation and a demonstration, then Scripture must be re-interpreted in order to harmonize with demonstration. Demonstration yields truth with certitude, while scriptural interpretation can be made in many ways, as St. Augustine and the other church fathers recognized.[14]

---

12. Blackwell identifies several Scripture passages that seem to imply geocentrism, including Ps 104:5, 1 Chr 16:30, Gen 1:17, and Josh 10:12. See Blackwell, *Galileo, Bellarmine, and the Bible*, 60, 65.

13. Galileo, "Letter to the Grand Duchess Christina," 175.

14. St. Augustine mentions at least four senses of Scripture: history, etiology, analogy, and allegory. See "De Utilitate Credendi," 5. In his letter to the Grand Duchess, Galileo also quotes St. Jerome's remarks in his *Epistola ad Paulinum* about the

Believing that Copernicus shares this view, Galileo writes:

> For Copernicus never discusses matters of religion or faith, nor does he use arguments that depend in any way upon the authority of sacred writings which he might have interpreted erroneously. He stands always upon physical conclusions pertaining to the celestial motions, and deals with them by astronomical and geometrical demonstrations, founded primarily upon sense experiences and very exact observations. He did not ignore the Bible, but he knew very well that if his doctrine were proved, then it could not contradict the Scriptures when they were rightly understood.[15]

Far from accepting the criticisms of the theologians who condemned heliocentrism on the basis of Scripture, Galileo argued that the onus was on those theologians to devote their attention to falsifying heliocentrism. Scientific claims should only be condemned after they are falsified and not before, as Galileo writes in the following passage:

> Now if truly demonstrated physical conclusions need not be subordinated to biblical passages, but the latter must rather be shown not to interfere with the former, then before a physical proposition is condemned it must be shown to be not rigorously demonstrated—and this is to be done not by those who hold the proposition to be true, but those who judge it to be false."[16]

Galileo holds the view that theologians should be concerned not only with scriptural interpretations *per se*, but also with the implications of these interpretations. Those individuals who would condemn scientific claims on the basis of Scripture should do so only after those scientific claims have been shown to lack certitude. So it is not the case that theologians are to concern themselves only with Scripture and not with science; theologians ought indeed to be concerned with science. Of course, if a theologian held a particular scriptural interpretation with restraint, it is unlikely that he or she would condemn a particular scientific view on the basis of that interpretation.

---

ways in which the meaning of Scripture can be variously (and sometimes perversely) interpreted.

15. Galileo, "Letter to the Grand Duchess Christina," 179.
16. Ibid., 194–95.

HARMONIZATION OF SCIENTIFIC THEORIES WITH SCRIPTURE

Thus far, we have examined how Galileo subordinates scriptural re-interpretation to scientific demonstration. Under the principle of the harmonization of scientific theories with Scripture, Galileo argues that undemonstrated scientific claims are to be subordinated to the existing scriptural interpretation. He writes:

> In the books of the sages of this world there are contained some physical truths which are soundly demonstrated, and others that are merely stated; as to the former, it is the office of wise divines to show that they do not contradict the holy Scriptures. And as to the propositions which are stated but not rigorously demonstrated, anything contrary to the Bible involved by them must be held undoubtedly false and should be proved so by every possible means.[17]

Galileo assumes that since truth does not contradict truth, scientific demonstrations will not contradict Scripture. Those scientific claims that lack demonstration, which we would probably identify as hypotheses, can be expected to be proved false if they contradict Scripture. Thus, this principle subordinates scientific claims to Scripture, provided that those claims lack demonstration. Once again, it is the role of the theologian to preserve the authority of Scripture by showing that scientific demonstrations do not contradict Scripture, and that contradictory scientific claims are falsified.

Notice that there is nothing in this principle that would rule out the possibility of a hypothesis achieving certitude in the future. At such a time, according to Galileo, this scientific claim would be governed by a different hermeneutical principle, i.e., the principle of harmonization with demonstration. In 1615, the year in which Galileo wrote his letter to the Grand Duchess, Copernicanism had not been demonstrated.[18] So even if his interlocutors had agreed to follow his principle of harmonization, they would have no reason to apply it to Copernicanism since Copernicanism did not meet the conditions specified in the principle. Moreover, Galileo does not suggest how one is to distinguish between those scientific claims that are in principle demonstrable but have yet to be demonstrated, and those claims that are absolutely indemonstrable.[19] Although he was confident that heliocentrism was demonstrable, he did not articulate criteria that would have

---

17. Ibid., 194.
18. Blackwell, *Galileo, Bellarmine, and the Bible*, 79.
19. Ibid., 82.

justified that confidence. In terms of his conflict with the theologians, Galileo was on shaky ground: before he could persuade anyone to re-interpret Scripture on the basis of heliocentrism, he would have to produce a scientific demonstration. Galileo was therefore unable to use his own model to solve the conflict between theology and science.[20]

CHURCH AUTHORITY AND SCRIPTURAL INTERPRETATION

The final hermeneutical principle that I will address is the principle of church authority over scriptural interpretation. The influence of the Council of Trent on Galileo's views cannot be underestimated. In fact, he cites the articles of the Fourth Session of Trent directly:

> To control petulant spirits, the Council decrees that, in matters of faith and morals [including practical matters that extend beyond morals] pertaining to the edification of Christian doctrine, no one, relying on his own judgment and distorting the Sacred Scriptures according to his own conceptions, shall dare to interpret them contrary to that sense which Holy Mother Church, to whom it belongs to judge of their own sense and meaning, has held and does hold, or even contrary to the unanimous agreement of the Fathers, even though such interpretations should never at any time be published. Those who do otherwise shall be identified by the ordinaries and punished in accordance with the penalties prescribed by the law.[21]

Galileo acknowledged the authority of the Council of Trent, but argued that Copernicanism was outside its purview because church authority governed only matters of faith and morals.[22] However, the church maintained that her authority governed matters that were implied by Scripture, including Copernicanism.[23] As a result, Galileo found himself in an extremely precarious position: an argument over the correct application of church authority was not an argument he was likely to win. In 1616, the church condemned Copernicanism and Cardinal Bellarmine ordered Galileo to abandon it.[24]

20. Blackwell makes this point in *Galileo, Bellarmine, and the Bible*, 69.
21. Blackwell, "Decrees of the Council of Trent Session IV," 183.
22. Galileo, "Letter to the Grand Duchess Christina," 203.
23. Blackwell, *Galileo, Bellarmine, and the Bible*, 19, 37–39.
24. Ibid., 125–27.

CONCLUSION

Although Galileo's model was not applicable to his own situation due to the status of Copernicanism at the time, some aspects of his model look promising for contemporary debates between theology and science. For example, according to Galileo both scientists and theologians have the freedom to pursue their own research within their areas of specialization. Galileo affirms the truth of both science and Scripture when science is adequately demonstrated and Scripture properly interpreted. A degree of reflexivity is allowed between theology and science, depending on the status of the claims within each discipline. More specifically, if there is a conflict between a scientific demonstration and an interpretation of Scripture, then it is the role of the theologian to examine the relevant Scripture passages in light of the demonstration. In order for a proposition to be contrary to the Christian faith, it must first be proven false.[25] The theologian is then faced with a choice: either prove the demonstration false or reinterpret Scripture. Galileo believes that if the demonstration cannot be proved false, then the theologian will eventually be able to find the actual meaning of Scripture and it will not conflict with the demonstration. With respect to scientific hypotheses, since such hypotheses lack demonstration, there is no need for scriptural interpretation to conform to them. Galileo follows St. Augustine in urging theologians to advocate for their positions with restraint, recognizing that at least some scientific hypotheses have the potential to achieve demonstration.

Galileo includes within his model a number of provisions. He is aware of the fact that science and religion cannot always be reconciled easily;[26] he believes that it is possible to reconcile the two disciplines, but that such reconciliation can be challenging.[27] Additionally, Galileo is keenly aware of the fact that human reason has its limitations, conceding, "I have no doubt that where human reasoning cannot reach—and where consequently we can have no science but only opinion and faith—it is necessary in piety to comply absolutely with the strict sense of Scripture."[28]

According to Galileo, human reason is not to be substituted for faith. Reason is to coexist with faith, continuing where human reason cannot reach. Piety and obedience to Scripture are also, in his view, key ingredients to human life; however, they should not prevent human reasoning from

---

25. Galileo, "Letter to the Grand Duchess Christina," 206.
26. Blackwell, *Galileo, Bellarmine, and the Bible*, 167.
27. Ibid.
28. Galileo, "Letter to the Grand Duchess Christina," 197.

attempting to discover things about God's creation or to reach the threshold of its rational ability.

Nevertheless, there is a significant problem with Galileo's model. Since Galileo focuses so narrowly on demonstration, and since few, if any, scientific claims ever achieve that level of certitude, the issue remains of reconciling with scriptural interpretation those scientific hypotheses accepted by the scientific community as indubitable but perhaps not demonstrable. Since demonstration cannot resolve the conflict in these cases, one is left with the priority of Scripture over science, which is exactly the position that the theologians took against Galileo.

In conclusion then, Galileo's model is neither simplistic nor reductionistic. It is a product of its historical context and of the theological and scientific worldviews that Galileo adopted. But in Galileo's model scientists and theologians who are inclined to admit that their disciplines are not incommensurable are offered a tenuous beginning to the process of reconciliation.

BIBLIOGRAPHY

Augustine, Saint. *De Genesi ad litteram*. Translated by John Hammond Taylor SJ. New York: Paulist, 1982.

———. "De Utilitate Credendi." In *Seventeen Short Treatises of St. Augustine, Bishop of Hippo*, translated by C. L. Cornish and H. Browne, 85–158. Oxford: Parker, 1982.

Blackwell, Richard J., trans. "Decrees of the Council of Trent Session IV: Decree on the Edition and on the Interpretation of the Sacred Scriptures." In *Galileo, Bellarmine, and the Bible*. Notre Dame: University of Notre Dame Press, 1991.

———. *Galileo, Bellarmine, and the Bible: Including a Translation of Foscarini's Letter on the Motion of the Earth*. Notre Dame: University of Notre Dame Press, 1991.

Drake, Stillman. *Discoveries and Opinions of Galileo*. New York: Doubleday, 1957.

Finocchiaro, Maurice. *Galileo on the World Systems*. Berkeley: University of California Press, 1997.

Galilei, Galileo. "Letter to the Grand Duchess Christina." In *Discoveries and Opinions of Galileo*, edited and translated by Stillman Drake, 173–216. New York: Doubleday, 1957.

McMullen, Ernan. "Galileo on Science and Scripture." In *The Cambridge Companion to Galileo*, edited by Peter Machamer, 271–347. Cambridge Companions to Philosophy, Religion and Culture. Cambridge: Cambridge University Press, 1998.

Weed, Jennifer Hart. "*De Genesi ad litteram* and the Galileo Case." In *Go Figure! Essays on Figuration in Biblical Interpretation*, edited by Stanley D. Walters, 148–60. Eugene, OR: Wipf & Stock, 2007.

14

Philosophical Hermeneutics and the Natural Sciences

A Conflict in Progress

Jason C. Robinson

INTRODUCTION

The subtitle of this chapter, "A Conflict in Progress," has two meanings. The first points to the ongoing conflict—the antagonism through time—between the so-called hard sciences and the soft sciences, in which hermeneutics is typically situated as the study, theory, and art of interpretation. There appears to be a conflict at a fundamental level, an irreconcilable difference, between the interpretive and the objective—one that exists at the very marrow of each and maintains a proverbial gap between them. This, I argue, is created by the scientific ethos, not the hermeneutic consciousness.

The second meaning—better phrased "a conflict over progress"—refers to the specific problem of progress and its proper meaning. Are we to understand that the best form of progress in human understanding is the accumulation of knowledge and objective facts about the world? Or is there another sense in which humans may be said to move forward in understanding, one in which we do something rather anti-objective? These two meanings of progress are related in important if still uncertain respects. This chapter offers a venue for dialogue by situating my interpretation of philosophical hermeneutics alongside some of the major claims of progress in the natural sciences. My hope is that by doing so I may deepen the appreciation for an ontology of hermeneutics that reaches much deeper into our perceptions of reality than a purely foundational-objective approach.

One of the most important of current debates in hermeneutics has to do with its relationship (or lack thereof) with the natural sciences, and its response to the entrenched dichotomy between objectivity and subjectivity that has taken hold throughout the West. While hermeneutics was initially seen as something distinct from the natural sciences, with Wilhelm Dilthey it became a foundational approach to the humanities believed to be just as credible and objective as the natural sciences—albeit unique in subject matter and approach. This separate-but-equal approach has been welcomed by some as a vindication of the soft sciences. That view of hermeneutics, however, was quickly challenged by others such as Martin Heidegger and Hans-Georg Gadamer, both of whom saw hermeneutics as something quite unlike the natural sciences—something in many respects more robust, universal, and relevant. While hermeneutics may be present in the hard sciences as a general theory or description of human understanding, it is not the methodological practice of science *per se*, nor the prescribed rational basis for making scientific decisions. Science and hermeneutics are not separate-but-equal, with the superior form of understanding belonging to hermeneutics. Rather, they are in many important respects separate-and-unequal. Thus, the task that remains for Heidegger and Gadamer was one of finding the right place for scientific and technological activities so that we do not surrender our natural mode of understanding in exchange for artificial and inhibiting forms of investigation, i.e., foundational-objectivity. This, I believe, remains one of the principal tasks for hermeneutics today, and for philosophy more generally.

Conversations about (philosophical) hermeneutics remain isolated from the natural sciences despite the focused efforts of accomplished scholars such as Patrick Heelan, Martin Eger, Don Ihde, Theodore Kisiel, Joseph Kockelmans, and others.[1] Importing elements of hermeneutics as a descriptive mechanism of human thought and action in science has become increasingly popular among sociologists and philosophers of science, but it often remains at the level of cultural interpretation rather than phenomenological description. That is, the full force of the claims of hermeneutics remains unappreciated, even within circles open to the interpretive nature

---

1. For an outstanding introduction to the main debates over the possibility of a hermeneutics of the natural sciences, involving many of the major thinkers in this area, refer to *Continental Philosophy Review* [formerly *Man and World*] 30 (1997).

of the hard sciences. Much of the difficulty stems from the lack of clarity around what might be meant by "progress."

I am interested in three interrelated questions:

1. What might one mean by scientific and hermeneutic progress?
2. How might we situate an understanding of the human self within the major positions on progress?
3. If we grow antagonistic toward a description of progress that relies heavily on foundational objectivity, what are the benefits of a hermeneutical description of progress that rejects linear, permanent, and epistemic-representational progress?

This, of course, assumes that it is possible to speak meaningfully of progress in hermeneutics. Many would forcefully reject this claim.

PROGRESS AND SCIENTIFIC KNOWLEDGE

The celebrated label "science" (one I am associating with the hard sciences, especially physics) is widely recognized as belonging only to those human activities that may be said to progress. Science has earned its reputation for success because of its nature as an ever-expanding body of knowledge and explanation of reality. More than this, however, science has become the effectual authority for deciding what counts as credible knowledge and therefore progressive knowledge. The connection between credibility and progress is most often argued through variations of the no-miracles argument. It would be a miracle, so it goes, if there were no direct affinity or contact between scientific theories and the world.[2] Given how empirically successful science has been in predicting experimental outcomes and generating a great assembly of theories that work, as evidenced by its technological applications and achievements, we must accept it as uniquely capable of progressing rather than merely changing; that is to say, its history of progress shows that science is, at least in part, trans-historical and transcultural. Simply stated, science explains because it works, so we must believe its reputation of progress.

There are two cautionary points I would like to make up front. First, we do not need to ask the question of success and progress in the same breath. Science may very well be successful *in spite of* its particular means of progress as advertised in textbooks and to the general public, namely,

---

2. This is famously presented by Hilary Putnam. "The positive argument for realism is that it is the only philosophy that doesn't make the success of science a miracle." See Putnam, *Mathematics, Matter and Method*, 73.

objective-foundationalism. Kuhn and many others have belaboured this point, showing, for example, that its success may be because of social, psychological, and/or historical influences. Second, the question of progress is not necessarily a question about the value of science. It is possible that science may be valuable whether or not it is genuinely progressive as it defines itself. If one rejects the claim of linear scientific progress, one need not simultaneously reject the success of science. Both points merit attention that I cannot properly give them here.

In the last fifty years alone, notions of how and what we know have changed significantly among philosophers of science, and so too have notions of what constitutes progress. An understanding of progress as "ever better contact with reality" has been and continues to be challenged, sometimes radically. The old-order ways of positivist ideology, in which interpretation-free observations and neutral theories are meant to match reality, are something of a "Golden Age" that never happened. There is growing acceptance that interpretation occurs constantly at every level of human thought, but the antagonism between the purposes of science and the existence of relative human thought (interpretation) in those same sciences is so sharp that few know how to accommodate both. Meanwhile, at least for now, the dominant view of practicing scientists remains one steeped in objectivity and a pre-Kuhnian version of progress.[3] Thus, our first difficulty in discussing progress is arriving at a meaningful and current description of knowledge.

Here are five of the most common views present in contemporary literature on the subject of scientific knowledge:

1. *Scientific knowledge is simply true.* It is universal, necessary, and certain knowledge, never particular, contingent, and probable.[4] Facts are reliable and unchanging, so long as we have read and understood the proverbial Book of Nature correctly.

2. *Science is true in what it says, although it is presently incomplete.* Genuine knowledge is achieved when we have filled in all the gaps.

---

3. On a similar point about philosophers of science see, for example, Ginev, "A (Post)Foundational Approach," 58. He writes: "Although the dominant account of science's cognitive specificity has increasingly been put in question within neopragmatism, hermeneutic philosophy, and some branches of the (post)analytical tradition, the majority of philosophers of science still believe that only by reconstructing an epistemological and/or methodological and/or metaphysical and/or transcendental 'essence' of science, one can defend its cognitive specificity in a coherent manner." Ginev goes on in his paper to show why this is not the necessary conclusion.

4. What is real has come to be associated with what is certain. On this point see, for example, Heidegger's "Science and Reflection."

3. *Scientific knowledge is most likely true.* In this sense scientific facts are conceived of in terms of frequency probabilities and (to a lesser degree) belief-type probabilistic explanations.[5] That is, scientific knowledge is the most frequent value we get when we tally the results of long-term studies, observations, and the like, even though the results do not all agree. True knowledge ignores the weird things because they are least likely to be true. To be objective requires that one gamble in some way.

4. Science tries to possess the absolute truth but is seeking an impossible goal. *Tentative approximation or truth-likeness is the best we may achieve.*

5. *Scientific knowledge is what is useful,* in that it is able to solve problems. It is not ultimately true in a permanent sense, nor does it need to be to work.

In fact, there are a dizzying array of competing "isms," and versions thereof, regarding scientific knowledge, including constructivisms, realisms, anti-realisms, empiricisms, structuralisms, and more. The proper response to the question of scientific knowledge should be bewilderment. On the surface of the debate the championed view of knowledge seems relatively static, having something to do with objectivity and permanent facts. However, even a brief overview of the history of scientific revolutions (fundamental changes in knowledge claims) ripples that surface.

What should we think now that the once material and mechanical nature of reality has dissolved into a paradoxical quantum reality; when the shortest distance between two points is no longer a straight line but a curved one;[6] or when time itself ceases to flow and becomes one already complete manifold within which our consciousness unfolds while the universe stands still and unchanging?[7] What should we do when the Earth ceases to be the

---

5. Raymond Nickerson makes a supporting point in *Cognition and Chance*, 16, when he writes: "That atoms decay spontaneously and that the probability that a given atom will decay instantaneously is constant over time are sufficiently well established in modern physics to be viewed as facts and are invoked to explain a wide range of other phenomena. Why atoms have this probabilistic property—why one cannot tell that a particular atom is more or less likely than others of the same type to decay in a given time—remains a mystery." This claim is distinct from the belief-type probability that refers to degrees of belief in a proposition or state of mind. Probability in this latter sense is connected with actual properties of things and not merely a reflection of our lack of knowledge of an otherwise determinate world.

6. Before the eighteenth century it was the accepted view that the structure of space was Euclidean. Lobachevsky, Gauss, and Riemann demonstrated that non-Euclidean constant-curvature geometries were possible. They went on to show that variably curved space was possible. Euclid's axioms, it seems, are not axioms after all.

7. Some physicists, e.g., Paul Davies, have found block-time or manifold theories

center of the universe; when light turns out to be made up of both particles and waves (two very different things) until we look; or when dark energy, dark matter, and dark flow make up the vast majority of reality (according to the Standard Model of Cosmology) even though we cannot observe, measure, or quantify them?

We must, at the very least, be tentative about connecting correct and immutable knowledge with progress, and progress with empirical success. Moreover, whereas the most popular view of scientific progress as the accumulation of knowledge presupposes static knowledge, science routinely changes its definitions—of energy, space, time, gravity, and so on—for the sake of new explanatory concepts and theories. It is true that scientific progress yields ever more precise definitions, but these are not real if by real we mean changeless. Thus, if we accept that scientific knowledge not only changes but is often fully superseded and replaced, then our idea of progress must be broadened to account for this.[8]

Indeed, there are a number of different, often conflicting, interpretations of scientific progress. It may be any one or a combination of the following (and more):

1. the generation of true stories about a mind-independent world through increasingly complete and literal descriptions

2. an increase of approximate truth (verisimilitude), meaning that science may approach the truth but should avoid claiming that it has arrived fully. While nearness to truth is perhaps not as satisfying, it is still very useful.

3. an increase in the articulation and specialization of knowledge; in other words, the more precision and detail about reality, the more progress.

4. the solving of problems or fulfillment of functions; science that works, true or not.

5. demonstration of shortcomings and inconsistencies in theories, rather than proving them correct by confirming them with evidence.[9]

---

of time to be very promising. These hold that the past, present, and future are all equally real. Time does not flow but simply is already, all at once; like space, it is just there. This view is necessary to account for the relativity of "nows" gained from Einstein's physics.

8. We might think of an example like the Laws of Motion and Universal Gravitation, said to explain all motion in the heavens and on Earth until they were challenged by the Special and General Relativity theories.

9. Popper is famous on this point of rejecting empirical verification for methodological falsification, according to which knowledge is provisional and hypothetical.

SITUATING PROGRESS AND THE SELF

Hermeneutics has many different faces. For some, such as Dilthey and Habermas, it is a tradition that has dreamt of the day when the soft human sciences could rise confidently to greet the hard natural sciences eye-to-eye, and share in the venerated status conferred upon distinct forms of objectivity, rationality, and socially accepted reliability. For others, such as Heidegger, Gadamer, and Richard Rorty, the tradition of hermeneutics sees the human self as participating in a way of being that frustrates standards for quantifiable measurement and evaluation, including forms of quasi-objectivity, ideal speech situations, and the like. For them, it would seem, there is very little in the way of reliable criteria to identify progress, for the self far exceeds the popularly conceived measure of scientific progress.

Conversely, the many faces of science have shared a unifying ethos of progress in objectivity since at least the 1840s.[10] Objectivity, having no specific definition in the literature, tends to be understood as the purposeful eradication of subjectivity through methods and techniques. In simple terms, objectivity is anti-subjectivity; it is the belief that the self is a hindrance to truth. This makes science a matter of achieving "freedom from" the prejudice, bias, desire, will, social influence, and so on that inhere in the self; science is said to progress by an ever-vigilant eradication of the self and its finitude for the sake of attaining value-free facts.[11] Bauman sums up this peculiar if not miraculous movement of "freedom from" for the sake of "freedom toward" knowledge when he writes of scientists as:

> informed of *contingency* while believing themselves to narrate *necessity*, of particular *locality* while believing themselves to narrate *universality*, of tradition-bound interpretation while believing themselves to narrate the extraterritorial and extra-temporal truth, of undecidability while believing themselves to narrate transparency, of the provisionality of the human

---

10. On the history of objectivity see Daston, "Objectivity and the Escape from Perspective." For a more prolonged discussion see Daston and Galison, *Objectivity*.

11. Daston is worth quoting at length on this point: "Experience we have always had with us, but facts as a way of parsing experience in natural history and natural philosophy are of seventeenth-century coinage. Aristotelian experience had been woven of smooth-textured universals about 'what happens always or most of the time'; early modern facts were historical particulars about an observation or an experiment performed at a specific time and place by named persons. What made the new-style facts granular was not only their specificity but also their alleged detachment from inference and conjecture. Ideally, at least, 'matters of fact' were nuggets of pure experience, strictly segregated from an interpretation or hypothesis that might enlist them as evidence. Daston, "Fear and Loathing of the Imagination in Science," 75.

condition while believing themselves to narrate the certainty of the world, of the ambivalence of man-made design while believing themselves to narrate the order of nature.[12]

Hermeneutics recognizes what the natural sciences do not yet fully appreciate, namely, that the problem of progress resides chiefly in our view of the self and its abilities, not the subjugation of the self. For hermeneutics the radical nature of the self and its ability to understand frustrates attempts to refine it through method and to compartmentalize it through dichotomies such as objectivity and subjectivity. The human self and therefore human understanding is fundamentally misconceived when we attempt to control and dominate it. Instead, a hermeneutics of progress begins when we move beyond objectivity and subjectivity and free the self to know and experience the world as it naturally seeks to do—in the very manner of being that is said to destroy access to genuine scientific knowledge.[13]

At the risk of partly oversimplifying things: it seems that the self is believed, not only by the idealized scientific self but also by the average everyday research scientist, to impede genuine progress, whereas for the hermeneut, on the other hand, progress is embodied in the self. In its pure form, objectivity—as the undergirding ethos of progress—refuses to cross the invisible boundary between experience and "truth," between what we know by virtue of our living in the world, and what we know through designed and applied methods. Where scientific progress relies on enforcing and accentuating this fracture, a hermeneutics of progress heals it, drawing attention to its artificiality and showing that the worlds of self and reality exist naturally together as one.

SCIENTIFIC AND HERMENEUTIC PROGRESS

The following four subsections compare and contrast scientific themes with hermeneutical ones, outlining the progressive self-understanding of the natural sciences and philosophical hermeneutics. A portion of this provisional map is admittedly something of a positivistic caricature, resulting primarily from the need to generalize the infinitely varied natural sciences and their

---

12. Bauman, *Modernity and Ambivalence*, 231–32. Bauman is referring to the modern social sciences, but these same ironies exist across the natural and social sciences.

13. Hermeneutics is hardly anti-method. Rather, the point is that method has been greatly exaggerated as a means to truth about the world, self, and others. The danger in this is the use of method to enforce the separation of self and world, self and "genuine" understanding.

corresponding standards and criteria of progress;[14] even so, it is a helpful way of aligning comparative values, means, products, and self-descriptions.

Values and Means

Science

Scientific progress is said to be continuous, successive, linear, and dependent almost exclusively on rejecting and overcoming a flawed and less accomplished past, for scientific knowledge is cumulative and increasingly comprehensive.[15] Progress is achieved through applied methods, procedures, and ideals of objectivity, including measurement, universal codification (communicability), and empirical certainty. Success is largely by virtue of the skill and technique of the scientist, whose actions are judged in terms of instrumental effectiveness and adherence to scientific values. In its purest form progressive science is disinterested, seeking knowledge for its own sake rather than for "the good" of the human condition, quality of life, or social justice. Application of knowledge or judgments of its relevance are not strictly scientific questions; they are ancillary concerns to an ever better literal reading of the book of nature.

Progress often occurs in situations where naturally and unnaturally occurring variables and events are isolated and controlled for the sake of an anticipated (hypothesized) outcome. In such situations the scientist relies on the universal acceptance of such values as simplicity, reliability, consistency, scope, testability, and repeatability.[16] And while science may routinely admit that current answers (facts and theories) are not yet final or comprehensive, the guiding ethos is to pursue the one true image of the world, believing that there is a finale to the work. Scientific progress is finite:

---

14. I hesitated initially to rely on features of an old positivist portrait of science to characterize today's science but, as it turns out, it is hardly old at all. Indeed, one need not look far to find residual positivistic images of science still being taught boldly in major science textbooks and classrooms. For an interesting paper that examines this concern, see Rowbottom and Aiston's "Myth of 'Scientific Method.'"

15. The persistent belief in cumulative and comprehensive knowledge remains even for some who try to describe a hermeneutics of progress. For example, Reinoud Bosch recently proposed a hermeneutical method claiming that the "importance of subjective judgments of relevance, plausibility, and accuracy together with the iterative process of improvements on preconceptions implies an accumulation of subjective interpretations of knowledge throughout history, offering increasingly comprehensive ideas." Bosch, "Pragmatism," 196. Such an approach seems confused.

16. Versions of Popperian falsification and others could be included; still, this is an adequate account of core values.

it will end when a complete picture has been achieved and there is nothing left to be said.

Scientific progress is often a response to aggressive competition and the antagonism of other scientists. Certain incentive structures, inherent in the way scientific research is conducted, generate these competitive attitudes. Being the first to publish, the first to secure grants and research funding, the first to attract promising new recruits, etc., is often paramount to scientific survival (i.e., one's own progress). While science is in large part a group activity, the primacy of the self over the collective is evident at key points along the way toward collective progress. The extent and significance of this particular dynamic is beyond the scope of this discussion.

Hermeneutic Progress

Hermeneutic progress is discontinuous, non-linear, and circular, for it relies on an ever new relationship with the past and a projection into the future. Our pasts and anticipated futures are constantly at work within us, changing us and our beliefs about the world, others, and ourselves. Progress is achieved through practical reasonableness in everyday engagements, i.e., our ability to live well by applying general theory to practical affairs. Success is by virtue of openness, vulnerability, and a willing exposure to and search for the truth of "the other"—the other person, text, work of art, or tradition, and progress means that at any moment one may be utterly devastated or thrilled by that truth.[17] A hermeneutics of progress also makes a universal claim on all human understanding, but its claim is for the prioritization of asking questions, listening, accepting personal responsibility, and seeking solidarity with the other. Thus, truth is most often discovered in situations where one cannot or does not isolate and control naturally and unnaturally occurring variables and events; it often surprises and even frustrates us by being entirely unpredictable and contrary to our assumptions (theories). Hermeneutic progress also admits that answers (facts and theories) are not final, but that is because progress has no end and resides within evolving individuals and communities. It is often a response to practical demands, such as something breaking or someone wanting to be understood. Moreover, hermeneutic progress is an implicit search for "the good" of the human condition, quality of life, and social justice;[18] knowledge for its own

---

17. Schmidt makes this point in a helpful paper arguing that "the otherness of the other is preserved in hermeneutic conversations, and that Gadamer's concern for the other is not a recent phenomenon." Schmidt, "Respecting Others," 360.

18. For example, when asked by Riccardo Dottori, "To what extent must we admit

sake lacks a necessary connection to human purpose. The disconnection of theory and practice as two separate activities makes no sense; rather, at every moment in our lives theory and practice simultaneously co-determine our experiences.

The Progressive Self

Science

The ideal self of science, one that exists perhaps nowhere in practice, is an impartial and passive observer, a *tabula rasa*. The ideal knower is a blank slate—neutral, unbiased, disinterested, and detached, waiting for nature to inscribe herself. We need not assume that this is what actually goes on in scientific practice, only that it is the ideal according to which practice is judged and purports to be corrected.[19] Scientists are expected to be active in eradicating vestiges of self in collecting data, performing experiments, developing hypotheses, and so on. Once the negative elements of self are removed, the naked scientific observer is free to see the world as it is in itself.[20] This new "objective observer" self employs language as a tool to transliterate rather than interpret nature. It is an expert or specialist in a given field who accepts a paradigm of principles and foundational concepts. It pays attention only to those questions that seem answerable and whose answers are, therefore, at least partially already known.

---

to ourselves that we engage in politics?" Gadamer responds: "To the extent that we recognize that our actions are always purposeful. And if a person wants to achieve a purpose, then he or she must also persuade others of it and, moreover, gain their consensus. Nevertheless, we have to be clear about whether we want to persuade others because we think it would be something good or whether we simply want to persuade them because it suits our purposes—without even asking whether this would be anything good. What I want to show is that, whether we can answer it or not, we should always begin from the idea of posing the question of the *agathon*, the good. The question is always whether it's simply a matter of what's better or whether it is really a matter of what lies beyond every particular purpose." He adds, "I admit that when we search for the good we can, at most, perhaps find the better." Gadamer, *A Century of Philosophy*, 44.

19. On the point that most of what goes on in science is not objective, see Boyd, "Scientific Realism" and Sismondo, "Social Constructions."

20. This is somewhat different when it comes to unobservables that are believed to be real.

Hermeneutics

The hermeneutical self fosters an ever deeper and ongoing recognition of one's finitude, with meaningful activities emerging from a historically and linguistically mediated context. There is no *tabula rasa*, for all progress must be written in the middle of an ongoing narrative or conversation. Progress depends on whether and to what degree we know ourselves as largely unknowable and take our tradition seriously, i.e., on our self-understanding.[21]

The self of hermeneutics is an active participant in the co-determination of understanding. This is not social constructivism or subjective relativism but an ongoing negotiation between what is universal and particular, between one's horizon and that of another—not a surrender of meaning for gain, but a reworking, refashioning, revaluing. The self of hermeneutics speaks through language, itself something that is both historical and cultural, which simultaneously limits understanding and makes it possible. This self is not an expert or specialist, for hermeneutics is more than merely a skill, technique, or body of knowledge to be learned. And yet, like the scientist, the hermeneut is already inculcated into a pre-existing ethos or web of beliefs that determines what counts as legitimate understanding. This self of radical openness and vulnerability aims to ask questions whose answers are genuinely unknown, or which are perhaps unanswerable, although in practice it is most difficult to question honestly and deeply.

Product of Progress

Science

The product of scientific activity emerges among colleagues of like rational mind, specifically those initiated into and committed to closed communities, i.e., academic disciplines. The product of science is true stories about a mind-independent world, generated by the accumulation of increasingly complete information and descriptions. Semantic correctness, scope, and precision are highly valuable to attaining products of progress. The product

---

21. Gail Soffer succinctly describes Gadamer's hermeneutical progress: "Progress in the human sciences, he claims, does not consist in the quasi-Hegelian dialectical resolution of differences, the synthesizing of partial perspectives into a whole, but rather in the prevention of the loss of meaning, the preservation of the tradition against sinking into oblivion. Thus for Gadamer the hermeneutical disciplines make 'progress' so long as the past continues to say something to us, even if we fail to agree upon what it says." Soffer, "Gadamer, Hermeneutics, and Objectivity," 244.

contributes to an ordered and atemporal body of knowledge that may be codified, packaged, and distributed. It fills in gaps of understanding and smooths over inconsistencies and contrary meanings. It offers superior prediction, control, efficient action, and the determination of universal constants and quantitative laws.

The product of science is the acceptance of newly established facts and theoretical revisions that more accurately reflect observed phenomena, and achievements that meet criteria of universalized objectivity, e.g., standardized communicability and terms of measurement. It falls within the predetermined range of acceptable knowledge claims. The products of progress may also give rise to creative ideas that cause reinterpretation of accepted paradigms and the generation of new insights into phenomena; however, progress may ultimately require that such ideas be ignored if they present anomalies for which the theoretical framework cannot offer an account.[22]

Hermeneutics

The results of a hermeneutic consciousness emerge among deeply interested and engaged dialogue partners, whether they are laypeople or specialists. Progress is rational inasmuch as each individual is responsible for finding "the better," but made possible insofar as we allow the other, however foreign, to influence our preconceptions. The product takes the form of ongoing identification and articulation of prejudices, tacit assumptions, and beliefs through conversation with others and one's own tradition in the hope of distinguishing the inappropriate from the appropriate, the impeding from the enabling. By challenging our preconceptions rather than ignoring their influence we are able to see what emerges in light of them. Progress is possible to the extent that we are able to continue questioning and testing the familiar and alien.

The products of hermeneutic understanding are embodied, temporal (i.e., historical and changing), and most often unquantifiable. They aid us in learning to live well with undecidability and the absence of knowledge or certainty. Understanding is an attempt to fill in gaps and clear up inconsistencies and contrary meanings while simultaneously respecting the radical otherness and difference to which we are exposed. To borrow from Grondin, an experience of hermeneutic understanding is "as much a knowing as

---

22. This is more akin to Kuhn's view of "normal" science. During times of "revolutionary" science, the theoretical paradigm—the then reigning ethos of a scientific community—would change radically so as to account for new ideas and anomalies that did not fit under the old model.

a 'not-knowing.' It is actually less a form of knowledge than a mode to find one's way around in the absence, as it were, of such a knowledge."[23]

When achieved, the product of hermeneutical progress is largely a matter of self-forgetting. Only when an object of study is so close that we forget ourselves in our experience of it may we say we know something. Gadamer writes:

> [B]eing present has the character of being outside oneself . . . In fact, being outside oneself is the positive possibility of being wholly with something else. This kind of being present is a self-forgetfulness . . . Here self-forgetfulness is anything but a private condition, for it arises from devoting one's full attention to the matter at hand [or object].[24]

The products of hermeneutical consciousness are creative ideas that cause reinterpretations of the familiar and engagement with the foreign. Progress may mean that these are negative experiences insofar as conversations are unpredictable and often contrary to expectation. Progress does not establish facts but recognizes emergent artifacts—social and cultural meanings and interpretations. It is progressive to the degree that we, with Aristotle, find "the right measure" of a concrete situation and take responsibility for making decisions necessary to meet practical demands.[25] How well we act in terms of practical reasonableness is a response to our own self-understanding and the *logos* of the situation.

The product of hermeneutics is achieved through identifying and fostering local solidarities. When we are able to recognize deep solidarities by freely engaging others in open discussion, allowing them to influence and condition us, self-understanding is developed and matured. Hermeneutic progress is achieved wherever there is a shared willingness to question and to find a common accord. For Gadamer, rational self-responsibility emerges

---

23. See Grondin, "Continental or Hermeneutical Philosophy," 79.

24. Gadamer. *Truth and Method*, 125–26.

25. In describing the hermeneutical dimension of ethics and practical reason, Gadamer writes: "What is rational in the sense of the right thing to do in this situation is not prescribed to you in the general orientations you have been given about good and evil in the same way that the instructions for use that come with a tool tell you how to use it. Rather, you have to determine for yourself what you are going to do. And to do this you have to arrive at a comprehension of your situation, reach an understanding with yourself about it. In other words, you have to *interpret* it!" Gadamer, *A Century of Philosophy*, 79.

to the degree that we recognize the dialogical nature of all our *praxis*[26] and find "the paths of solidarity and of reaching understanding."[27]

Theoretical Progress

Science

Theoretical progress means better access to reality by more accurately generalizing, classifying, systematizing, and explaining causal phenomena. This relies on empirical verification as the incremental confirmation of the disclosure of a mind-independent reality and the accumulation of knowledge. Scientific theory is meant to get behind experience, i.e., behind the effect, in order to discern a cause. The better the theory the more it accounts for observations. An enormous amount of scientific effort is spent bringing theory and nature into closer agreement. Since Kuhn, theoretical progress is increasingly seen as a matter of better problem-solving. Both versions are possible only when there is a high standard of clarity and agreement.

Hermeneutics

Theoretical progress is a matter of practical application. Discovery is possible through concretizing the general, e.g., text, to the particular or to one's horizon. Theoretical progress is a "play" of circularity in which we move between theory and experience, universal and particular, while gradually spiraling outward into new and unpredictable experiences. To truly progress is to question more, experience more, engage more, dialogue more. These are possible only when we risk ourselves through exposure to the challenging and strange.

BENEFITS OF A HERMENEUTICS OF PROGRESS

Where might a hermeneutics of progress get us if it cannot prescribe a clear-cut means to achieving that progress? Unlike the progress of science, hermeneutics cannot offer specific rules or methods. One of the main advantages is that the hermeneutical description of progress matches experienced reality

---

26. "Praxis" for Gadamer is not merely this or that specific activity but encompasses all we do, think, say, feel, and so on. It may refer to both action and understanding, or draw attention to one or the other, depending on its use.

27. Gadamer, *A Century of Philosophy*, 80.

more closely than the objectivist depiction, both the reality of what we do in our daily lives and, more controversially, the reality of what scientists are already doing in the lab. As a description of lived experience with its many practical demands, hermeneutics is able to appreciate the kind of overall progress achieved in the lab, namely its multifaceted nature (historical, social, linguistic) that relies upon self-understanding as the basis for a description of the world—a world that is always more than merely a composite of discrete objects in themselves. In this regard, there are two case studies that are particularly well known for having challenged the standard view of daily scientific practice. The first is Karin Knorr-Cetina's one-year study of a science laboratory at UC Berkeley. The second is Bruno Latour's and Steven Woolgar's study of Roger Guillemin's neuroendocrinology laboratory at the Salk Institute in La Jolla, California.[28]

Let me briefly survey the relevant conclusions from Knorr's research. A well known proponent of social constructivism (also "constructionism"), Knorr is a sociologist of science who has had a major influence on the view that scientific reality is, at least in part, constructed through selective and contextual practices in the laboratory, practices that are governed by social and historical conditions.[29] In her own laboratory studies Knorr claims to have observed the emergence of scientific facts through constant negotiations and interpretations among scientists. These, for Knorr, go a long way toward showing that scientists create scientific reality in the lab rather than passively observe it through highly controlled experiments designed to filter out the self. The process of discovering facts, itself a process of manufacturing according to Knorr, seems to involve far more than descriptions of what is real, i.e., of what is comprehensible as separate and distinct from one's self-understanding. Rather, the activity of establishing facts or the truth of one's research clearly reflects the unique socio-historical context in which those claims were born, as well as the surrounding opportunities and possibilities of the situation. And like the meaning of all other artifacts, their meaning often changes to fit emerging contexts.

Knorr's initial work involved the observation of lab researchers working in basic and applied research in chemical, physical, microbiological,

---

28. We might also consider Lynch's *Art and Artifact in Laboratory Science*.

29. Knorr (subsequently known as Knorr-Cetina) describes her "constructivist" interpretation of knowledge when she writes, "I do not maintain that reality is produced (constructed) in the sense that its appearance has no independent existence. Rather, this approach claims that once we see scientific products as selectively carved out, transformed and constructed from whatever is, we will also see that there cannot be any warrant in the claim that we have somehow captured (subject to progressive improvement) what is." Knorr, "Tinkering Toward Success," 369.

toxicological, technological, and economic areas. Most of the scientists had degrees in at least one of these areas as well as biochemistry. In all there were some 300 potential subjects involved in one way or another in the ongoing function of the lab in question, but Knorr's observations focused on those working with plant proteins. During the one-year period those most involved with the work on plant proteins produced nine new publications, five of which were original research results that appeared in relevant journals. In addition, group leaders often had strong reputations in the field at an international level. In short, the work observed by Knorr was not that of a small lab with little or no association with the larger scientific community; her observations were of many active, contemporary, and widely respected researchers.

In "Tinkering toward Success: Prelude to a Theory of Scientific Practice," Knorr draws out some of the connections between her observations at Berkeley and the nature of hermeneutical understanding. In the course of her study she identified a number of surprising features about laboratory life, answering her own question, "is there any evidence from a direct observation of the laboratory which would substantiate the hermeneutical nature of inquiry in the hard sciences?"[30] In addition to the problem of value-laden theories, language games, and other common hermeneutical features of human understanding, Knorr discovered specific ways in which scientists were routinely required to make evaluative judgments and interpretations—required, in other words, to be hermeneuts. This was perhaps most evident in the development of local idiosyncrasies in the interpretation of scientific methods and rules. These idiosyncrasies were used to determine the best way of performing in the lab and of negotiating the meaning and significance of results. That is, according to Knorr, actual lab work was accomplished by making choices and interpretations that were not universally standardized among other biochemists (objective) but were developed to meet the unique needs, limitations, and goals of the local situation.[31]

Decisions in the lab were constantly required in terms of (1) the selection of specific ingredients and instrumentation; (2) how much of a substance was to be used, how long it was to be maintained, and when a measurement was to be taken; and (3) what kind of control in method was best, such as "simplicity of composition vs. complexity as an approximation of practice, or strict vs. indirect comparability in the case of potential

---

30. Ibid., 351.

31. Without attempting to define the specific case in greater detail, one might go so far as to suggest the development of phronetic insight (practical wisdom), i.e., the proper relation to one's situation and the practical demands it makes, as the basis for this lab's successful research.

interaction between the instrumentation and the experimental material."[32] According to Knorr, these choices were not governed by clearly prescribed laws or rules meant to secure an objective result so much as by the need to work within the limits of available resources and respond to the widely shared desire for success in the form of notoriety, publications, potential research grants, etc. Generating scientific truth, according to Knorr, was not a chief criterion driving success in the lab—that is, unless one is willing to include hermeneutical insights to allow for a broad conception of truth capable of supporting actual lab practices in which truth and success arise through negotiations and interpretations that are both limited and enabled by local opportunities. And, in fact, these wider notions of success and truth were precisely what Knorr observed.[33] Scientific facts were attained through negotiations and interpretations that had value largely because of the role they played in responding to the particulars of the situation. In short, scientific facts were relative, at least in part, and had a great deal of practical relevance. Discovered in the context of judgments about how, what, why, and when, the research produced was not objective in the traditional sense but, Knorr argues, distinctive, i.e., marked by the idiosyncrasies of its production. For Knorr, even the language of truth and success bore obvious marks of the self-understanding of scientists.

> The laboratory site is the cell which breeds the facts and the fields of empirical science, and the collective "faith" which sustains its form of life. Nowhere within this site do we seem to find the worlds of ideas we are looking for, nor the cognitive objects and interests generally identified with research. The laboratory site is a practice.[34]

To summarize, Knorr's point is that the practice of science in laboratory research is dependent upon local opportunities, judgments, and interpretations, just as we see in other human activities. Scientific practice, at least among these select biochemists, was not rigidly mechanistic, highly rational, and unified across the disciplines. For our purposes there are four important claims about laboratory practice that, while not conclusive, are highly compelling:

---

32. Knorr, "Tinkering toward Success," 361.

33. Knorr writes, "In the *research process*, however, success leads a peculiarly phantasmagoric existence. Always projected or retrospectively interpreted (cash-outs are the breaks between projection and reinterpretation), success can never be fully tracked down and given permanent identity." Ibid., 368.

34. Ibid., 348.

1. Ideals of objective rationality, impartiality, and evidence do not play the dominant regulative roles in scientific practice that they are often believed to play.
2. Rigid mechanisms of procedure, technique, and method required in order to gain and secure new insights are surprisingly lacking.
3. In their more productive moments, scientists rely on practical reasoning and creative problem-solving—thinking outside the proverbial box or textbook—to make things work.
4. Accepted values are not merely simplicity, reliability, consistency, scope, but are often very much a reflection of who will get the next research grant, how to get published and made visible to peers, and similar human needs in the context of "reliable" science.

In short, very little of what goes on in scientific practice seems to fulfill the criteria for objectivity.[35] If this is true, then perhaps a hermeneutics of progress will allow scientists to speak authentically as interested and involved individuals, without the need for layers of mechanism and technique that are meant to bolster an image of neutrality and distance. Perhaps most importantly, by acknowledging the role of interpretive limitations and fallibility we are better positioned to be self-correcting in light of the conditions and elements on which we rely to make sense of the world.

CONCLUSION

The idea of hermeneutical progress does not signal an onslaught of sophisticated banter for postmodern relativism or skepticism. Philosophical hermeneutics agrees that what we see is real, and what we touch, taste, and smell are also real. These are also "real" as linguistically mediated and therefore historically and socially conditioned experiences. Such is not a corrupted or deluded existence, for these features of reality make human experience possible. They are not unwanted viruses or infections but the glorious primordial stew from and by which we first emerge and are later sustained. Moreover, its concern for "the real" is one that escapes the long-drawn-out and ultimately unhelpful realism debate, whose eventual answer probably would not change much of anything.[36] Hermeneutics unhinges the dog-

---

35. On this point see also Boyd, "Scientific Realism" and Sismondo, "Social Constructions."

36. On this point see McArthur, "The Anti-Philosophical Stance." He argues, following Fine, Rouse, Rorty, and others, that the realism debate does not yield insight into the actual practice of science.

matic connection between what is real and what is certain, a connection on which science has relied to define and protect its own version of the ideal of scientific investigation. The real, for hermeneutics, need not be certain, but must be apprehended within the practical and real-world interactions we know tentatively, relatively, and often ambiguously.

Progress in hermeneutics is a matter of finding a new, more helpful relationship with the present by reconsidering the past and allowing the other to influence us wherever we encounter it (or them). A hermeneutics of progress is both progressive and regressive as the giving up or modifying of cherished beliefs. Hermeneutics expects to revisit and revise self-understanding routinely, indeed requiring such revision in order to find "the better." Objectivity attempts to explain away the rejection of theories, beliefs, and ideals as merely adaptations to what remains basically the same.

A hermeneutics of progress provides an account of rational-scientific understanding that has no need either to rely on or to reject a progressive realist ontology—the notion of a separate immutable reality—to justify its actions. Instead, it succeeds by virtue of critical self-awareness and self-understanding, and by looking for artifacts of meaning. For hermeneutics, once we are able to get over the preoccupation with seeing things as they are, we may begin to hear what things are saying; a hermeneutics of progress is one of attunement, a progress in which we are not passive recipients of knowledge but active participants in seeing and hearing the truth in others and the world. By allowing ourselves to be thus involved in the world we find a more progressive relationship with it. The self of hermeneutics allows for a complete conception of progress, for while science relies on the removal of self, a hermeneutics of progress relies on clarifying the self within what is understood. A hermeneutics of progress need not be arbitrary if understanding is underdetermined, incomplete, and largely circular. It needs to be self-forgetting, vulnerable, and temporally flexible.

BIBLIOGRAPHY

Bauman, Zygmunt. *Modernity and Ambivalence*. Cambridge: Polity, 1991.
Bosch, Reinoud. "Pragmatism and the Practical Relevance of Truth." *Foundations of Science* 12 (2007) 189–201.
Boyd, Richard N. "On the Current Status of the Issue of Scientific Realism." *Erkenntnis* 19 (1983) 45–90.
Daston, Lorraine. "Fear and Loathing of the Imagination in Science." *Daedalus* 127 (1998) 73–95.

---. "Objectivity and the Escape from Perspective." *Social Studies of Science* 22 (1992) 597–618.
Daston, Lorraine, and Peter Galison. *Objectivity*. Boston: Zone, 2007.
Gadamer, Hans-Georg. *A Century of Philosophy: Hans-Georg Gadamer in Conversation with Riccardo Dottori*. Translated by Rod Coltman and Sigrid Koepke. New York: Continuum, 2004.
---. *Truth and Method*. Translated by Joel Weinsheimer and Donald G. Marshall. 2nd rev. ed. New York: Continuum, 2002.
Ginev, Dimitri. "A (Post)Foundational Approach to the Philosophy of Science: Part II." *Journal for General Philosophy of Science* 38 (2007) 57–74.
Grondin, Jean. "Continental or Hermeneutical Philosophy: The Tragedies of Understanding in the Analytic and Continental Perspectives." In *Interrogating the Tradition: Hermeneutics and the History of Philosophy*, edited by Charles E. Scott and John Sallis. New York: State University of New York Press, 2000.
Heidegger, Martin. "Science and Reflection." In *The Question Concerning Technology: An Other Essays*, 155ff. Translated by William Lovitt. Martin Heidegger Works. New York: Harper & Row, 1977.
Knorr, Karin D. "Tinkering Toward Success: Prelude to a Theory of Scientific Practice." *Theory and Society* 8 (1979) 347–76.
Knorr-Cetina, Karin D. *The Manufacture of Knowledge: An Essay on the Constructivist and Contextual Nature of Science*. Oxford: Pergamon, 1981.
Latour, Bruno, and Steven Woolgar. *Laboratory Life: The Construction of Scientific Facts*. 2nd ed. Princeton: Princeton University Press, 1986.
Lynch, Michael. *Art and Artifact in Laboratory Science*. London: Routledge, 1985.
McArthur, Dan. "The Anti-Philosophical Stance, the Realism Question, and Scientific Practice." *Foundations of Science* 11 (2006) 369–97.
Nickerson, Raymond. *Cognition and Chance: The Psychology of Probabilistic Reasoning*. Mahwah, NJ: Erlbaum, 2004.
Putnam, Hilary. *Mathematics, Matter and Method*. Cambridge: Cambridge University Press, 1975.
Rowbottom, Darrell Patrick, and Sarah Jane Aiston. "The Myth of 'Scientific Method' in Contemporary Educational Research." *Journal of Philosophy of Education* 40 (2006) 137–56.
Schmidt, Lawrence. "Respecting Others: The Hermeneutic Virtue." *Continental Philosophy Review* 33 (2000) 359–79.
Sismondo, S. "Some Social Constructions." *Social Science Studies of Science* 23 (1993) 515–53.
Soffer, Gail. "Gadamer, Hermeneutics, and Objectivity in Interpretation." *Praxis International* 12 (1992) 231–68.

15

Muhammad Iqbal
A Reformist Islamic Philosophy of Science

H. Chad Hillier

The early twentieth-century Indian-Muslim poet-philosopher Muhammad Iqbal is arguably the first truly modern Muslim thinker. Born in 1877 in the Punjab region of the British Raj into a middle-class family of Sufis, Iqbal began his early education in the local madrasa. Recognizing Iqbal's intellectual gifts, however, his teacher taught him a Western curriculum alongside his traditional Islamic studies. This led to Iqbal's studies at a local missionary college and further studies at university in Lahore, where he obtained a bachelor's degree in liberal arts and a master's degree in philosophy by 1899. He became an accomplished poet, publishing several popular poems, including one lauded as the unofficial national anthem of the Indian nationalist movement. He was also a successful lecturer at Oriental College, where he was encouraged to further his education in England. Leaving for Europe in 1905, by 1907 he had earned a bachelor's degree in Islamic studies from Trinity College at Cambridge, was called to the bar at Lincoln's Inn, and completed a doctorate in philosophy from the University of Munich. He returned home to India in 1908.[1]

Before his studies in Europe, Iqbal had been a committed pan-Indian nationalist. However, his experiences in England and Germany soured him

---

1. This biographical sketch is drawn largely from Mir, *Iqbal*, 1–21.

on the prospect of a pluralistic Indian society and on the heart of Western modernity. Known as the "spiritual father of Pakistan," he committed the rest of his public life to promoting the ideal of a Muslim state in northwest India. He was also involved in both the Indian Parliament and the Muslim League.

While continuing to write poetry, he published a series of lectures in 1934 that he had delivered at various universities in India. The resulting book, *The Reconstruction of Religious Thought in Islam*, established his impact as a modern Muslim philosopher.[2] Perhaps a Muslim Spinoza, Iqbal arguably set forth the first comprehensive effort at modernizing Islamic thought and society through the assimilation of Western science and philosophy. Although Iqbal has often been wrongly interpreted as a Nietzschean, a label he personally rejected but was unable to shake, his genius is in his assimilation of the diverse elements of nineteenth-century European idealism in interpreting Islamic thought as consistent with trends in modern scientific thought.

This essay outlines Iqbal's Islamic challenge to scientific naturalism/materialism—an ideological system he finds inconsistent with religion—as well as his assimilation of other systems of natural philosophy to articulate a more modernized Islamic understanding of science. In doing so Iqbal add his own voice, a uniquely Muslim voice, to the critics of naturalism. This paper will also present Iqbal's resolution of the epistemological crisis that he perceived to be facing his community.

IQBAL AND THE CRITICISM OF SCIENTIFIC MATERIALISM

The Western philosophical doctrine of scientific materialism (i.e., naturalism), the belief that our sensory observation of nature is the sole source of knowledge or that the observable world is the only reality, is obviously contrary to the Islamic intellectual tradition. It is anathema to the Qur'anic worldview of a divinely created universe full of creatures, both seen and unseen. It is therefore no surprise to find a devout Muslim thinker like Iqbal rejecting this Western doctrine out-of-hand. At the same time, modern science, a tradition in its own right, does offer explanations for significant elements of our human experience.

In addressing the problem of science, Iqbal reveals that, for him, the tension between religious knowledge and the philosophical assumption of materialism as the basis from which all is learned, discovered, or formed

---

2. See Esposito and Voll, *Makers of Contemporary Islam*.

is significant in terms not only of the future of Islam but also of religious knowledge itself. In reading Iqbal's *Reconstruction*, we find a protracted defence of the validity of religious knowledge.

The foundation of Iqbal's criticism of scientific materialism comes from the French philosopher Henri Bergson. Bergson, in his landmark book *Creative Evolution*, seeks to challenge the Darwinian theory of natural selection. As Michael Vaughan notes,[3] Bergson believes that mechanistic natural selection and dissociation cannot account for the entire evolution of all biological entities, only for their extinction. Evolution, a process of gradual mutation, has to be a process of creative change. Biological life cannot be explained merely as a series of biochemical processes. Instead, evidence suggests that something within matter—a vitality—drives its creation, its organization, and its growth. This is not a mere force like any other material force in the universe; rather, it is an inherent aspect within all matter.[4]

In Hegelian fashion, Bergson argues that the power of this creative process is time itself,[5] what he calls "duration" or "élan vital." Time is more than a simple measure of movement; it is a real force in the universe. Our minds, however, as products of evolution, tend to divide and segment the world we encounter to establish intellectual relations with it;[6] this is why nature appears to be mechanical. Scientific mechanicalism, therefore, divides reality into parts and isolates them, producing only a partial view of reality. Although such a methodology has proven helpful in certain fields of human inquiry, Bergson argues, it cannot explain the whole of biological and psychological life and experience.[7] Here Bergson invokes his famous doctrine of "intuition," knowledge derived from a direct experience of reality; and here Iqbal finds his connection to Islam.

The importance in noting Iqbal's assimilation of Bergson, however, is not whose thought he feels is compatible with Islamic tradition (even though that is also important) but how he assimilates it. Iqbal argues that the Qur'an reveals the reality of time and of the dual source of human knowledge. He argues that human knowledge derives from both sensory observation and intuition,[8] intuition being knowledge based on the mystical "direct association with reality as it reveals itself within" the human—called "heart" (*fu'ad* in the Qur'an). The division between the two sources of knowledge leads to

3. See Vaughan, "Henri Bergson's *Creative Evolution*."
4. Bergson, *Creative Evolution*, 101.
5. Vaughan, "Henri Bergson's *Creative Evolution*," 11.
6. Bergson, *Creative Evolution*, 101.
7. Ibid., 345–67.
8. Iqbal, *Reconstruction*, 15.

an isolation of intuition, confining it to the sphere of religious experience, with real knowledge being solely that which is experienced by the senses.[9] Iqbal immediately criticizes this regulation of intuition in intellectual history and argues that the prominence and early priority of mystical knowledge in human history demands that the modern mind not dismiss it as an equal source of human knowledge.[10]

Along with Hegel, Iqbal states that the dominant epistemological theory since Kant conceives a metaphysical division between subject and object, "an unbridgeable gulf between the ideal and the real."[11] He argues that it is philosophically possible to conceive of thought or mind not simply as a principle of organization and integration of experiential information from outside the person but as "a potency which is formative of the very being of its material."[12] If thought or mind is a power that can form matter, thought cannot be foreign to reality; rather, it shares the same essence. Thus, it is a power that moves reality towards a particular end or purpose. This idea does more than bridge the Kantian chasm; it does away with the chasm by uniting the two sides.

Iqbal conceives of three levels of being: matter, mind, and life, which correspond to the scientific disciplines of physics, psychology, and biology, respectively. The reality of each is also reflected in the Qur'an.

Matter

Iqbal observes that modern physics is fixated on sensory experience of the material world. The physicist may *hypothesize* about imperceptible entities such as atoms or molecules, but "he does so because he cannot otherwise explain his sense-experience."[13] This entails, naturally, the exclusion of a whole range of human experience from the scope of physics. Moreover, according to its own presuppositions, modern physics maintains that the "things" that the observer perceives are only the "qualities" of an object (e.g., color, taste, texture, shape, size, etc.), not its real essence. This dichotomy forces physics to embrace a theory of pure matter, which is essence minus

---

9. Ibid., 16.

10. Ibid., 17. Iqbal notes a hadith from the Bukhari collection in which Muhammad observes the mystical experiences of a local Jewish youth (Ibn Sayyid) and questions him about them. Iqbal contends that this was the first psychological test in Islamic history.

11. Ibid., 31.

12. Ibid.

13. Ibid., 32.

qualities. Implied in this theory, however, is that "qualities" are not objective but subjective experiences dependent upon the senses of a perceiver (e.g., the book is blue because it impresses that color upon the observer's mind through the eyes). Because qualities are not objective but are, according to the most recent theories, a product of imperceptible (i.e., unverifiable) ether or sound waves, the experiences of nature that we actually have may be illusory.[14]

If this is the case, then science can no longer support a theory of matter or of radical materialism, for the gulf between observer and the observed world can only be bridged by maintaining non-verifiable ideas of matter and quality. Inklings of this conclusion, Iqbal argues, are seen in thinkers like Einstein and Alfred North Whitehead, who challenge the modern scientific conception of absolute matter floating in absolute space and argue that matter is a dynamic "structure of inter-related events" and a creative progressive flow throughout non-serial time.[15]

For example, according to Einstein's theory of relativity, "space is real, but relative to the observer."[16] Thus, in rejecting Newtonian absolute space, Einstein argues that mass, shape, and size are relative to the observer's speed and position, meaning that movement and rest are also relative to the observer. In other words, "no such thing as a self-subsistent materiality of classical physics"[17] exists. This does not lead to "monadistic idealism," however, for "the space-time frame does not depend on the observer's mind; it depends on the point of the material universe to which his *body* is attached."[18]

Although this supports the idea that the ultimate nature of reality is spiritual, Iqbal argues that Einstein's theory cannot give any information on that ultimate nature. Philosophically, it can only make two definite claims: "It destroys, not the objectivity of nature, but the view of substance as simple location in space";[19] and it asserts that space is dependent upon matter, expanding with the expanding material universe so that any concept of "empty space" is denied. The problem with relativity theory, however, is its conception of time as unreal, as a fourth dimension of space rather than as

---

14. Ibid., 32–3.
15. Ibid., 34.
16. See Einstein, "Moving Bodies."
17. Iqbal, *Reconstruction*, 37.
18. Ibid., 38

19. Ibid. Substance in Einsteinian physics is not a "persistent thing with variable states, but a system of inter-related events." Iqbal notes that in Whitehead's philosophy "matter" is replaced by the notion of "organism."

the "free creative movement" of pure duration or serial time. As such, it is not really time.[20]

Mind or Consciousness

Iqbal argues that because humans can only conceive of the consciousness from the effects of our sensory experiences, science has mistakenly believed consciousness is simply an effect that arises from the union of those experiences. Therefore, scientists like Newton and Darwin conceive of natural history in mechanistic terms, where "all life, thought, will and feeling" can be explained by natural physical laws.[21] Thus, the commitment of science to the sole priority of sense-knowledge is in opposition to the view of the ultimate nature of reality given by religion (intuition). As Iqbal admits, while science does produce genuine knowledge, "we must not forget [that] what we call science is not a single systematic view of reality. It is a mass of sectional views of reality—fragments of a total experience which do not seem to fit together." Therefore, although science has something to say about matter, about life, and about mind, it cannot address how each of these relates to the others. Iqbal states that "natural science is by nature sectional; it cannot, if it is true to its own nature and function, set up its theory as a complete view of reality."[22] Science is simply too variegated to provide a holistic view of reality. This makes science an artificial endeavor.

As such, it can only offer a selective organization of knowledge,[23] which is why religion need not be suspicious of science and should welcome the data it produces: religion, because it deals with the whole of reality, must occupy a central place in the synthesis of all "data of human experience" into a coherent whole. Moreover, such holistic synthesis, Iqbal argues, reveals the human mind as a dynamic and independent thing having no defined

---

20. Ibid., 38–40. Iqbal states, "Ouspensky describes our time-sense as a misty space-sense and argues . . . that to one-, two-, or three-dimensional beings, the higher dimension must always appear as succession in time. This obviously means that, what appears to us three-dimensional beings as time, is in reality an imperfectly sensed space-dimension which in its own nature does not differ from the perfectly sensed dimension of Euclidian space. In other words, time is not a genuine creative movement; and what we call future events are not fresh happenings, but things already given and located in an unknown space."

21. Ibid., 39.

22. Ibid., 42.

23. Ibid. Iqbal gives the example of the notion of "cause," which gives priority to effect and is therefore "relative to the subject-matter of physical science which studies one special kind of activity to the exclusion of other forms of activity observed by others." The concept of cause fails at the levels of life and mind, which require new concepts.

edges, able to expand and contract as needed. It is the "luminous point" that moves biological life in a teleological way, and can selectively distinguish between mental processes (e.g., memories) that have impact on that teleological process. It is a purely spiritual energy, an organizing principle of life, not a substance or an "epi-phenomenon" of material processes within the body.[24]

Organic Life

The weakness of modern science is seen especially at the third level of being. Here materialistic theories like causation cannot apply, Iqbal argues, because causality operates differently in the teleological action of living organisms. Because concepts of purpose are essential in biological life, physics and chemistry, which can explain certain aspects of life, are not sufficient to explain its totality. Biological life differs from machines in that it is "self-maintaining and self-reproducing"[25] and experiences growth and adaptation. Thus, biological life has some "spiritual" aspect beyond the mere repetition of certain physical and chemical bodily processes essential to its evolution. The totality of biological life cannot be explained through naturalistic evolutionary theory.

IQBAL AND THE CONSTRUCTION OF TRUE SCIENCE

After outlining his criticism of modern science, Iqbal attempts construction of a philosophy of science more consistent with both specific trends in European science and the Qur'anic worldview. He begins by arguing that a true philosophy of science begins with a proper metaphysical understanding of reality.

Metaphysical-Theological Foundation of Science

Iqbal asserts that the universe is not something static; rather, it is a "structure of events possessing the character of a continuous creative flow."[26] This view of reality is consistent with the Qur'an, which characterizes reality as succession and alternation or as change itself (10:6; 23:80; 25:62; 31:27; 39:5).

24. Ibid., 40.
25. Ibid., 43.
26. Ibid., 45.

Iqbal argues that we require more than mere sensory observation to understand the universe. However, given that humans are spatio-temporally limited, how can we discover a source of knowledge beyond our senses? Iqbal contends that the only way we can have a deeper understanding of reality is for there to be an element within that reality that can be fully possessed by human understanding, and that the only such thing is human consciousness. An observation of our own consciousness reveals that, like the universe, our minds are existences characterized by change, succession, alternation, duration, or time itself.[27]

This dynamic temporal existence of the consciousness reveals two kinds of temporality: serial and non-serial time, or linear succession and metaphysical duration.[28] These two kinds of temporality reflect two sides of human consciousness: the temporal, serial, spatial, and practical *efficient side* and the non-serial, temporal, and mystical *appreciative side*. The first we experience in our daily lives; the other is only rarely experienced during moments of profound meditation.

The temporality of the appreciative self,[29] however, transcends linear time, perceiving everything as a "single now."[30] The temporality of the efficient self is "hardly distinguishable from space," a spatialized time; but this is not true time. Like a string of beads, it "pulverizes" all movement into a series of "nows." The appreciative self, however, is only found in "moments of profound meditation" when the efficient self is set aside and we can find the center of experience. Iqbal notes, then, that it is impossible even to describe "this inner experience of pure duration" in words because language itself is shaped by the serial time of our efficient self.[31] At this level, the "states of consciousness melt into each other," creating a unity of the ego where every

---

27. Ibid., 47. Iqbal observes, "Thus there is nothing static in my inner life; all is a constant mobility, an unceasing flux of states, a perpetual flow in which there is no halt or resting place."

28. Ibid.

29. Ibid., 48. Iqbal coined the term "appreciative" as a descriptor of this side of consciousness.

30. This distinction between serial and non-serial time is reflected in the Qur'an. For instance, the scriptural metaphorical axiom in which one day for God is equal to a thousand years on earth reveals that although creation may take many years in serial time, it is a "single indivisible act" in non-serial time. Iqbal cites 25:59, "[He] . . . Who in six days created the Heavens and the earth, and what is between them, then mounted his Throne," and 54:49–50, "All things We have created with a fixed destiny: Our command was but one, swift as the twinkling of an eye."

31. For instance, Iqbal states, a ray of light, which comprises billions of particles that would take thousands of years to observe individually, is observed by the eye in an instant.

experience is felt by the whole consciousness. At this level, "there is change and movement, but this change and movement are indivisible; their elements inter-penetrate and are wholly non-serial in character."[32] The appreciative self is thus a corrective to the efficient self, taking a divided existence and making it into an "organic whole."[33]

This whole is "pure time," or "moments in the life of reality," where past and present move together and the future presents itself as an open possibility, not a fixed future.[34] This is the true meaning of the Qur'anic notion of destiny (*taqdir*).[35] Destiny is not some unrelated fate or preordained events dripping forth across time, but an inward reach from the innermost being that "forms the very essence of things" and becomes actualized in serial time. Time must be understood as absolutely and creatively free, original, novel, and unforeseeable. This is why it cannot be explained via mechanism and, consequently, why naturalistic science cannot comprehend life.[36]

If consciousness is an analogy for reality, then our examination of the mind reveals that "the universe is a free creative movement." The material universe is not an inert thing, not a "collection of solid stuff occupying a void" but *act*; it is the permeation of life and thought that allows for the synthesis of all elements into a growing organic whole moving teleologically towards an end.[37]

At this point, however, Iqbal and Bergson part. Despite Bergson's theory of creative life, he fails to see in the universe a teleological drive towards the future.[38] This view of reality as a process through organically connected stages moving forward to actualize all the open possibilities within its destiny is Qur'anic.

To "exist in pure duration" is to be a self-aware mind.[39] The degree to which we intuit that consciousness (our I-amness) in relation to non-self

---

32. Iqbal, *Reconstruction*, 48.

33. Ibid., 47.

34. Ibid., 49.

35. Ibid. Destiny is "time regarded as prior to the disclosure of its possibilities . . . time freed from the net of causal sequence . . . it is time as self and not as thought and calculated." In affirming the notion of possible worlds, Iqbal illustrates: "If you ask me why the Emperor Humayun and Shah Tahmasp of Persia were contemporaries, I can give you no causal explanation. The only answer that can possibly be given is that the nature of reality is such that among its infinite possibilities of becoming, the two possibilities known as the lives of Humayun Shah Tahmasp should realize themselves together."

36. Ibid., 50.

37. Ibid.

38. Ibid., 51.

39. Ibid., 52.

determinates is the point we occupy within a scale of being. Also contrary to Bergson, Iqbal argues that because self-aware consciousness (or ego) is prior to absolute time (or duration) and stands at the highest level of being, reality itself must be conceived as an all-embracing and concrete ego; for to exist in pure duration is to exist as such an ego. This ego is God. God is the ultimate reality of the universe for Iqbal.

The scientific importance of this realization lies in the fact that ego-hood characteristically possesses "a uniform mode of behaviour."[40] When we posit this characteristic of God, the Ultimate Ego and Ultimate Reality of the universe, we realize that the "structure of events [and] systematic mode of behaviour" displayed by nature is really divine activity or, as the Qur'an reveals, "the habit of Allah."[41] Like the ego-consciousness, the universe "must be understood as a living, ever-growing organism" whose only limitation is the internal limitation of the ego-consciousness that animates it. As such, science has a spiritual meaning in that knowledge of the universe is knowledge of God and his activity.[42]

Two Examples of True Science

Iqbal offers two contemporary theories as examples of true science: emergent evolutionary theory and Gestalt psychological theory. We explore both below.

Emergent Evolutionary Theory

This theory conceives of the world as an orderly sequence of events; evolution is the "comprehensive plan of sequence in all natural events."[43] It is "the orderly advance of natural events without restriction."[44] Specifically, Iqbal suggests, attention should be focused upon "integral clusters of events

---

40. Ibid., 56.

41. Ibid., 57. Iqbal cites Surah 50:14, "And verily unto thy Lord is the limit."

42. Ibid., 56. Iqbal writes, "The not-self does not present itself as a confronting 'other,' or else it would have to be, like our finite self, in spatial relation with the confronting 'other.' What we call nature or not-self is a fleeting moment in the life of God. His 'I-amness' is independent, elemental, absolute. Of such a self it is impossible for us to form an adequate conception. As the Quran says, 'Naught' is like Him; yet 'He hears and sees.'"

43. Morgan, *Emergent Evolution*, 1.

44. Morgan, "Emergent Evolution," 70.

which we call entities." These "items of stuff go together on some specific plan in substantial unity or, briefly, in substance."[45]

Emergent evolution stresses the "incoming of the new" within natural entities and its unpredictability, as evidenced in everything from the atom and on up to the mind itself.[46] Emergent evolution is founded in the observation from chemistry and biology that the addition or subtraction of something causes a new and unpredictable result.[47] Additionally, it comes from the theories concerning how a living organism can evolve from a nonliving thing through incremental changes or additions. Thus, evolution always moves forward and upward rather than regressing under dissolution.[48] Morgan states, "When there is increased complexity, with variety and multiplicity of the items of stuff, and increased richness . . . in the substance (or substantial unity) in virtue of which the entity is an indivisible whole, there is evolutionary advance."[49] For Morgan, evolution occurs not in steps but in leaps, however small or numerous, and with each such leap "there are in evidence new qualities and properties which characterise the new entity which leaps into being without loss of some at least of its old traits."[50]

Emergent evolution is thus a protest against, or rather, the antithesis of, scientific mechanicalism. Morgan posits that emergent evolution, while it does not necessarily generate new scientific facts, puts new questions to the interpretations of scientific facts.[51] Scientific mechanicalism maintains that all elements in the natural order are part of the same "tissue of events" and are therefore equally subject to scientific methods.[52] Although scientific materialism omits any supernatural explanations, nothing within emergent evolutionary theory excludes an acknowledgment of God. This is because the philosophy of science does not supersede science but supplements it, and such admission of the divine requires support only by the methods of philosophy.[53]

Emergent evolution accepts naturalism, meaning that all physical and psychological events fall within "one order of nature." However, that does

---

45. Iqbal, *Reconstruction*, 71.
46. Morgan, *Emergent Evolution*, 2.
47. Ibid.
48. Ibid., 7.
49. Morgan, "Emergent Evolution," 70.
50. Ibid., 71.
51. Ibid.
52. Morgan, *Emergent Evolution*, 2.
53. Ibid.

not mean that God "falls within the emergent scheme as a limiting concept at the upper end of the emergent scales."[54]

Mechanicalism does not go beyond measurable effects, ignoring anything beyond it that might be said to be emergent. As such, mechanicalism "regards a chemical compound as only a more complex mechanical mixture, without any kind of relatedness of its constituents. It regards life as a regrouping of physio-chemical events with no new kind of relatedness expressed."[55] Emergent evolution rejects this limited explanation and argues that scientific materialism holds this belief dogmatically, in defiance of the evidence.[56] Although the facts demand a certain agnosticism, any ultimate *philosophical explanation* of the facts requires supplemental interpretation that posits the existence of the divine.[57]

Borrowing from Samuel Alexander, Morgan posits a pyramidal scheme of the natural order. At the bottom, although Iqbal and Morgan disagree with him on this point,[58] Alexander places "space and time."[59] From there, evolution moves from matter into life into mind and, finally, into deity, the highest level of being: "Each higher entity in the ascending series is an emergent "complex" of many entities of lower grades, within which a new kind of relatedness gives integral unity."[60] Within the scheme, a divine activity is posited.

Emergent evolution envisions the involvement of lower forms within the higher forms of being. That is, without matter, there is no life; and without life, there is no mind. Each level is dependent upon the previous one. Each emergent at any given level presents a "new kind of relatedness of which there are no instances at lower levels."[61] This is to be accepted via natural piety.

But what is dependence? Morgan argues that, clearly, if a key characteristic of a particular level of existence (e.g., consciousness) is omitted, that existent drops to a lower level. Thus the new relations emerge at each

---

54. Morgan, "Emergent Evolution," 73. This is in contradistinction to Samuel Alexander's view of God or deity as the highest emergent form within a single Spinozist cosmology.

55. Morgan, *Emergent Evolution*, 7.

56. Ibid., 8.

57. Ibid., 10.

58. Iqbal will argue that Ego or Self is prior to space-time, while Morgan argues that there is no solid evidence to show that space-time exists without physical events (see Morgan, *Emergent Evolution*, 22).

59. Alexander, *Space, Time and Deity*, 1.

60. Morgan, *Emergent Evolution*, 11.

61. Ibid., 15.

higher level, and that level is sustained with this emergent characteristic. For example, through the pyramid of mental evolution in living organisms, we see the development of sensory perception, then naïve perception, and finally contemplative thought. Each characteristic quality depends upon the former, yet it is a new quality altogether.[62]

Deity is the highest emergent quality in the natural system. Although in Alexander's conception this natural system is characterized by space-time, where time is the mind of space, Morgan (and Iqbal) conceive of any physical system as also psychological: "All systems of events are in their degree psycho-physical. Both attributes, inseparable in essence, are pervasive throughout the universe of natural entities . . . Every natural entity, say from atom to man, expresses both attributes while still preserving its substantial identity, in some sense of this phrase."[63] Humans experience psychophysical events in two ways, each acquainted with physical or psychological aspects of man. We call psychological experience "intuition"[64] or "enjoyment"[65] (in the vocabularies of Bergson and of Alexander, respectively); physically, the same event is sense experience. For Morgan, the world is independent from the human mind and God becomes a directive activity within the natural scheme.[66] This means that, for Morgan, God is an active agent in the system, while for Alexander, God is simply an emergent quality, like mind: an ideal that is always becoming.[67]

Gestalt (Configuration) Psychological Theory

The early proponents of Gestalt psychological theory (i.e., Wertheimer, Kohler, and Koffka) argue that psychology, like modern science, has become too fixated on the "systematic collection of data."[68] Students of psychology believed that mimicking the presumptions of modern science would make

62. Ibid., 17.
63. Ibid., 26.
64. Bergson, *Creative Mind*, 175.
65. Alexander, *Space, Time and Deity*, 12.
66. Morgan, *Emergent Evolution*, 27.
67. Alexander, *Space, Time and Deity*, 12.
68. Wertheimer, "Gestalt Theory," 1. Kohler adds that the mainstream psychological view taught in universities was "that all psychological facts (not only those in perception) consist of unrelated inert atoms and that almost the only factors which combine these atoms and thus introduce action are associations formed under the influence of mere contiguity. What had disturbed us was the utter senselessness of this picture, and the implication that human life, apparently so colorful and so intensely dynamic, is actually a frightful bore." See his "Gestalt Psychology Today," 728.

it a "real science" also. Koffka, citing the Latin adage *multum non multa*, states that according to the dominant scientific paradigm, the "person who knows twenty items knows ten times as much as the person who knows only two items."[69] He challenges this by positing that the latter person, "if he knows those two items in their intrinsic relation, so that they are no longer two but one with two parts, knows a great deal more than former, if he knows just twenty items in pure aggregation."[70]

In all this, Kohler argues, psychology has lost something important—something vital, in fact.[71] Some argue that there are areas of life that simply cannot be examined by science; others argue that there is a methodological distinction between the natural and human sciences. Have we limited science? Wertheimer asks, "Perhaps science already embodies methods leading in an entirely different direction, methods which have been continually stifled by the seemingly necessary, dominant ones."[72] Koffka continues in this vein, arguing that science has already begun to employ a different methodology contrary to the encyclopedic accumulation of data, a method striving for increased simplification. Such a simplification is not achieved by making science easier to learn but by having the scientist master the system of science so well that it becomes a progressively more "cohesive and unitary whole."[73]

The central philosophical notion of Gestalt theory is holism. Whereas Western sciences divide and isolate nature into component elements to discover its laws and then reassemble them, Gestalt scientific theory argues that the natural order comprises wholes that cannot be understood piecemeal or in partial processes. Natural science has added support to the idea that sense perception exhibits particular characters as wholes over their parts. Within physical systems pervaded by interactions, it appears that "these interactions affect the parts of the system until, eventually, in a steady state, the characteristics of all parts are such that remaining interactions balance one another."[74] Gestalt theory contends, based on observation, that "we often experience things that are not part of our simple sensation."[75] Wertheimer asks us to consider hearing a piece of music: What in the human mind allows one to recognize the same tune later even when played in a different

69. Koffka, *Gestalt Psychology*, 3.
70. Ibid.
71. Kohler, "Some Gestalt Problems," 57.
72. Wertheimer, "Gestalt Theory," 1.
73. Koffka, *Gestalt Psychology*, 4.
74. Kohler, "Gestalt Psychology Today," 729.
75. Boeree, "Gestalt Psychology."

key or produced by different instruments? It is not the recognition of each note but the recognition of the whole by virtue of some ability in the mind. It is not the sum of individual tones (pieces of data) that is the foundation of our experience; rather, "what I experience at each place in the melody is a part which is itself determined by the character of the whole."[76] This also applies to looking at a connect-the-dots picture, a neon sign in Las Vegas that appears to move, or a motion picture: what we experience is greater than the sum of its parts (i.e., individual dots, lights, or photos). In his original article Wertheimer states, "I stand at the window and see a house, trees, sky. Theoretically, I might say there were 327 nuances of colour. Do I have '327'? No. I have sky, house, and trees."[77] He also maintains, "It is the hope of Gestalt theory to determine the nature of such wholes"; it looks for the "dynamic functional relationship to the whole."[78]

Therefore, as Wolfgang Kohler adds, "we cannot assume that the perceptual scene is an aggregate of unrelated elements because underlying processes are already functionally interrelated when that scene emerges and now exhibits corresponding effects."[79] What are important are the *relations* between objects, not the naïve perception of results (i.e., physical sense experiences).

This can be seen in the psychological problem of the ego. Is the ego a mere sum of its mental parts, or something else? Gestalt theory conceives of the ego as "a functional part of the total field" of mind and experience. Such a view implies a need to reconfigure our understanding of the ego-organism in relation to its environment and other egos.[80] Contrary to the claims of behaviorism and vitalism, both of which consider the ego's engagement with nature to be piecemeal, nature does "exhibit numerous instances of physical wholes in which part events are determined by the inner structure of the whole."[81] These occur both in biology and other sciences, so the "fundamental question can be very simply stated: Are the parts of a given whole determined by the inner structure of that whole, or are the events such that, as independent, piecemeal, fortuitous and blind, the total activity is a sum

---

76. Wertheimer, "Gestalt Theory," 5.
77. Wertheimer, "Laws of Organization," 71.
78. Wertheimer, "Gestalt Theory," 4.
79. Kohler, "Gestalt Psychology Today," 728.
80. Wertheimer, "Gestalt Theory," 6.
81. Kohler, "Gestalt Psychology Today," 729.

of the part-activities?"[82] Wertheimer supports the possibility of teleology in natural order.[83]

Koffka argues that one's scientific theory does affect morality: "In other words, whereas the world of primitive man had directly determined his conduct, had told him what was good, what bad, the scientific world proved all too often a failure when it came to answering such questions. Reason seemed to reveal truth, but a truth that would give no guidance to conduct; but the demand for such guidance remained and had to be filled. Thus arose eventually the dualism of science and religion, with its various phases of

---

82. Wertheimer, "Gestalt Theory," 7.

83. Ibid., 10. According to Kohler, "drive" or "motivation" is another example from "human experience." Although an apparent "need" is sometimes a motivating factor, it is something greater than a mere felt physical need. Rather, Kohler speaks of a "dynamic relation" an individual has with an object, whereby the individual is either attracted or repelled by the object: "In other words, an object may have characteristics which establish a dynamic relation between the subject and that object. According to common experience, it is this dynamic relation which makes the subject move toward, or away from, the object." It is for this relation that we should reserve the term "motivation." Kohler asks, "How would a Gestalt psychologist handle motivation in the present sense? He would begin with the following psychological facts. I do not know up to what point Lewin would have accepted what I am now going to say. My facts are these: (*a*) In human experience, motivation is a dynamic vector, that is, a fact which has a direction and tends to cause a displacement in this direction. (*b*) Unless there are obstacles in the way, this direction coincides with an imaginary straight line drawn from the object to the subject. (*c*) The direction of the experienced vector is either that toward the object or away from it. In the first case, the vector tends to reduce the distance in question; in the second, to increase it. (*d*) The strength of both the need present in the subject and of the valence exhibited by the object can vary. Both in man and in animals it has been observed that, when the strength of the valence is low, this reduction can be compensated for by an increase of the need in the subject; and, conversely, that, when the need is lowered, an increase of the strength of the valence may compensate for this change. When considering these simple statements, anybody familiar with the elements of physics will be reminded of the behavior of forces: (*a*) In physics, forces are dynamic vectors which tend to change distance between one thing (or event) and another. (*b*) Unless there are obstacles in the way, force operates along a straight line drawn from first object (or event) to the other. (*c*) The direction in which a force operates is either that of attraction or of a repulsion, of a reduction or of an increase of the given distance. (*d*) The formula which the intensity of a force between two objects is given contains two terms which refer to the sizes of a decisive property (for instance, an electric charge) in one object and in the other. It is always the product of these two terms on which, according to the formula, the intensity of the force depends. Consequently, a reduction of the crucial term on one side can be compensated for by an increase in the term on the other side." Given this, it appears that motivation is the same power as "force" in physics: "Gestalt psychologists are, therefore, inclined to interpret motivation in terms of such forces or, rather, of forces which operate between certain perceptual processes and processes in another part of the brain, where a need may be physiologically represented." See Kohler, "Gestalt Psychology Today," 732–33.

double-truth theory, bitter enmity, and sentimentalisation of science, one as unsatisfactory as the other."[84] Science must build a systematic and rational system, Koffka argues; therefore, it must admit only the facts that permit the security of the system. When scientists realize this truth, such ideology is not dangerous; it is only when scientific triumphalism assumes that it adequately interprets reality, and therefore fails to realize areas it has neglected as valid, that it becomes dangerous.[85]

In his brief advocacy of Gestalt theory (what he calls configuration psychology), Iqbal also contends that modern psychology and its debate over determinism and freedom of the ego are products of their "slavish imitation of [the] physical sciences."[86] Psychology is ignorant of its own freedom as a unique science. Iqbal contends that "the view that ego-activity is a succession of thoughts and ideas, ultimately resolvable to units of sensation, is only another form of the atomic materialism which forms the basis of modern science."[87] Rather, he argues in support of Gestalt theory, "A careful study of intelligent behaviour discloses the fact of 'insight' over and above the mere succession of sensations. This 'insight' is the ego's appreciation of the temporal, spatial, and causal relation of things—the choice, that is to say, of data in a complex whole, in view of a goal or purpose which the ego has set before itself for the time being. It is this sense of striving in the experience of purposive action and the success which I actually achieve in reaching my 'ends' that convince me of my efficiency as a personal cause."[88]

CONCLUSION

Iqbal's discussion of science arises within his larger defense of religious knowledge as true knowledge of reality. Iqbal seeks to show how intuition has been gradually maligned in Western intellectual history and relegated to the sphere of religion. In early human history, however, intuition was the primary source of knowledge of reality, as humans turned to those charismatic members of society whose insights into reality were supported by their experience. We have come to call such individuals "prophets," and in the prophetic experience we find genuine knowledge of reality as a whole, not as merely isolated parts. Iqbal's criticism of scientific materialism and the search for a science compatible with Islam, then, fits into the larger goals

84. Koffka, *Gestalt Psychology*, 7.
85. Ibid.
86. Iqbal, *Reconstruction*, 37.
87. Ibid., 107.
88. Ibid., 108.

of *Reconstruction*. While admitting that an "intellectual stupor" has fallen upon Islamic civilization over the last five centuries, he holds out hope for reform as Muslim thinkers turn intellectually towards the West;[89] and since the West is simply the inheritor of medieval Islamic science, streams within it run consistently with its origins. In those streams, Islamic thought can find revitalization.

BIBLIOGRAPHY

Alexander, Samuel. *Space, Time and Deity: The Gifford Lectures at Glasgow 1916–1918, Volume 1.* London: MacMillan, 1927.

Bergson, Henri. *Creative Evolution*. Translated by Arthur Mitchell. New York: Henry Holt, 1913.

———. *Creative Mind*. Translated by Mabelle L. Andison. 1946. Reprint. New York: Citadel, 1992.

Boeree, C. George. "Gestalt Psychology." 2000. No pages. Online: http://webspace.ship.edu/cgboer/gestalt.html.

Einstein, Albert. "On the Electrodynamics of Moving Bodies." In *The Principle of Relativity*. Translated by George Barker Jeffery and Wilfrid Perrett. London: Methuen, 1923.

Esposito, John L., and John O. Voll. *Makers of Contemporary Islam*. New York: Oxford University Press, 2001.

Iqbal, Muhammad. *The Reconstruction of Religious Thought in Islam*. Dubai: Kitab al-Islamiyyah, 1934.

Koffka, Kurt. *Principles of Gestalt Psychology*. 1935. Reprinted, London: Routledge, 2001.

Kohler, Wolfgang. "Gestalt Psychology Today." *American Psychologist* 14 (1959) 727–34.

———. "Some Gestalt Problems." In *A Source Book of Gestalt Psychology*, edited by Willis D. Ellis, 55–70. 1938. Reprinted, New York: Harcourt, Brace, 1939.

Mir, Mustansir. *Iqbal*. Matrix: Makers of Islamic Civilization. London: Tauris, 2006.

Morgan, C. Lloyd. *Emergent Evolution*. Gifford Lectures 1922. London: Williams & Norgate, 1923.

———. "Emergent Evolution." *Mind* 34 (1925) 70–74.

Vaughan, Michael. "Introduction: Henri Bergson's *Creative Evolution*." Special Issue 114 *SubStance* 36 (2007) 7–24.

Wertheimer, Max. "Gestalt Theory." In *A Source Book of Gestalt Psychology*, edited by Willis D. Ellis, 1–12. 1938. Reprinted, New York: Harcourt, Brace, 1939.

———. "Laws of Organization in Perceptual Forms." In *A Source Book of Gestalt Psychology*, edited by Willis D. Ellis, 71–88. 1938. Reprinted, London: Routledge, 1999.

---

89. Ibid., 7.

www.ingramcontent.com/pod-product-compliance
Lightning Source LLC
Chambersburg PA
CBHW051637230426
43669CB00013B/2339